TIJUANA, ENSENADA & VALLE DE GUADALUPE WINE COUNTRY

JENNIFER KRAMER

Contents

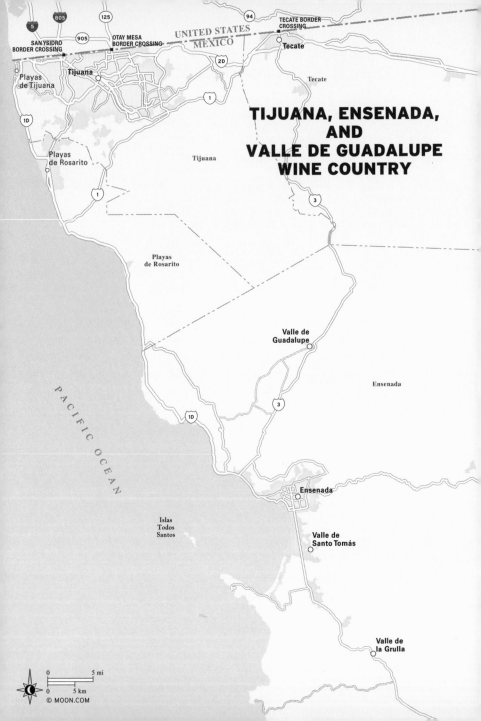

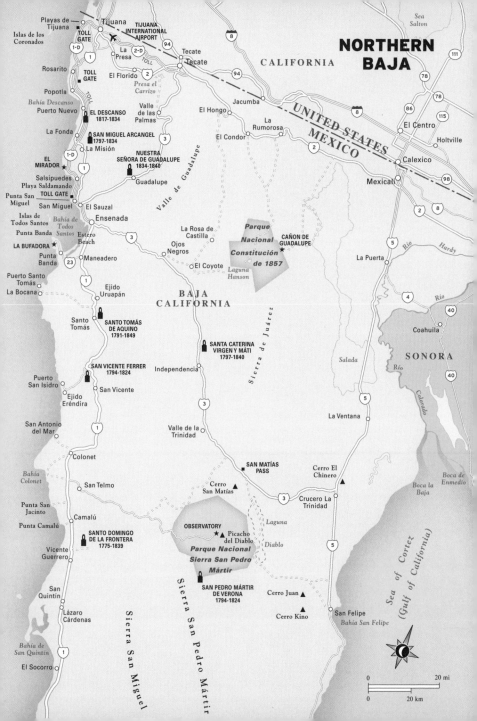

Tijuana, Ensenada & Valle de Guadalupe Wine Country

Northern Baja has a unique flavor. The influence of the United States, just over the border, can be felt everywhere as the region balances the two cultures with a subtle finesse. While many peninsula road-trippers skip this region in favor of destinations farther south, just as many make it their final destination thanks in part to a thriving culinary scene whose food, craft beer, and wine are being recognized worldwide.

The five regions that define this area—Tijuana, Tecate, Rosarito, Ensenada, and Valle de Guadalupe—are as different from each other as they are from the rest of the peninsula. Tijuana is the big city (the largest on the entire peninsula), with a population of 1.7 million. The infamous party town of yore has reinvented itself in recent years as a culinary and cultural destination that should not be missed. Young creative types and entrepreneurs are turning vacant dance clubs into tech offices, art galleries, and craft breweries. Regional chefs are leading a food movement emulated around the world by renowned chefs such as Rick Bayless.

To the east of Tijuana, the tranquil border town of Tecate is a designated *Pueblo Mágico*. The small town is set amid the mountains and ranchland that

Clockwise from top left: food at Finca Altozano in Valle de Guadalupe; Mercado Hidalgo in Tijuana; Quinta Maria hotel in Valle de Guadalupe; beer in Ensenada with ocean views; Baja California cuisine, made with fresh local ingredients; outdoor dining in wine country.

characterize the region. Down the coast past Tijuana on Mexico 1 is the beach town of Rosarito, popular for a weekend of sipping margaritas at sunset, feasting on seafood, and relaxing. An hour south of Rosarito, the port town of Ensenada is a destination for road-trippers and cruise travelers with a sophisticated culinary scene.

Just east of Ensenada, the serene Valle de Guadalupe is home to over 150 wineries and quickly becoming the new tourist draw for Baja California. The restaurants have followed the wineries, and many of the well-known chefs from Tijuana and Ensenada have opened their own *campestre* restaurants in the valley. While the valley has grown incredibly in the past few years and is gaining worldwide recognition, it remains a tranquil destination marked by dirt roads, boutique wineries, and specialty accommodations.

Come enjoy the unique flavor of northern Baja. You'll find yourself returning for another taste.

Clockwise from top left: Valle de la Grulla; inventive dish at Tras/Horizonte in Tijuana; casual outdoor setting at Troika restaurant in Valle de Guadalupe; oak trees at Casa Magoni winery.

5 TOP
EXPERIENCES

1 Go wine-tasting: Visit the highly acclaimed wineries in Valle de Guadalupe (page 118), as well as lesser-known Valle de la Grulla and Valle de Santo Tomás (page 138).

2 **Savor the local cuisine:** Tijuana is famous for its street food (page 40), while seafood reigns supreme in Ensenada (pages 95 and 104). Enjoy gourmet farm-to-table food at outdoor *campestre* restaurants in wine country (page 129).

3 Sample craft beer: Get a taste of Baja's growing craft beer scene in the local breweries and tasting rooms of Tijuana (page 38) and Ensenada (page 103).

<<<

4 Catch a wave: Ensenada (page 101) and Rosarito (page 75) are home to both epic surf spots and milder waves for beginners.

>>>

5 Join the action downtown: Take in the vibrant bustle of Tijuana's Avenida Revolución (page 27), Tecate's Plaza Parque Hidalgo (page 55), and Ensenada's Avenida López Mateos (page 96).

<<<

Planning Your Trip

Where to Go

Tijuana

Tijuana is undergoing a cultural renaissance with **exquisite restaurants, street food, craft breweries,** and **art galleries** taking over the spaces where the nightclubs and bars used to be. The **large, buzzing city** attracts adventurous foodies in search of the **best street tacos** and beer aficionados who frequent the craft breweries along Avenida Revolución.

Tecate

The small town of Tecate is a **sleepy destination** where visitors can relax around the town plaza, check out the **growing culinary scene,** visit the nearby **cave paintings of El Vallecito,** or enjoy a stay at one of the region's **ranches.** As the "gateway" to the Ruta del Vino, many travelers pass through Tecate for the **easy border crossing,** stopping for a meal or to get some goodies at the town's **famous bakery.**

Rosarito and the Northern Baja Coast

Rosarito is most famous for its **beautiful beaches,** fresh **seafood,** and **relaxed vibe.** The region sprawls along the **picturesque coastline** and comprises a number of smaller communities, each with their own offerings. Convenient to Tijuana, Valle de Guadalupe, and Ensenada, Rosarito can be used as a **jumping-off point** for exploring the region.

Ensenada

Down the Pacific coast, Ensenada draws foodies

Deckman's en el Mogor restaurant in Valle de Guadalupe

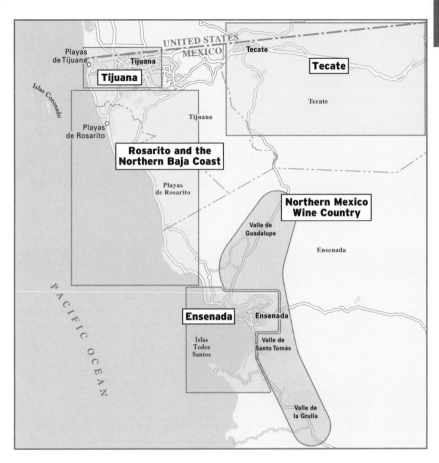

to its **high-end restaurants,** famous **street carts, fish taco stands,** and **craft breweries.** With an easy ambience, gorgeous coastline, and **world-class surfing,** Ensenada has a variety of experiences to offer and is a **popular weekend destination.** Many visitors who want to **tour the nearby Valle de Guadalupe wine region** stay in Ensenada, which is just a 30-minute drive from the valley.

Northern Mexico Wine Country

Ensenada's **Ruta del Vino** takes travelers east into the nearby **Valle de Guadalupe,** Mexico's premier wine region, popular for its charming **boutique wineries,** *campestre* **restaurants,** and **intimate hotels.** South of Ensenada is a second, smaller wine region, the **Antigua Ruta del Vino,** comprising **Valle de la Grulla** and **Valle de Santo Tomás** and offering a handful of wineries and **fewer crowds.**

Know Before You Go

High and Low Seasons

Spring and fall are generally considered the **best seasons for traveling anywhere in northern Baja,** when the weather is pleasant throughout the region. The week before Easter, called *Semana Santa,* is a very popular time for Mexicans to travel; reservations for this period should be made in advance and beach areas will be very busy.

TIJUANA

Tijuana has **temperate weather** year-round. There aren't high or low seasons here; hotels may be slightly more expensive in the summer months, and the city will be quiet around the holidays and in January.

TECATE

Temperatures reach over 100°F (38°C) in **Tecate** during the summer, making **late** summer the **low season** for this region. Hotels may offer specials during the month of August when temperatures are highest. The cooler **winter** months are the **high season** for this region.

ROSARITO AND THE
NORTHERN BAJA COAST

Summer is **high season** for **Rosarito.** Hotel rates will be the most expensive during summer weekends, but be aware that the Rosarito coast can experience the marine layer during early summer, with "May Gray" and "June Gloom" causing cloudy, cool weather along the coast. **Winter** is **low season** for tourism in Rosarito. The temperatures are pleasant here year-round so most businesses will still be open during the winter, although a few restaurants may close for a few weeks in January. You'll get cheaper rates on hotel rooms in the winter.

seafood tostadas at Ensenada's Sabina Restaurante

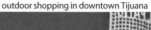
outdoor shopping in downtown Tijuana

Quinta Monasterio, a small winery in Valle de Guadalupe

ENSENADA

Summer is also **high season** for visiting **Ensenada.** Hotel rates will be the most expensive during summer weekends, especially during the Valle de Guadalupe Fiestas de la Vendimia wine harvest festival in July and August, when many visitors stay in Ensenada. **Winter** is considered more of a **low season** for Ensenada. The temperatures are pleasant year-round so most businesses will still be open, but you'll get cheaper rates on hotel rooms.

NORTHERN MEXICO WINE COUNTRY

Summer is the **high season** for **Valle de Guadalupe** and the Northern Wine Region, although the temperatures can reach well over 100°F (38°C). Be prepared for large crowds, especially on weekends and during the three weeks of the annual Fiestas de la Vendimia wine harvest festival in July and August. **Winter** is considered the **low season** and hotel rates may be lower. All of the wineries will still be open,

but the outdoor seasonal restaurants will be closed.

Passports and Visas

Passports are required to visit Baja California. Non-Mexican citizens must also obtain a *forma migratoria múltiple* **(FMM) tourist permit** in order to travel in Mexico. If you are flying into northern Baja from outside of Mexico, this will be included in your ticket. If crossing by land, you can obtain your permit at the border crossing.

Transportation

Many travelers explore northern Baja by car. **Mexican auto insurance** is required by law, so don't forget to purchase it before you leave on your trip.

It's best to reserve a **rental car** for use during your trip if you are flying into northern Baja; the only commercial **airport** in this region is **Tijuana**'s General Abelardo L. Rodríguez International Airport (TIJ).

The Best of Northern Baja

The northern coastal border region is one of the most fascinating and culturally interesting on the Baja peninsula. The beautiful beaches and countryside provide the perfect backdrop for an incredible culinary scene, world-class wine region, and bourgeoning craft beer industry.

Day 1: Tijuana
29 KM (18 MI)
1 HOUR

Get an early start to cross south at the **San Ysidro border crossing** into **Tijuana.** Head to **Mercado Hidalgo** to explore the market's stalls of fresh produce, regional spices, and local artisan goods. Tijuana has some of the best **street food** in the world, so get some *birria* at nearby **Tacos Rio,** or enjoy street tacos at **Las Ahumaderas.** After lunch, catch an exhibit at **CECUT Cultural Center.** For dinner, try a nice restaurant like **La Justina** or **Misión 19** to get a taste of Tijuana's incredible **culinary scene.** If you like **craft beer,** cap off your night at **Plaza Fiesta,** Tijuana's collection of craft beer tasting rooms.

Day 2: Ensenada
105 KM (65 MI)
1.5 HOURS

Head to breakfast at the original **Foodgarden** and then drive down the coast along Mexico 1 to **Ensenada.** Check out the **Mercado de Mariscos** and grab some of Ensenada's famous **fish tacos** at one of the stalls outside the market, or walk over to **Muelle 3** for incredible **ceviche** and **fresh seafood.** Spend the afternoon shopping and taking in the sights on **Avenida López Mateos** (Calle Primera). Enjoy dinner at one of Ensenada's prime restaurants like **Boules** or **Manzanilla.** After dinner, stop in at the long-established **Hussong's Cantina** for a beer or margarita.

Tijuana Arch, one of the city's most recognized landmarks

Vinos Pijoan, a relaxing place to spend the afternoon in wine country

Day 3: Valle de Guadalupe
29 KM (18 MI)
30 MINUTES

Grab a breakfast featuring local cheeses and other products at **Casa Marcelo** before driving east to the **Valle de Guadalupe**. Stop in at the **Museo de la Vid y el Vino** to learn about the history of winemaking and the valley. Enjoy lunch alfresco at the *campestre* **Finca Altozano** and visit a **winery** such as **Vinos Paoloni** to enjoy your wine with beautiful views. Enjoy a gourmet six-course dinner while looking out at the garden at the famous **Corazón de Tierra restaurant.**

Day 4: Wine-Tasting

Enjoy a hearty breakfast of *huevos con machaca* at **La Cocina de Doña Esthela** before heading off for a day of **wine-tasting** at boutique wineries like **Vena Cava, Vinos Pijoan,** or **Lechuza.** Enjoy a Mexican-style late lunch/early dinner at **Malva.** Then catch **sunset** with incredible

dramatic ocean views at the cliff-top **Bar Bura** at **Cuatrocuatros.**

Day 5: Tecate
79 KM (49 MI)
1 HOUR

Drive north on Mexico 3 to the *Pueblo Mágico* town of **Tecate** and grab some fresh-baked goods for breakfast at **El Mejor Pan de Tecate.** Head to the **Museo Comunitario de Tecate** to learn about the history and culture of the region. Grab a carne asada taco for a quick bite at **Taqueria Los Amigos** and enjoy a stroll around the town plaza, savoring the shade of the mature trees and listening to the **mariachis.** If you want to have a drink before dinner, head to the locals' spot **Bar Diana,** right on the plaza, for a beer or margarita. Then go to **El Lugar de Nos** to enjoy a memorable meal before crossing back to San Diego through the laid-back Tecate border crossing.

Tijuana Weekend

Tijuana is a gritty and vibrant city with an incredible culinary scene and plenty of cultural attractions to make it well worth a weekend getaway. From street tacos to fine dining, the city has been luring foodies for years, and with a new craft beer scene emerging, beer aficionados are now flocking to the city as well.

Day 1

Drive or walk across the **San Diego/Tijuana border** at **San Ysidro** and head to the center of the action on **Avenida Revolución** in Zona Centro. Explore the *pasajes,* do some artisanal shopping, and get your photo taken with one of Tijuana's famous zonkeys. For lunch, duck into **Caesar's Restaurante,** where you can have a Caesar salad prepared tableside in the very spot it was invented. After lunch, sample some craft beers at one of the many breweries on Revolución such as **Norte Brewing Co.** or **Teorema/Lúdica**

Co-Tasting Room. Enjoy a delightful gourmet dinner nearby at **Verde y Crema** or **La Justina.** If you're in the mood for a nightcap, head to **Dandy del Sur** or **La Mezcalera** before heading back to your hotel.

Day 2

Head west to Playas de Tijuana and enjoy a fresh breakfast with the locals at **El Yogurt Place.** Spend some time walking along the expansive Playas boardwalk and check out **El Parque de la Amistad (Friendship Park)** before heading back to Zona Rio to grab some gourmet tacos for lunch at **Tras/Horizonte.** Spend the afternoon checking out an IMAX movie or the current exhibits at **CECUT Cultural Center.** Don't miss your reservation for dinner at **Misión 19,** one of Tijuana's top restaurants. After dinner, head upstairs to **Bar 20** for cocktails, or go to **Plaza Fiesta** if you're looking for a boisterous beer scene.

Patrons can sip on craft beer and enjoy excellent views of Tijuana from Norte Brewing Co.

Day 3

Head to Tijuana's famous market, **Mercado Hidalgo.** Take in the sights and smells of the produce, spices, and artisanal goods before checking out some of the awesome street food around the market such as **Tacos el Franc** or **Los Perrones.** Head north to **Estación Federal** to grab a coffee or drink before getting in line at the border to cross back to the United States.

Wine-Tasting Getaway

Valle de Guadalupe is Mexico's premier wine country and is home to unique boutique hotels, incredible *campestre* restaurants, and over 150 wineries. The area is perfect for a tranquil or romantic getaway and is drawing visitors from all around the world who are starting to hear about the award-winning wines and fantastic food.

Day 1

121 KM (75 MI)
2 HOURS
Drive across the **San Diego/Tijuana border** at **San Ysidro** and keep going two hours south to arrive at the **Valle de Guadalupe.** Check into your intimate B&B at **La Villa del Valle** or **Casa Mayoral.** Start your explorations in the valley with a quick visit to the **Museo de la Vid y el Vino** to learn about wine and the history of the region. Check out a few boutique **wineries** like **Vinícola 3 Mujeres, Vena Cava,** or **Alximia.** Enjoy a six-course gourmet meal at chef Diego Hernandez's **Corazón de Tierra.**

Day 2

Have breakfast at your B&B before heading out to your first **winery** such as **Lechuza** or **Bodegas F. Rubio.** Then enjoy a lunch of octopus, brussels sprouts, or lamb *birria*

Enjoy a multicourse menu and beautiful garden views at Corazón de Tierra in Valle de Guadalupe.

at Javier Plascencia's *campestre* restaurant, **Finca Altozano.** Leave enough time before or after your lunch reservation to enjoy a glass of wine atop one of the giant wine barrel lookouts perched around the property. After lunch, enjoy another **wine-tasting** at a boutique winery like **Vinos Pijoan** or **Vinos Paoloni.** For **sunset,** head to the cliff-top **Bar Bura** at **Cuatrocuatros,** where you'll bask in stunning Pacific Ocean views. Finish off the day with a memorable dinner at **Fauna.**

Day 3
80 KM (50 MI)
1 HOUR

For your last morning, enjoy a delicious homemade Mexican breakfast of corn pancakes or *huevos con machaca* at the famous **La Cocina de Doña Esthela.** Enjoy one last **wine-tasting** at **Viña de Frannes** or **Torres Alegre y Familia** on your way up Mexico 3 to Tecate. Grab some baked goods at **El Mejor Pan de Tecate** before crossing back over the border to the United States.

Ensenada Beach Getaway

Two hours south of the U.S. border, the town of Ensenada is a prime getaway with a lot to offer visitors, including beautiful beaches, delicious seafood, craft beer, and a lively downtown area.

Day 1

Drive across the **San Diego/Tijuana border** at **San Ysidro** and keep going two hours south on toll road Mexico 1 to arrive at **Ensenada.** Along the way, stop at **El Mirador,** a half hour north of Ensenada, to take in the impressive Pacific views. Once you get into Ensenada, head downtown to the **Mercado de Mariscos** fish market to see the day's catch and walk along the *malecón.* Walk a few blocks inland to **Avenida López Mateos** (Calle Primera)

a view of Ensenada's harbor

Northern Baja has turned into a globally recognized culinary hot spot with its fresh and flavorful food, growing craft beer scene, and popular wine region. Here's where to go to find what.

STREET FOOD

Tijuana

From excellent fine dining to some of the best street food in the world, Tijuana is leading Baja California's culinary movement. Alongside chefs like Javier Plascencia and Miguel Angel Guerrero and their gourmet restaurants are taco stands and *mariscos* street carts that have been around for decades. Tijuana is famous for its savory and affordable street tacos, but tamales, tortas, and seafood all abound in street carts and stands throughout the city.

Ensenada

Home to the fish taco, Ensenada has numerous fish taco stands and there are *mariscos* carts throughout the city as well. Serving up fresh seafood, La Guerrerense was called the best street cart in the world by the late Anthony Bourdain—and it lives up to its reputation.

SEAFOOD

Rosarito

Rosarito and the surrounding areas are home to many well-known seafood spots like the lobster village of Puerto Nuevo and the daily fresh fish coming in at Popotla. Seafood lovers can also get their fix at fish taco stands and sit-down restaurants in Rosarito proper.

Ensenada

Seafood reigns supreme in Ensenada, from fish tacos and ceviche tostadas sold at street carts to nice sit-down restaurants like Manzanilla or Boules. This fishing town provides some of the freshest ceviches and seafood cocktails you'll ever find.

BEER AND BREWERIES

Tijuana

There are a few independent *cervecerías* (breweries) that have tasting rooms in Tijuana, and the old Plaza Fiesta mall has reinvented itself as a collection of small beer tasting rooms, drawing breweries from Mexicali, Ensenada, and Tijuana to open up shop there. Many of the region's

battered fish tacos in Ensenada

best breweries have now opened their own tasting rooms along Avenida Revolución, such as beloved Border Psycho and Insurgente.

Ensenada

There are a handful of craft breweries in Ensenada that have their own tasting rooms, many with ocean views. Some, such as Wendlandt and Doble C, are located in downtown Ensenada, while others like Agua Mala are located north of town in El Sauzal.

WINE

Just inland from the town of Ensenada is Mexico's bourgeoning wine region. In Valle de Guadalupe, east of Ensenada, there are over 150 wineries and a growing number of *campestre restaurants* where the food is cooked over wood fires. The result is a region being recognized worldwide for its rustic but charming atmosphere, beautiful boutique wineries, and gourmet restaurants like Finca Altozano and Corazón de Tierra. South of Ensenada are two more wine regions: Valle de la Grulla, smaller and lesser-known than Valle de Guadalupe but quickly making a name for itself, and Valle de Santo Tomas, home to the oldest winery in Baja California.

La Bufadora, a natural sea geyser

fresh local seafood at Ensenada's Mercado de Mariscos

and grab a ceviche tostada at the famous **La Guerrerense** food cart. Check into your hotel just north of town at **Torre Lucerna** or **Las Rosas** and take some time to enjoy the pool area and the beautiful sunset over the Pacific. Enjoy craft cocktails and dinner at **Manzanilla** restaurant.

Day 2

Spend the morning catching waves. Experienced surfers will enjoy the break at **San Miguel,** while beginners can take a lesson with **Surf Ensenada.** Post-surf, grab some fish tacos at **Tacos El Fenix** for lunch. Then spend time discovering some of Ensenada's craft breweries like **Agua Mala** and **Wendlandt.** When you get hungry, head to **El Trailero,** one of Ensenada's most popular taco stands, open 24/7.

Day 3

Get an early start and drive south out of Ensenada to the **Antigua Ruta del Vino** in **Valle de la Grulla.** Savor **wine-tastings** at **MD Vinos** and **Palafox.** Then head to the **Valle de Santo Tomás** to visit the first winery in Baja California, **Bodegas de Santo Tomás,** established in 1888. Return to Ensenada to have a memorable dinner at **Cocina Madre.**

Day 4

Have an early breakfast at **Casa Marcelo** before driving one hour south of town to check out Ensenada's natural sea geyser, **La Bufadora.** Enjoy the beautiful drive along the way, and when you get there, do some artisanal shopping at the stalls that line the street out to the geyser. Then drive north on Mexico 1 back up to the border.

Tijuana

With a gritty honesty and buzzing energy,

Tijuana is both the largest city on the Baja peninsula and also the most misunderstood. The raw vitality of Tijuana hits you as soon as you cross the border from San Diego, and it's something that people either love or hate. The city is full of neglected buildings punctuated with graffiti and street art and avenues crazed with disorderly traffic. It's also a city brimming with world-class art and culture, fascinating history, and incredible cuisine—from street carts to fine dining.

Tijuana first came to the attention of Americans during Prohibition, when it was a playground for U.S. citizens indulging in the drinking and gambling that were outlawed on the other side of the border. Tijuana maintained its party city image over the years, in later

Highlights

Look for ★ to find recommended sights, activities, dining, and lodging.

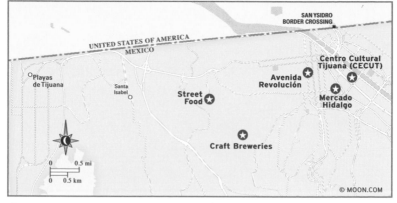

★ **Take a walk down busy Avenida Revolución,** buzzing with restaurants, breweries, shops, and the city's famous *pasajes* (page 27).

★ **Catch an art exhibition** or an IMAX show at **Centro Cultural Tijuana (CECUT),** Tijuana's impressive cultural center (page 32).

★ **Shop at Mercado Hidalgo,** the city's famous market, for fresh produce and artisanal goods (page 32).

★ **Sample Tijuana's craft brewery scene,** which echoes the one just over the border in San Diego and is gaining a strong following from both locals and visitors (page 38).

★ **Get a taste** of some of the best **street food** in the world, from tacos to tortas, tamales, and tostadas (page 42).

decades crawling with college students and young members of the U.S. military who came to take advantage of the young drinking age, dance clubs, bars, and anything-goes attitude.

All of that has changed. When the violence of the drug wars started ramping up in Mexico the late 2000s, the tourists stopped coming to Tijuana. One by one the businesses that relied on tourism shuttered their doors, and the city grew quiet. But then something beautiful happened. A cultural renaissance took place as the Tijuanenses rebuilt their city as a mecca for chefs, artists, and entrepreneurs. Businesses converted to art galleries, craft breweries, and high-tech offices. New restaurants started opening each week with unbelievably creative and delicious local cuisine. And the tourists eventually began to return as well. With its new culinary and cultural reputation, Tijuana is now drawing trendsetting crowds from both sides of the border.

PLANNING YOUR TIME

Because Tijuana is just across the border from San Diego, Southern Californians frequently explore the city in a day trip. A weekend will give you enough time to check out the city's main sights and allow ample opportunity to eat and drink at some of the best spots in the city.

ORIENTATION

The main tourist areas in Tijuana are Zona Centro and Zona Río. Zona Centro comprises Avenida Revolución and is home to many restaurants, breweries, and cafés. Zona Río is adjacent and just to the east of Zona Centro and is where CECUT and a number of other tourist attractions are located. The El Chaparral San Ysidro border crossing is located in Zona Río. West of downtown Tijuana is Playas de Tijuana, where restaurants and bars are clustered along the coast.

Sights

ZONA CENTRO

The buzzing energy of **Zona Centro,** Tijuana's downtown area, is centered on Avenida Revolución.

TOP EXPERIENCE

★ Avenida Revolución

A trip to Tijuana isn't complete without spending time on one of the city's most famous streets: **Avenida Revolución,** running through Zona Centro. Affectionately dubbed "Revu" by locals, the large avenue anchors the tourist zone and stays busy night and day with locals and visitors who come to take advantage of many of the great restaurants, bars, breweries, and shops that Tijuana has to offer. While the street was once home to all of the dance clubs and

nightlife of the city, most of those businesses have become artisanal restaurants, craft breweries, art galleries, and Tijuana's famous *pasajes.*

While many of the more touristy signs of Tijuana's past are slowly disappearing, you'll still spot the town's famous **zonkeys** on Revolución. These donkeys, painted with black and white stripes to look like zebras, have been ready and waiting for photo ops with tourists since 1914.

Pasajes Rodríguez and Gomez

Avenida Revolución's *pasajes* are enclosed alleyways supporting small art galleries, cafés, bars, and shops. **Pasajes Rodríguez and Gomez** are the two most well known, located across the street from one another on Revolución between Calles 3 and 4. They're

---

Previous: Mercado Hidalgo, Tijuana's famous produce market; Telefónica Gastro Park, offering a wide range of food stalls and craft beer; taco from a Tijuana taco stand.

Downtown Tijuana

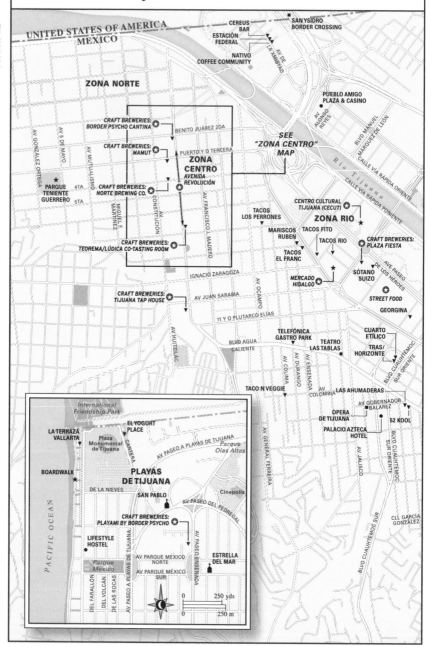

UNITED STATES OF AMERICA
MEXICO

CEREUS BAR
ESTACIÓN FEDERAL
NATIVO COFFEE COMMUNITY
SAN YSIDRO BORDER CROSSING
AV DE LA AMISTAD

ZONA NORTE

PUEBLO AMIGO PLAZA & CASINO
AV ALONSO REYES
BLVD MANUEL MARQUEZ DE LEON

CRAFT BREWERIES: BORDER PSYCHO CANTINA
BENITO JUÁREZ 2DA
SEE "ZONA CENTRO" MAP
CALLE VÍA RÁPIDA ORIENTE
Río Tijuana
CALLE VÍA RÁPIDA PONIENTE

CRAFT BREWERIES: MAMUT
PUERTO Y O TERCERA
ZONA CENTRO
AVENIDA REVOLUCIÓN

AV GONZÁLEZ ORTEGA
AV 5 DE MAYO
AV MUTUALISMO

PARQUE TENIENTE GUERRERO
4TA
5TA

CRAFT BREWERIES: NORTE BREWING CO.
MIGUEL F. MARTÍNEZ
AV CONSTITUCIÓN
AV FRANCISCO I. MADERO

CENTRO CULTURAL TIJUANA (CECUT)
ZONA RIO

TACOS LOS PERRONES
MARISCOS RUBEN
TACOS FITO
TACOS RIO
CRAFT BREWERIES: PLAZA FIESTA

CRAFT BREWERIES: TEOREMA/LÚDICA CO-TASTING ROOM
TACOS EL FRANC

IGNACIO ZARAGOZA
MERCADO HIDALGO
SÓTANO SUIZO
AV PASEO DE LOS HEROES

CRAFT BREWERIES: TIJUANA TAP HOUSE
AV JUAN SARABIA
AV OCAMPO
STREET FOOD
GEORGINA

11 Y O PLUTARCO ELÍAS

AV HUITZILAC
TELEFÓNICA GASTRO PARK
BLVD AGUA CALIENTE
TEATRO LAS TABLAS
CUARTO ETÍLICO
TRAS/ HORIZONTE
BLVD CUAUHTÉMOC SUR ORIENTE

AV DURANGO
AV ENSENADA
AV COLIMA

TACO N VEGGIE
AV COLOMBIA
LAS AHUMADERAS

ÓPERA DE TIJUANA
AV GOBERNADOR BALAREZ
52 KOOL

PALACIO AZTECA HOTEL
BLVD CUAUHTÉMOC SUR ORIENTE
AV JALISCO

CLL GARCÍA GONZÁLEZ

BLVD CUAUHTÉMOC SUR

Inset map

International Friendship Park

LA TERRAZA VALLARTA
EL YOGURT PLACE
Plaza Monumental de Tijuana
CANTERA
AV PASEO A PLAYAS DE TIJUANA
Parque Olas Altas

BOARDWALK

PLAYAS DE TIJUANA
DE LA NIEVES
SAN PABLO
Cinepolis
AV PASEO DEL PEDREGAL

PACIFIC OCEAN

AV GENERAL FERREIRA

CRAFT BREWERIES: PLAYAMI BY BORDER PSYCHO

LIFESTYLE HOSTEL

AV PASEO ENSENADA

Parque México

ESTRELLA DEL MAR

DEL FARALLÓN
DEL VOLCÁN
DE LAS ROCAS
AV PASEO A PLAYAS DE TIJUANA

AV PARQUE MÉXICO NORTE
AV PARQUE MÉXICO SUR

0   250 yds
0   250 m

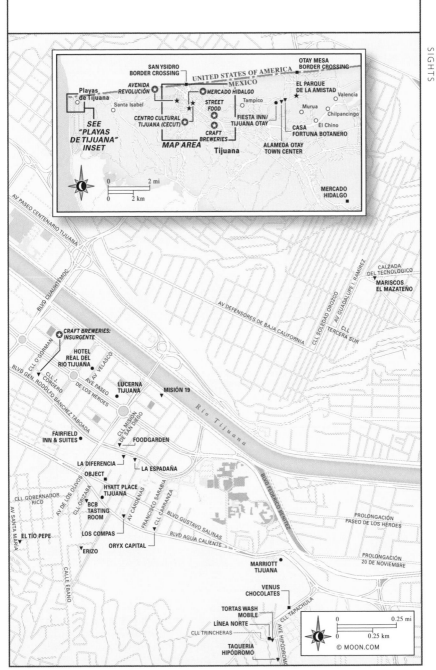

Best Restaurants and Accommodations

RESTAURANTS

★ **Verde y Crema:** Savory dishes, a chic atmosphere, and friendly service keep locals and foodies coming back to this Tijuana favorite (page 40).

★ **La Justina:** This gastropub on Avenida Revolución serves well-crafted food and cocktails (page 41).

★ **Los Compas:** This small but excellent eatery is run by two of Mexico's top chefs, who bring a fresh take to traditional Mexican dishes made with corn (page 42).

★ **Las Ahumaderas:** Also dubbed "taco alley," this collection of taco stands has been serving up TJ's favorite street food since 1960 (page 42).

★ **Misión 19:** Chef Javier Plascencia's sleek, upscale restaurant offers some of the best dining in Baja (page 45).

ACCOMMODATIONS

★ **One Bunk:** Hipsters will love the cool vibe and the central location of these accommodations located right on Avenida Revolución (page 47).

★ **Grand Hotel Tijuana:** Visitors can look forward to luxury accommodations and personalized service in the heart of Tijuana's Zona Río (page 48).

★ **Hyatt Place Tijuana:** Travelers will feel comfortably right at home with all of the services and amenities at this large hotel (page 48).

★ **K Tower Urban Boutique Hotel:** Luxurious finishes and amenities keep upscale clientele happy at this modern hotel (page 48).

covered in vibrant street art with impressive murals from some of Tijuana's best artists. The *pasajes* generally attract a young, bohemian crowd and come alive in the evenings and on weekends.

ART GALLERIES

Located in Pasaje Rodríguez, the small gallery **206 Arte Contemporáneo** (Ave. Revolución #942, no tel., www.206artecontemporaneo. com, 4pm-7pm Thurs.-Fri., 3pm-6pm Sat.) is home to rotating exhibits as well as workshops and lectures.

Tijuana Arch and Plaza Santa Cecilia

At the northern end of Avenida Revolución is a landmark visible from most parts of Tijuana. The large **Tijuana Arch,** similar to the one that graces the skyline of St. Louis, was built to celebrate the new millennium in 2000 and has since become one of the city's most recognized landmarks. Tucked away near the arch is **Plaza Santa Cecilia,** home to shops and carts selling souvenirs and handicrafts as well as small restaurants and bars, cafés, and pharmacies.

Parque Teniente Guerrero

Located a few blocks west of the hustle and bustle of Avenida Revolución is **Parque Teniente Guerrero** (Calle 3ra and Ave. 5 de Mayo), where mature trees offer substantial shade, and nice benches surround a central

Zona Centro

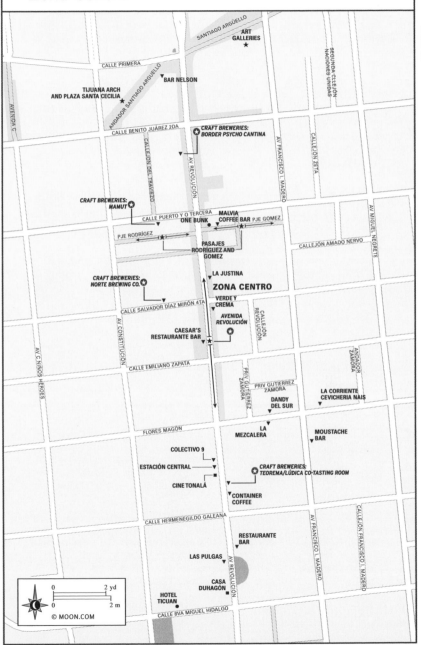

SANTIAGO ARGÜELLO

ART
GALLERIES ★

SEGUNDA CALLEJÓN
NACIONES UNIDAS

CALLE PRIMERA

BAR NELSON

AVENIDA C

ANDADOR SANTIAGO ARGÜELLO

TIJUANA ARCH
AND PLAZA SANTA CECILIA ★

CALLE BENITO JUÁREZ 2DA

AV FRANCISCO I. MADERO

CALLEJÓN ZETA

CRAFT BREWERIES:
BORDER PSYCHO CANTINA ✪

CALLEJÓN DEL TRAVIEZO

AV REVOLUCIÓN

CRAFT BREWERIES:
MAMUT ✪

CALLE PUERTO Y O TERCERA
ONE BUNK

MALVIA
COFFEE BAR PJE GOMEZ

AV MIGUEL NEGRETE

PJE RODRÍGUEZ ★

PASAJES
RODRÍGUEZ AND
GOMEZ

CALLEJÓN AMADO NERVO

CRAFT BREWERIES:
NORTE BREWING CO. ✪

LA JUSTINA

AV CONSTITUCIÓN

CALLE SALVADOR DÍAZ MIRÓN 4TA

ZONA CENTRO

VERDE Y
CREMA

CALLEJÓN
REVOLUCIÓN

*Avenida
Revolución*

AV C NIÑOS HÉROES

CAESAR'S
RESTAURANTE BAR ★

*AVENIDA
REVOLUCIÓN* ✪

CALLE EMILIANO ZAPATA

PRIV GUTIERREZ
ZAMORA

PRIV GUTIERREZ
ZAMORA

ANDADOR
ZAMORA

LA CORRIENTE
CEVICHERIA NAIS

DANDY
DEL SUR

FLORES MAGÓN

LA
MEZCALERA

MOUSTACHE
BAR

COLECTIVO 9

ESTACIÓN CENTRAL

CINE TONALÁ

CRAFT BREWERIES:
TEOREMA/LÚDICA CO-TASTING ROOM ✪

AV FRANCISCO I. MADERO

CALLEJÓN FRANCISCO I. MADERO

CONTAINER
COFFEE

CALLE HERMENEGILDO GALEANA

RESTAURANTE
BAR

LAS PULGAS

AV REVOLUCIÓN

CASA
DUHAGÓN

HOTEL
TICUAN

0   2 yd
0   2 m

© MOON.COM

CALLE 8VA MIGUEL HIDALGO

zocalo. The small park has a playground for kids and nice lawns and tables for picnicking.

ZONA RÍO

The **Zona Río neighborhood** is a fashionable middle-class area where many of Tijuana's restaurants, bars, and shops are located. The large Paseo de los Héroes is the heart of the neighborhood. The CECUT, Mercado Hidalgo, Plaza Río shopping mall, and Plaza Fiesta beer-tasting rooms all call this area home.

★ Centro Cultural Tijuana (CECUT)

The **Centro Cultural Tijuana (CECUT)** (Paseo de los Héroes 9350, tel. 664/687-9600, www.cecut.gob.mx, 10am-7pm daily, US$3) is a distinctive landmark thanks to the large spherical planetarium (that now functions as an IMAX theater) that fronts the building. The cultural center houses permanent and temporary exhibitions, art galleries, a 1,000-seat performing arts theater, the aforementioned IMAX theater, a café, bookstore, and shops. World-class rotating exhibitions feature art and photography by local and visiting artists. Many of Tijuana's large events and festivals take place at CECUT. There's a restaurant, **Cubo Bistro** (tel. 664/210-7455, www.cubobistro.com, 11am-10pm Tues.-Thurs., 11am-11pm Fri.-Sat., 11am-8pm Sun.), where visitors can enjoy a wide range of dishes from salad to pastas or steak. On Sunday there's free admission to everything except the IMAX theater and the concert hall.

★ Mercado Hidalgo

Since 1955, restaurateurs and other Tijuanenses have been buying their produce at Tijuana's best market: **Mercado Hidalgo** (Sanchez Taboada 9351, tel. 664/684-0485, 6am-6pm daily). It's a popular spot for travelers to browse the regional produce and products and eat at some of the nearby taco stands. Peruse the stands full of piles of dried chilies, local spices, regional cheeses, and fresh fruits and vegetables. When you're hungry, grab a tamale, *chicharrón, carnitas,* or taco from any of the stands in the market. Just outside the market on the surrounding streets are a number of famous taco, *birria,* and seafood stands as well. There's parking in the center of the market (US$1).

Art Galleries

Located near Hipódromo, **La Caja Galeria** (Callejón de las Moras #118-B, tel. 664/686-6791, www.lacajagaleria.com, 10am-6pm Mon.-Fri.) is one of Tijuana's most beloved art galleries, representing some of the city's best artists as well as some international artists. Its front covered by striking and vibrant murals, this former industrial warehouse was renovated with reused materials to house the rotating exhibits in the sleek gallery, as well as to host workshops and classes.

PLAYAS DE TIJUANA

Separated geographically from the rest of the city, the community of **Playas de Tijuana** is situated on the beach on the west side of town. It's a peaceful area, with a very different vibe from the rest of the city. The large beach stretches out in the background with small restaurants and cafés on the boardwalk looking out at the Pacific. Behind the boardwalk, the Plaza Monumental Bullring by the Sea sits quiet for most of the year except when the bullfights take place certain summer weekends. To get to Playas from Zona Centro in Tijuana, take the Mexico 1D scenic toll road west and exit at Playas de Tijuana. Playas is about 10 kilometers (6.2 miles) and a 15-minute drive from Zona Centro.

Boardwalk

South of the international border fence, the boardwalk heads along the beach, lined with colorful street art and a string of cafés, bars, restaurants on one side and the Pacific Ocean on the other.

1: Mercado Hidalgo 2: produce at Mercado Hidalgo 3: Pasaje Rodríguez, home to cafés, galleries, and vibrant street art 4: Centro Cultural Tijuana (CECUT)

El Parque de la Amistad

It's hard to ignore the rust-colored border fence that separates Tijuana from San Diego and runs all the way into the Pacific Ocean. **El Parque de la Amistad or Friendship Park** (www.friendshippark.org) sits beneath the lighthouse just adjacent the beach. The park has both a Mexico and a U.S. side. This is a spot where families and close friends reunite from either side of the fence. The park is open 24 hours on the Tijuana side, but is only open 10am-2pm Saturday-Sunday on the U.S. side. On the Tijuana side is the famous "Monument 258" and a small garden.

Recreation

BEACHES

Playas de Tijuana is home to Tijuana's **main beach.** Located right on the border with the United States, the large and beautiful beach is most famous for the border fence that continues into the ocean. There's a nice boardwalk lined with cafés, bars, and restaurants that all boast nice ocean views.

Visitors to Tijuana can also easily visit Rosarito Beach, which is a 25-minute drive from Playas de Tijuana.

SPECTATOR SPORTS

Tijuana has three professional sports teams. Arguably the most popular is its *fútbol* (soccer) team, **Club Tijuana Xoloitzcuintles de Caliente** (www.xolos.com.mx), nicknamed the Xolos. The 33,000-seat stadium, **Estadio Caliente** (Boulevard Agua Caliente), fills with spirited fans and the entire city is abuzz when there's a game. Tijuana's baseball team, the **Toros** (www.torosdetijuana.com, tickets US$2-7), play in the Mexican League. The baseball stadium, **Estadio Chevron** (Calle Estadio Tijuana s/n, tel. 664/635-5600), is located in eastern Tijuana. The city's basketball team, the **Zonkeys** (www.tijuanazonkeys.com.mx), play at **Tijuana Auditorio Fausto Gutiérrez Moreno** (Boulevard Gustavo Díaz Ordaz, tel. 664/321-6385, tickets US$8-24).

Recognized for its colorful costumes and masks, **Lucha Libre** (www.facebook.com/LuchaLibreDeTijuana) wrestling takes place at the Auditorio Municipal Fausto Gutierrez

the Playas de Tijuana boardwalk

The History of Friendship Park

In 1849, following the Mexican-American War, a monument was put in place to signify the new international boundary between the United States and Mexico established by the Treaty of Guadalupe Hidalgo. This location next to the Pacific Ocean, called Monument Mesa, is considered the birthplace of the border. Crossings between the two countries were largely unregulated at this time, and only the monument demarcated the United States and Mexico.

A refurbished monument was placed in this spot in 1894. This new monument was dubbed Monument 258 (there are 258 of these monuments along the 2,000-mile Mexico-U.S. border) and is the one that stands there today. Its base sits directly on the international boundary, inscribed "Boundary of the United States" on one side and "Punto Límite de la Republica de México" on the other.

The border here has changed significantly over the years, from a wide-open space to a wire demarcation to a fence to the wall that stands there today. The space has always been a meeting place for separated friends and family, who reunite and spend time together in Friendship Park.

Moreno, Tijuana's municipal auditorium, on Friday nights. The controversial sport of **bullfighting** has many advocates pushing to ban it permanently from the city, but attempts to do so have failed thus far. The season takes place each summer at the iconic bullring by the sea in Playas de Tijuana and at a new bullring, Caliente Plaza de Toros, situated near the Hipódromo.

ORGANIZED TOURS

The burgeoning interest in Tijuana has fostered a number of tour outfitters that lead unique culinary and activity-based excursions to the city. Tijuana is a large city that can feel daunting to navigate on your own, so many day-trippers utilize these organized tours. Most tour operators will accommodate visitors departing from San Diego or those who are already in Tijuana. **Turista Libre** (www.turistalibre.com) attracts a young crowd that enjoys visiting destinations tourists normally don't make it to on their own, such as water parks, sporting events, and markets.

Baja Test Kitchen (www.bajatestkitchen.com) focuses on Tijuana's culinary side with a variety of food and craft beer tours. Its "Taste of TJ" tour visits the famous Mercado Hidalgo, features some of the best street food in Tijuana, and samples craft beer. They have regularly scheduled group tours available weekly and can also accommodate private groups.

Let's Go Clandestino (www.letsgoclandestino.net) leads monthly group tours to Tijuana and surrounding areas with a focus on regional food and drink.

Entertainment and Shopping

PERFORMING ARTS

CECUT (Paseo de los Héroes 9350, tel. 664/687-9600, www.cecut.gob.mx) is home to a few different theaters and stages that host frequent live performances such as opera, orchestra, dance, and theater.

Tijuana's **Casa de la Cultura** (Ave. Paris 7 Lisboa #5, tel. 664/687-2604, www.imac. tijuana.gob.mx) is a grand building with a nice theater that hosts performances in dance, live music, and theater. They also offer classes and workshops.

Film, food, and drink come together at **Cine Tonalá** (Ave. Revolución 1303, tel. 664/688-0118, http://tj.cinetonala.mx). Catch dinner and a drink on the upstairs terrace overlooking Revolución before catching an indie movie. The venue also hosts other performing arts like dance, comedy, dramatic performances, and live music.

For a smaller, more intimate venue, **Teatro las Tablas** (Calle Unión 2191, tel. 664/382-6183, www.teatrolastablas.com) is home to a resident theater company and independent productions that play to the 35-seat audience.

Each summer, the Colonia Libertad neighborhood is home to **Opera en La Calle** (Opera in the Street), put on by **Opera de Tijuana** (www.operadetijuana.org), which has performances throughout the year. Opera en La Calle is a free street performance that takes place on Calle 5ta; it's held on one Saturday evening in July with hundreds of artists performing throughout the evening.

NIGHTLIFE

Just the name *Tijuana* carries connotations of its past notoriety for dance clubs, tequila shots, and drunk college students. You won't find much of that anymore; in the past decade, many of the dance clubs have closed and the city has reinvented itself with and a more cultured and respectable nightlife scene.

In Zona Centro, **Calle Sexta** (6th Street) off of Revolución is where many of the bars can be found. At **Dandy del Sur** (Calle Sexta, tel. 664/688-0052, 10am-3am daily) you'll get a downright local dive bar experience. Across the street is **La Mezcalera** (Calle Sexta 8267, tel. 664/688-0384, 6pm-2am Tues.-Sat.), where local hipsters go to sip on mezcal.

A few blocks away near the arch on Revolución, the historic **Bar Nelson** (Ave. Revolución 721, tel. 664/685-4596, noon-2am daily) is a retro spot for cocktails. Try the "Especial," a salt-rimmed highball with lime, white rum, 7UP, and Coca-Cola.

For those still looking for the large dance clubs that used to dominate Zona Centro, **Las Pulgas** (Revolución 1127, tel. 664/685-9594, www.laspulgas.mx, 4pm-6am daily) is located on Revolución between Calles 7 and 8. The club has been one of the top spots for nightlife in Tijuana since 1988.

The lively **Sótano Suizo** (Paseo de los Héroes 9415, tel. 664/684-8834, 1pm-2am Tues.-Sun.) in Plaza Fiesta in Zona Río is a fun spot for beers or cocktails. If you order their famously huge half-meter hot dog, be ready to share it with a friend (or two!).

For live music, hip locals head to **Moustache Bar** (Calle Madero 1250, 2pm-midnight Sun. and Tues.-Thurs., 2pm-2am Fri.-Sat.) on the weekends. There's usually no cover, and the patio out back is lively when the weather is nice.

Located behind a hidden door in Oryx Capital restaurant is **Nórtico** (Agua Caliente 10750, tel. 664/611-0589), Tijuana's first modern speakeasy, where craft cocktails are served in a swanky and cozy setting. You'll need to make a reservation; only a few seats at the bar are reserved for walk-ins.

Another speakeasy in town is **Cuarto Etílico** (Rio Colorado #9650, U.S. tel. 619/616-1109, 7pm-1am Thurs., 7pm-2am Fri.-Sat.). Located behind the restaurant Tras/Horizonte, the clandestine bar serves artisanal cocktails while foreign films play in the background. The space only seats about 20 people, so call ahead to make a reservation.

Downstairs from Javier Plascencia's Misión 19 restaurant is **Bar 20** (tel. 664/634-2493, 3pm-11pm Mon.-Thurs., 3pm-1:30am Fri.-Sat.), offering craft cocktails. Sip on cocktails like the "Mezcalero" or "Sangria 20" in the sleek and swanky setting.

In La Cacho neighborhood, **Public House TJ** (Miguel Alemán Valdez #2664, tel. 664/681-7625, 3pm-11pm Mon.-Wed., 3pm-1am Thurs.-Fri., 1pm-1am Sat., 10:30am-10pm Sun.) is a locals spot with a variety of local craft beers on tap and gastropub fare. Located in a historic old house, the setting is cozy and inviting. Grab a seat at the bar, or one of the tables inside or outdoors. They are also open for Sunday brunch.

For a craft beer experience in a bar setting,

1: Cine Tonalá, where film, food, and drink come together 2: Teorema/Lúdica Co-Tasting Room 3: Public House TJ 4: Mamut, with a view of downtown Tijuana

BCB Tasting Room (Orizaba 3003-E5, tel. 664/699-3028, noon-2am Mon.-Sat., noon-midnight Sun.) has an impressive 42 beers on tap and about 300 more in bottles. The industrial but intimate space features local craft beers from both Baja and San Diego.

Another spot to try craft beers from all over Baja is **República Malta** (José Gorostiza #1143, tel. 664/363-7011, 4pm-midnight Tues.-Wed., 4pm-2am Thurs.-Sat., 2pm-10pm Sun.). They serve food and often have live music from local bands.

In the Otay area of Tijuana, **Casa Fortuna Botanero** (Lázaro Cárdenas #17102, tel. 664/623-2111, 11am-11pm Tues.-Wed., 11am-midnight Thurs.-Sat., 8am-8pm Sun.) is a fresh new space serving craft cocktails and *botanas* (snacks). Classic drinks like margaritas are accompanied by other agave liquor creations like the namesake Casa Fortuna cocktail made with mezcal and *tepache*, a fermented pineapple drink. The food menu features shared plates and a variety of tacos.

TOP EXPERIENCE

★ CRAFT BREWERIES

Tijuana is one of three locations on the peninsula where the craft beer scene is gaining popularity (the other two spots are Ensenada and Mexicali). It's no wonder, since the city borders San Diego, which many consider the craft beer capital of the United States.

The beer scene here consists of very small microbreweries, many too small to have their own tasting rooms. Enter Tijuana's **Plaza Fiesta** (Paseo de los Héroes 10001, tel. 664/200-2960, www.facebook.com/plazafiestatijuana), a defunct mall that sat basically deserted for years until microbreweries started moving in to provide folks with a way to sample their output. Breweries from Tijuana, Mexicali, and Ensenada, including Border Psycho, Fauna, Tres B, Insurgente, and Mamut, have tasting rooms in Plaza Fiesta, making this the go-to spot in northern Baja to get a taste of the peninsula's craft beer scene. There are no set hours, but most breweries

open around 5pm or 6pm. The scene skews young with loud music and boisterous crowds, especially on the weekends. A more refined beer-drinking experience can be found at the individual tasting rooms.

Mamut (Calle 3 8161, tel. 664/685-0137, 10am-midnight Mon.-Sat., noon-8pm Sun.) has its own tasting room outside of Plaza Fiesta. One part of the brewery is in Pasaje Rodriguez, and the other part (with a separate entrance) is on the 2nd floor of the outside block with an outdoor patio open to the downtown buzz of Tijuana. They have a large assortment of tasty craft beers as well as house-made pizzas and other snacks. They've recently added a mezcal bar.

Just down the street from Mamut is **Norte Brewing Co.** (Calle 4ta, tel. 664/638-4891, www.nortebrewing.com, 2pm-midnight Mon.-Sat., 2pm-9pm Sun.), a craft brewery featuring bold beers and epic views of Tijuana. The brewery is housed in what was once a strip club, and names of beers such as "Escort," "Cougar," and "Penthouse" reflect the location's past. The brewery can be difficult to find—it's on the fifth level of the Foreign Club parking structure. Entrance to the parking structure is on Calle 4 between Revolución and Constitución.

Just down the street from Norte Brewing Co. on Revolución is **Teorema/Lúdica Co-Tasting Room** (Ave. Revolución 1332, tel. 664/210-0390, 5pm-midnight Mon.-Wed., noon-midnight Thurs.-Sat., 3pm-10pm Sun.). The tasting room features craft beer from two breweries, Teorema and Lúdica, and serves up tasters and pints in a sleek and modern space.

Also on Revolución is the **Border Psycho Cantina** (Ave. Revolución 821, tel. 664/976-6359, www.borderpsychobrewery.com, 11am-midnight daily), a newer outpost for one of Tijuana's oldest and best craft breweries. The large space has dozens of beers on tap and serves pub food as well. The brewery also has an outlet in Playas de Tijuana, **Playami by Border Psycho** (Paseo Ensenada #795, tel. 664/524-7449, 8am-midnight Tues.-Sat., 8pm-10pm Sun., 2pm-10pm Mon.), with a beer garden serving craft beers from other local breweries in addition to their own. It also serves wine, coffee, and food.

The brewery Cervecería Tijuana now has a new presence on Revolución in the form of **Tijuana Tap House** (Ave. Revolución 1010, tel. 664/200-2894, 1pm-midnight Tues.-Sun.). Draft and bottled house beers are available, as well as guest brews. There's a menu offering bar food such as hot dogs and tacos.

One of Tijuana's most beloved craft breweries, **Insurgente** (Juan Cordero 10021, tel. 664/634-1242, www.cervezainsurgente.com, 4pm-midnight Thurs.-Sat., 1pm-9pm Sun.) has a sleek tasting room in Zona Río with over 20 of their beers on tap as well as an upper-level terrace with views of the city. They also have a new taproom in Zona Centro, **Insurgente Tap Room Centro** (Ave. Revolución 933, no tel., 1pm-midnight Tues.-Thurs., 1pm-2am Fri.-Sat., 1pm-10pm Sun.).

EVENTS

Tijuana is a city that thrives on festivals and events. Almost every weekend brings culinary fests, art fairs, beer festivals, and concerts. The state tourism website, www.bajanorte.com, is a great resource for Tijuana events. The **Baja** **Culinary Fest** (www.bajaculinaryfest.com) in October is a series of dinners, workshops, and parties highlighting Tijuana's burgeoning culinary scene. **Entijuanarte** (www.fundacionentijuanarte.org) is a large cultural and arts fest that takes place every fall at CECUT with art booths, live entertainment, food, and drinks.

SHOPPING

For artisan crafts and souvenirs, **Avenida Revolución** has a number of small shops as well as a collection of stalls near the arch in **Plaza Santa Cecilia.** Don't be afraid to bargain for a lower price. Tijuana's large **Plaza Río Mall** (Ave. Paseo de los Héroes 96 and 98, www.plazariotijuana.com.mx) in Zona Río has a Sears, Cinépolis movie theater, and a number of specialty stores.

The **Mercado de Artesanías** (between Negrete and Ocampo north of Calle 2) is an area of shops where you can find artisan goods for prices lower than what you'll pay at the souvenir stands. Leather shoes, colorful Talavera pottery, glassware, home decor items, and other arts and crafts are all available here.

Right in the heart of Revolución, showroom **Casa Duhagón** (Ave. Revolución 1143, tel. 664/638-4849, www.casaduhagon.

shopping off of Avenida Revolución

com, 10am-6pm Mon.-Fri.) offers a modern selection of colorful accessories, art, and furniture. It's a full-service design studio as well.

For a beautifully curated collection of home decor, furniture, and accessories, visit Object (Amado Paniagua 3017, tel. 664/685-1595, www.objectmexico.com, 10am-8pm Mon.-Fri., 11am-7pm Sat.). Everything sold in the store is made by a Mexican artist or designer. Another home decor store, Línea Norte (Calle Trincheras #25, tel. 664/859-6896, www.linea-norte.com, 10am-7pm Mon.-Fri. 10am-2pm Sat.) specializes in tableware and glassware with a chic selection that any home entertainer will adore.

For a tasty treat that also makes a great gift, Venus Chocolates (Tapacula #5-A, tel. 664/972-9338, 10am-9pm Mon.-Fri., 10am-8pm Sat., 11am-7pm Sun.) in the Hipódromo neighborhood, specializes in exquisite truffles in various flavors indicative of the region (tequila, chile, mezcal, wine from the Valle de Guadalupe) as well as other confections.

If you want to take home a bottle of Mexican wine or some Baja craft beer, head to La Contra (Amado Paniagua 3017, tel. 664/634-2452, www.lacontravinos.com, 11am-8pm Mon.-Tues., 11am-9pm Wed.-Sat., noon-6pm Sun.) or GSalinas (Jalisco 2511, tel. 664/200-2771, www.gsalinasvinos.com, noon-9pm Mon.-Thurs., noon-10pm Fri.-Sat.). You can do tastings at both spots.

Mercado Hidalgo (Sanchez Taboada 9351, tel. 664/684-0485, 6am-6pm daily) not only provides an entertaining way to spend the afternoon exploring one of the city's best markets, but is also a great place to buy fresh produce, local spices, regional cheeses, and souvenirs like pottery, serving ware, and glassware.

Many Tijuanenses cross the border to the United States to visit Las Americas Premium Outlets (4211 Camino de la Plaza, San Diego, CA, U.S. tel. 619/934-8400, www.premiumoutlets.com, 10am-9pm daily) in the San Ysidro district of San Diego. The large mall features outlet stores such as Kate Spade, Armani, J Crew, New Balance, and The North Face as well as a variety of dining options. The Pedestrian West border crossing is located right across the street from the mall, making for a quick and easy crossing to get to and from the mall.

Food

Tijuana has the best food in Baja and is quickly turning into a world-recognized culinary destination. From fine dining to street food, there are plenty of savory options for every budget.

ZONA CENTRO

Mexican

The chic ★ Verde y Crema (Ave. Revolución 1010-A, tel. 664/207-2072, 1pm-11pm Tues.-Wed., 1pm-1am Thurs.-Sat., 1pm-8pm Sun., US$13-15) is the Tijuana restaurant of chef Jair Tellez, who also helms the famous Laja restaurant in the Valle de Guadalupe. The menu changes on a regular basis depending on what's fresh and available but features foods like tacos, tostadas, and sliders with fresh and unique ingredients and flavors.

Seafood

If the weather is warm, sit on the front patio at La Corriente Cevicheria Nais (Calle 6 at Ave. Madero, tel. 664/685-0555, 11am-10pm daily, US$3-10). This hip and casual spot serves great *mariscos*. Order the special red snapper tostada, ahi tuna tostada, or the taco "Kalifornia" with shrimp stuffed into a chile, served in a taco.

Colectivos

In recent years *colectivos,* collections of food

Baja Med

You may hear the term "Baja Med" in reference to the emergent culinary movement in Baja California. The term is actually trademarked by Tijuana chef Miguel Angel Guerrero. It's his way of describing the fusion of fresh regional Baja ingredients, Mexican flavors, and a twist of Mediterranean and Asian influence.

stalls or food trucks, have become popular in Tijuana.

Just off of Revolución is Colectivo 9 (Ave. Revolución, tel. 664/123-1234, www.colectivo9.com, 1pm-8pm Tues.-Thurs., 1pm-10pm Fri.-Sat., 1pm-8pm Sun.), a gathering of nine food stalls. They have an eclectic assortment of food, from burgers to Asian food to empanadas. The *colectivo* can be easy to miss, as it's down a narrow *pasaje*. Watch for the entrance on the west side of the street between Calles 6 and 7.

Located near the PedWest pedestrian crossing, Estación Federal (Larroque 271, tel. 664/514-5894) isn't a traditional *colectivo*, but the mixed-use space is home to a variety of chic food and drink places including Nativo Coffee Community (tel. 664/607-3922, 6:30am-9pm Mon.-Sat., 8:30am-5pm Sun.), Cereus Bar (tel. 664/906-5079, noon-10pm Mon.-Thurs., 11am-1am Fri.-Sat., 11am-10pm Sun.), and Tacos Kokopelli Foodtruck (tel. 664/622-5062, www.kokopelli.mx). The compound is housed in a remodeled gas station and offices that were abandoned in the 1950s.

International

Many people may not know that Tijuana is the original home of the Caesar salad. While the exact details of the story depend on which person you ask, there's no doubt that the salad was invented at Caesar's Restaurante Bar (Ave. Revolución 8190, tel. 664/685-1927, 11:30am-10pm Mon.-Sat., 11:30am-8pm Sun., mains US$15-19), where it's still prepared tableside today. Other dishes like steak, seafood,

and pastas are served in this upscale bistro setting. Owned by the Plascencia family, this institution is worth a stop for a drink at the beautiful large bar or to enjoy one of Tijuana's most famous dishes.

In the heart of Revolución, chic ★ La Justina (Revolución #990 between Calles 3 and 4, tel. 664/638-4936, 2pm-1am Tues.-Thurs., 2pm-2am Fri.-Sat., noon-7pm Sun., mains US$11-15) is a welcome and fresh gastropub culinary experience. Everything on the menu is handcrafted and well executed, from the cocktails to the seasonally changing menu featuring dishes such as bone marrow, pork buns, and fresh seafood. The intimate space is filled with upcycled industrial materials that create a chic atmosphere—wooden tables and chairs, exposed brick walls, rope chandeliers, and hanging Edison bulbs. Weekend evenings are particularly busy, with hip Tijuanenses coming in for craft cocktails and dinner.

The vintage aesthetic at Estación Central (Ave. Revolución 241, tel. 664/688-1017, www.estacioncentraltijuana.com, 8am-10pm Mon., Wed.-Thurs., 8am-1am Fri.-Sat., 9am-8pm Sun.) has made it a popular spot on Revolución for food, cocktails, and coffee. The cantina is anchored by a large marble bar where mixology cocktails are served and an abbreviated bar menu is served. For patrons in the dining room, the extensive menu features classic dishes like oysters Rockefeller and carbonara, juxtaposed with Mexican dishes like octopus and *queso fundido*.

Cafés

Tijuana has a rising artisanal coffee scene, with roasters sourcing beans from Mexico to make the specialty elixir.

Situated in a shipping container on Avenida Revolución, Container Coffee (Ave. Revolución 1348, tel. 664/638-4471, 8am-9pm Mon.-Thurs., 8am-11pm Fri.-Sat.) serves small-batch-roasted coffee sourced from Mexico. They have a patio out front where guests can sip coffee while people-watching on Revu. Just down the street, tucked into Pasaje Gomez, is Malvia Coffee

Bar (Pasaje Gomez local 10, tel. 664/151-6038, 10am-9pm Mon.-Sat., noon-8pm Sun.). The quaint and colorful coffee shop draws a young and hip crowd.

ZONA RÍO
Mexican

Focusing on traditional Mexican dishes and Mexico's heirloom corn, ★ Los Compas (Centro Comercial Rocasa, tel. 664/208-8269, www.loscompastj.com, 1pm-10pm Mon.-Thurs., 1pm-midnight Fri.-Sat., US$12-15) is a fresh restaurant from two of Mexico's hottest young chefs, Mario Peralta and Juan Cabrera. The casual space features traditional Mexican dishes like tlacoyos, chalupas, and tostadas, as well as seafood dishes.

For a traditional Mexican breakfast, locals head to La Espadaña (Blvd. Sánchez Taboada 10813, tel. 664/634-1488, www.espadana.com.mx, 7:30am-10:30pm daily, US$8-11). From traditional posole and huevos ahogados to American-style omelets and hotcakes, the menu is extensive. Breakfast is served daily until 1pm. Don't miss the famous café de olla—Mexico's traditional preparation of coffee with cinnamon and sugar. They also serve lunch and dinner. Dishes include traditional Mexican plates as well as chicken and steaks (no seafood).

Another traditional Mexican restaurant near La Espadaña is La Diferencia (Blvd. Sánchez Taboada 10521, tel. 664/634-7078, 8am-10:30pm Mon.-Sat., 8am-6pm Sun., mains US$8-13). Guests dine in a hacienda-style courtyard surrounding a fountain with Talavera pottery. The traditional Mexican decor creates a welcoming ambience and the perfect setting for dishes like chilaquiles, chicken mole, and arrachera with cactus. The off-street parking and a family-friendly environment make this a comfortable spot for groups of locals and tourists.

For a unique taco experience in a sit-down restaurant, Tras/Horizonte by Kokopelli (Río Colorado 9680, tel. 664/622-5062, www.kokopelli.mx, 1pm-10pm Tues.-Thurs., 1pm-11pm Fri.-Sat., 1pm-7pm Sun., US$3-9) serves tacos with a unique twist on traditional flavors and ingredients. In addition to savory seafood tacos like octopus with melted cheese and pesto are vegetarian options such as the portobello taco with goat cheese and spinach. The menu is rounded out with dishes like aguachile, burgers, and craft cocktails. The funky setting creates a hip and casual vibe. The restaurant started as beloved taco spot Kokopelli, which was out of commission for a while but returned to the streets in 2019 as a taco cart at Estación Federal.

Seafood

For fresh ceviche and seafood, another one of Javier Plascencia's restaurants fits the bill. Erizo (Ave. Sonora 3808, 664/686-2895, www.erizobaja.com, 11am-9pm daily, US$3-8) is an open and airy restaurant with a nautical feel punctuated by boats, oars, and surfboards serving as decor. The menu is full of various tostadas, tacos, and ceviches, such as the special green shrimp ceviche—shrimp with serrano chile, tomatillo, cilantro, chives, and avocado. They also serve mixology cocktails and craft beer.

★ Antojitos and Street Food

Tijuana is home to some of the best street food in the world, from tacos to tortas to tostadas.

Founded in 1960, ★ Las Ahumaderas (Guillermo Prieto 9770) is a series of six adjacent taco stands. Also called "Taco Alley," this is a classic stop for those looking for a taste of street tacos. Carne asada and adobada (al pastor) are the favorites. Grab a seat at the counter and enjoy the experience.

For birria, there are two places near Mercado Hidalgo that are local favorites: Tacos Fito (Francisco Javier Mina 14, 5:30am-1pm daily), specializing in both beef birria and tripa, and Tacos Rio (Calle Guadalupe Victoria, 3am-2pm daily), also serving beef birria.

1: carving off meat for a taco adobada 2: Tras/Horizonte, with a funky vibe and gourmet tacos 3: Estación Federal, home to Cereus Bar and Nativo Coffee Community

Don't miss the tacos *adobada* at Tacos El Franc (Blvd. Sánchez Taboada, Calle 8, tel. 667/142-2955, 4pm-1am Mon.-Thurs., 3pm-3am Fri.-Sat.). A specialty here is the beef *suadero* tacos—a smooth meat taken from between the belly and the leg. Near Tacos El Franc is Mariscos Ruben (Calle 8 and Quintana Roo), a food truck serving delicious Sonoran-style seafood cocktails. Also in this area is Tacos Los Perrones (Sanchez Taboada, tel. 664/865-7360), open 24 hours and famous for its Sonoran-style *arrachera* (skirt steak) *perrones.*

El Tío Pepe (Calle Garcia 9925, tel. 664/972-9999, 7am-7pm daily) is a great spot to get a *torta ahogada* (a torta covered in a chile sauce), a specialty from Guadalajara. They also serve *birria* tacos and *carnitas.*

Taqueria Hipódromo (Ave. Hipódromo 14, tel. 664/686-5275, 8:30am-2am daily) has been serving up carne asada tacos and *mulitas* (two tortillas with cheese and taco filling inside) since 1971. Open until 2am, it's a favorite late-night spot.

Best known for its shrimp *enchilados* (chilied) tacos, Mariscos el Mazateño (Calzada Tecnologico 473-E, tel. 664/607-1377, 7am-8pm daily) also serves up great marlin tacos and tostadas. It can be a trek to the Tomas Aquino neighborhood location, but many foodies think it's worth it.

Serving up tortas since 1964, Tortas Wash Mobile (tel. 664/255-2349, 9am-9pm Mon.-Sat.) is a must for anyone who loves street food. The juicy steak sandwiches are available at their cart on Avenida Jalisco or their stand in Hipódromo.

Vegans can also enjoy the TJ taco scene thanks to Taco N Veggie (Calle Colima at Colombia, tel. 664/164-4615, 9am-3pm Mon.-Sat.), a street taco cart that serves up vegetarian and vegan taco options. With a wide variety of creative options, even meat eaters will love this spot.

Colectivos

The best known of Tijuana's *colectivos* is Foodgarden (Blvd. Rodolfo Sánchez Taboada 10650, tel. 664/634-3206, www. foodgarden.mx, 9am-9pm Mon.-Thurs., 9am-10pm Fri.-Sat., 9am-7pm Sun.), an array of stands from well-established restaurants around the city. The food stalls line the courtyard where guests dine alfresco. The rich and savory *chilaquiles* with white or avocado sauce from Los Chilaquiles stand are a local favorite. Vegetarians will love the tacos or veggie burgers from Veggie Smalls. There's a second location of Foodgarden in the Plaza Río Mall (tel. 664/634-1087) and a third location in the Alameda Otay Town Center (tel. 664/200-1938). There are different food stands in each location.

Telefónica Gastro Park (Blvd. Agua Caliente 8924, tel. 664/684-8782, 8am-10pm daily) also hosts a collection of food stalls. Seating is outdoors, and diners can choose from options like risotto and fish from the Creta truck or homemade sausages from Humo. There's a large indoor brewery space where patrons enjoy relaxing over a pint of craft beer.

International

Chef Miguel Angel Guerrero brings specialties like oyster shooters, carpaccio, *machacas,* and grilled octopus to guests at La Querencia (Ave. Escuadrón 201 #3110, tel. 664/972-9935, 1pm-11pm Mon.-Sat., US$11-16). The sleek setting features touches of stainless steel, wood, brick, and mounted animals, giving it an eclectic feel. Another one of chef Angel Guerrero's restaurants is El Taller (Ave. Rio Yaqui 296, tel. 664/686-3383, 1pm-11pm Tues.-Thurs., 1pm-midnight Fri.-Sat., 1pm-10pm Sun., mains US$9-16). The industrial decor honors the building's history as a garage. Craft pizza, steaks, and fresh fish are on the menu, along with a nice wine selection.

Gastropub Oryx Capital (Blvd. Agua Caliente 10750, tel. 664/686-2807, www. oryxcapital.mx, 2pm-1am Mon.-Sat., US$10-13) has a diverse menu that features Mexican dishes like gourmet tacos and tostadas alongside items such as bone marrow, grilled octopus, artisan mac and cheese, and rib eye.

The Plascencia Dynasty

Caesar's, home of the Caesar salad, is today part of the Plascencia empire.

Ask any Tijuanense who the most influential family in the Tijuana restaurant business is, and they are likely to respond with one name: Plascencia. Starting the empire in 1969 with their Italian restaurant, Giuseppis, the Plascencia family's properties now comprise multiple locations including Caesar's, Villa Saverios, and Casa Plascencia.

Javier Plascencia (son of the family's original restaurateur, Juan José Plascencia) is considered Baja California's most-recognized chef and independently manages his own string of popular restaurants including Misión 19 and Erizo in Tijuana, as well as Finca Altozano in the Valle de Guadalupe.

Speakeasy bar Nórtico is accessed through a hidden door at the back of the restaurant.

Foodies head to ★ **Misión 19** (Misión San Javier 10643, tel. 664/634-2493, www.mision19.com, 1pm-10pm Mon.-Thurs., 1pm-11pm Fri.-Sat., mains US$20) for some of the best fine dining in Baja. Housed in one of Tijuana's most upscale high-rise buildings, the sleek setting and sweeping city views set the scene for the sophisticated menu. Filet mignon, pork belly, bone marrow, octopus, tripe tacos—all are made with fresh ingredients and carefully crafted into savory treats. Reservations should be made in advance for this special dining experience.

Crowds flock to **Georgina** (Antonio Caso 2020, tel. 664/684-8156, www.georgina.mx, 8am-2pm and 5pm-10pm Mon.-Sat.,

8am-4pm Sun., US$14-17) for a modern twist on Italian food. The refreshing, minimalist atmosphere is dressed in tones of white. Delicate pasta dishes and a range of savory meat options grace the menu. They serve brunch and dinner every day except Sunday, when only brunch is served. Be aware that they close for a few hours each afternoon between brunch and dinner service.

The hip atmosphere and savory dishes at **52 Kool** (Miguel Alemán Valdez #2612, tel. 664/686-3361, www.52kool.mx, 1pm-11pm Tues.-Sat., 10am-6pm Sun., US$9-13) have made it a fast favorite among patrons from both sides of the border. Despite initial impressions, the name has nothing to do with the word "cool," but rather has Mayan origins meaning "milpa," a traditional small

vegetable garden centered on corn. The dishes are beautifully presented and range from Mexican to Italian to steaks. There is a good selection of Baja wines and craft beers as well as cocktails.

You don't have to be a health food fiend to appreciate **Alma Verde** (Ave. Brasil #8930, tel. 664/634-1716, www.almaverde.com.mx, 7am-10pm Mon.-Sat., 7am-6pm Sun. , US$5-7), where the ingredients are fresh, the food is healthy, and the atmosphere is bright and airy. It offers brunch, salad, sandwiches, espresso, cold-pressed juices, smoothies, and vegan options. There's a second location near the Hipódromo.

For breakfast, hip locals head to **Mantequilla** (Praga #4085, tel. 664/526-6458, 8:30am-1pm daily, US$5-7), which serves up dishes such as variations on eggs Benedict, avocado toast, and chilaquiles. With a bright and vibrant atmosphere, the eatery is a casual spot for dining with friends over a savory breakfast and mimosas.

PLAYAS DE TIJUANA

There are many little spots along the boardwalk that take advantage of Playas de Tijuana's ocean views. Hipsters hang out at **Café**

Latitud 32 (Paseo Costero, tel. 664/609-4200, 8am-10pm daily, US$2-3) for the vistas, funky atmosphere, and lattes. Nearby is **Sunset Lounge** (Ave. Pacifico 769, tel. 664/680-1863, www.sunsetlounge.com. mx, 1pm-10pm Mon.-Wed., 1pm-midnight Thurs.-Sat., noon-9pm Sun.), a restaurant and lounge with an outdoor space overlooking the ocean, perfect for catching sunset with a glass of wine in hand.

La Terraza Vallarta (Del Pacifico 343, tel. 664/680-0769, 10am-8pm daily, US$6-8) is a *mariscos* restaurant most famous for the replica of the *Titanic* on the roof and for being visited by Anthony Bourdain on his show *No Reservations.*

El Yogurt Place (Cantera 360, tel. 664/680-2006, www.elyogurtplace.com, 7:30pm-8:30pm daily, US$4-7) has plenty of healthy and organic options for dining, from granola and whole-wheat waffles for breakfast to salads and sandwiches for lunch and dinner. Just steps away from Friendship Park, the large restaurant has been a Playas institution since 1976, and the hearty dishes and warm atmosphere draw crowds of locals every day of the week. There's often a wait for a table, but the breakfast bar is first-come, first-served.

Accommodations

Because of the number of business travelers who come to the city, there are upscale hotels in Tijuana, and the prices are very affordable. It's possible to stay in nice accommodations— even by U.S. standards—for under $100 a night.

ZONA CENTRO
Under US$50

For budget accommodations, **Aqua Rio Hotel** (Ave. Constitución 1618, tel. 664/685-1914, www.hotelaquario.com, US$40) offers

nice and clean rooms with granite floors, modern bathrooms, flat-screen TVs, wireless Internet, and air-conditioning. Free coffee and fruit are available in the lobby. The hotel is walking distance to Revolución, but away from most of the noise of downtown.

US$50-100

With a sister location in San Diego, ★ **One Bunk** (Ave. Revolución 920, U.S. tel. 664/210-1824, www.onebunk.com, US$58) provides boutique accommodations in the heart of Revolución. The nine-room micro hotel, set just above La Justina restaurant, has features like a mezcal honor bar, a communal living

1: Taco N Veggie, serving up vegetarian and vegan tacos 2: El Yogurt Place in Playas de Tijuana 3: the original location of Foodgarden 4: craft beer hall at Telefónica Gastro Park

room, and a rooftop with yoga and other special events. Catering to a hip crowd, the vibrant and fresh decor perfectly captures the urban vibe of Tijuana. Bookings can be made through Airbnb.

US$100-150

Guests will find friendly staff and large, comfortable rooms at **Hotel Ticuan** (Ave. Miguel Hidalgo 8190, tel. 664/685-8078, www.hotelticuan.mx, US$120). A free breakfast is included in your stay (but only for one guest per room). Once you park your car in the secured parking garage, you can easily walk to restaurants and stores from this convenient hotel. Because of the central location, rooms that face Avenida Revolución can be noisy, especially on weekends when music booms from the clubs. Ask for a room away from Revolución for a quieter experience.

ZONA RÍO
US$50-100

The upscale ★ **Grand Hotel Tijuana** (Agua Caliente 4558, tel. 664/681-7000, toll-free U.S. tel. 866/472-6385, www.grandhoteltj.com, US$85-100) features large, clean, and modern rooms. Amenities include a pool and Jacuzzi, as well as self-parking (US$1). The restaurant has a breakfast buffet in the mornings, and the hotel is located within walking distance of many other great restaurants. There's a bar in the lobby with live music on the weekends. Their special "Grand Care" rooms are equipped with hospital beds, wheelchairs, and shower chairs for those visiting Tijuana for medical tourism.

Close to the cultural center and Plaza Río Mall, **Hotel Real del Rio Tijuana** (José María Velazco 1409, tel. 664/634-3100, www.realdelrio.com, $80-95) is a sleek hotel with modern rooms, a gym, and outdoor terrace. A modern restaurant and bar are located in the lobby.

Palacio Azteca Hotel (Blvd. Cuauhtémoc Sur 213, tel. 664/681-8100, www.hotelpalacioazteca.com, US$75) has clean, spacious rooms with nice bathrooms, minibars,

and air-conditioning. There's a restaurant and bar and a business center. The sleek **Pueblo Amigo Plaza & Casino** (Via Oriente 9211, tel. 664/624-2700, www.hotelpuebloamigo.com, US$89) is attached to the Caliente Casino. The location is close to the border and the hotel has a friendly and accommodating staff.

A good option in Otay near Rodriguez airport, **Fiesta Inn Tijuana Otay** (Rampa Aeropuerto 16000, tel. 664/979-1900, www.fiestainn.com, US$70-90) has large rooms with comfortable beds and nice sheets. There's a pool, gym, restaurant, and 24-hour room service.

US$100-150

Those looking for the nicest accommodations in town will want to stay at the ★ **Hyatt Place Tijuana** (Agua Caliente 10488, tel. 664/900-1234, www.hyatt.com, US$110-135). With 145 rooms, the hotel features all of the modern and convenient amenities that you would expect from Hyatt. Guests will enjoy plush, comfortable beds, friendly staff, a nice buffet breakfast, a 24-hour gym, and a convenient location. There's secure underground parking that's free for guests.

Although it's smaller than its sister property in Mexicali, **Lucerna Tijuana** (Paseo de los Héroes 10902, tel. 664/633-3900, www.hoteleslucerna.com, US$150) is up to par with the same amenities and service. Rooms are well appointed, the grounds are well maintained, and amenities include a nice pool area and gym. The hotel has a bar and two restaurants in addition to 24-hour room service.

The **Fairfield Inn & Suites** (Blvd. General Rodolfo Sanchez Taboada 10461, tel. 664/512-1300, www.marriott.com, US$104) is a Marriott property with modern rooms, a fitness center, free parking, fast Wi-Fi, and included breakfast, making it a popular choice for U.S. travelers.

US$150-200

Next door to Lucerna Tijuana, and operated by the same owners, is ★ **K Tower Urban Boutique Hotel** (Paseo de Héroes 10902, tel. 664/633-7500, www.ktowerhotel.com, US$196). This adults-only boutique hotel features hip and modern luxury accommodations and specializes in personalized service. Amenities include a rooftop pool and Jacuzzi, gym with panoramic views, butler service, and an on-site bar and sushi restaurant.

Travelers will find a hotel up to U.S. standards with Mexican hospitality at **Marriott Tijuana** (Agua Caliente 11553, tel. 664/622-6600, www.marriott.com, US$125). The staff is welcoming and friendly, and rooms are clean and modern with fast wireless Internet. There's an outdoor pool and a fitness center. A restaurant and café are on-site.

PLAYAS DE TIJUANA

Dali Suites (Colina 551, tel. 664/680-6369, www.dalisuites.com, US$85) is an intimate 19-room hotel close to the beach, restaurants, and shops. The property is secure and well maintained, and the staff members are friendly and accommodating. Located nearby is the 60-room **Del Mar Inn** (Paseo Playas de Tijuana 116, tel. 664/630-8830, www.delmarinn.com.mx, US$60), with basic accommodations, a small pool, and an on-site restaurant.

Just off of the *malecón* is the clean and modern **Lifestyle Hostel** (Ave. Del Pacifico 820, tel. 664/976-8244, US$17 dorm bed, US$39 private room). Offering shared dormitories as well as private rooms, the hostel is conveniently located near plenty of shops, restaurants, and cafés, as well as the beach. They also have a jiujitsu academy attached where guests can join a class or use the academy during off hours.

Information and Services

Tijuana is a large city with all of the major conveniences you would find anywhere in the world.

TOURIST INFORMATION

On Avenida Revolución, there's an office for **Baja State Tourism** (Ave. Revolución 868-1, between Calles 2 and 3, 664/682-3367, www.bajanorte.com) with brochures and information about Tijuana and the state of Baja California. Tourists can call 078 on any phone for 24/7 bilingual assistance in northern Baja.

FOREIGN CONSULATES

The **U.S. Consulate** (Paseo de la Culturas, Mesa de Otay, tel. 664/977-2000, 7:30am-4:15pm Mon.-Fri.) is in Tijuana near the airport and can help with lost passports, visa issues, or emergency services. It can also assist with notaries, births and deaths of U.S. citizens, and arrests of U.S. citizens in Baja. The **Canadian Consulate** (Germán Gedovius 10411-101, tel. 664/684-0461, tjuna@international.gc.ca, 9:30am-12:30pm Mon.-Fri.) helps Canadian citizens with passport issues and other emergency situations that may arise while traveling.

MONEY

Many businesses will accept U.S. dollars, but you'll get a better exchange rate by using pesos. There are ATMs, banks, and exchange houses all around the city. Many restaurants and hotels will accept credit cards, but smaller establishments may be cash only.

DRINKING

Tijuana has always had a party city reputation and is generally considered a safe place to enjoy a night out, especially in the tourist areas. As with drinking anywhere, always keep an eye on your drink and never drink and drive. There are taxis and Ubers available throughout the city.

SAFETY

There are no problems with violence in the tourist areas of Tijuana. As with any large city, use precautions and be aware of your personal surroundings.

MEDICAL SERVICES

Located in Zona Centro is **Hospital Guadalajara** (Calle 2da. #1413, tel. 664/685-8953, www.hospitalguadalajara.com). This large, modern hospital is open 24 hours and can handle emergency services as well as general health issues. In Zona Río, **Hospital Angeles Mexico** (Ave. Paseo de los Héroes #10999, tel. 664/635-1800, www.angeleshealth. com) offers a wide variety of services from surgeries to a cancer center and is a popular hospital for medical tourism with patients from the United States.

There are pharmacies located all over the city. **Gusher Farmacia** (www.gusher. com.mx) and **Farmacia Roma** (www.farmaciasroma.com) are two of the biggest pharmacies in the region, with multiple locations that are all open 24 hours.

Transportation

GETTING THERE
Border Crossing

Tijuana has two border crossings: **San Ysidro** in the heart of Tijuana and **Otay Mesa** farther east. San Ysidro is open 24 hours a day and is the busiest land port of entry in the world. Southbound crossings by car are relatively quick and easy. If you are crossing northbound back to the United States at San Ysidro in a vehicle, expect a long wait. Otay Mesa generally has a shorter northbound wait than San Ysidro, but travelers should still expect multiple hours at peak times. For more information as well as wait times for either border crossing, refer to the **U.S. Customs and Border Protection website** at www.cbp.gov.

CAR

The **San Ysidro** border crossing is located at the southern terminus of the I-5 and I-805 freeways, 20 miles (32 km) and 25 minutes from downtown San Diego. The **Otay Mesa** border crossing is at the terminus of the CA-905 freeway, 25 miles (40 km) and 30 minutes from downtown San Diego.

ON FOOT

Many San Diego residents park in San Diego and cross San Ysidro by foot to explore Tijuana for the day. Those crossing by foot at the **San Ysidro El Chaparral** border crossing will need to fill out a *forma migratoria multiple* (FMM) tourist permit. Visitors staying for seven days or fewer can get an FMM for free; stays of more than seven days require a payment of US$28. The paid FMMs are valid for up to 180 days. Once in Tijuana, it's easy to get around by Uber or taxi. Zona Centro and Avenida Revolución are best explored on foot and provide lots of options for food, shopping, and entertainment.

There are two **pedestrian crossings** at the San Ysidro El Chaparral border crossing—the **Pedestrian West (PedWest)** crossing, on the western side of the border crossing, and the **Pedestrian East (PedEast)** border crossing, which is on the eastern side of the northbound vehicle crossing.

Air

Tijuana's **General Abelardo L. Rodríguez International Airport** (TIJ, tel. 664/607-8200, www.tijuana-airport.com) is about 10 kilometers (6.2 miles) east of downtown in Otay Mesa. Many domestic and international flights arrive at the airport. There are car rentals and Uber and taxi service at the airport.

The new **Cross Border Xpress** (www. crossborderxpress.com) pedestrian bridge now makes it possible for ticketed passengers flying out of Tijuana to park in San Diego and walk across a pedestrian bridge to get to the airport (and vice versa). Tickets for the bridge are available for US$16 one-way and can be purchased on-site or in advance through the website. CBX is located on the eastern side of Tijuana near Otay Mesa and connects directly to Rodriguez airport.

Bus

The **Central de Autobuses de Tijuana** (tel. 664/621-2982) is on Lazaro Cardenas at Boulevard Arroyo Alamar south of the airport. Large bus lines such as Greyhound, **Autobuses de la Baja California** (ABC, tel. 664/104-7400, www.abc.com.mx), and **Aguila** (toll-free Mex. tel. 800/026-8931, www.autobusesaguila.com) have service out of Tijuana.

San Diego Trolley

The **San Diego Trolley** (U.S. tel. 619/233-3004, www.sdmts.com, US$2.50) blue line stops in San Ysidro at the border right next to San Ysidro's PedEast crossing. The trolley operates 5am-2am daily with trolleys running every 7-30 minutes, depending on the time of day.

GETTING AROUND

Tijuana is a large city but has pockets that are easily walkable. Zona Centro and Avenida Revolución are best explored on foot since there are enough things to see and places to eat and drink to keep you occupied for a full day.

Driving in Tijuana can be difficult for those not familiar with the orientation of the city or for those not used to driving in big cities with lots of traffic. Street parking is very difficult to find in tourist areas, so you'll want to look for paid parking structures or lots. Many restaurants will have their own parking lots for patrons.

If you aren't experienced at driving in large cities in developing countries, you may find it stressful to get yourself around Tijuana. Luckily, **Uber** (www.uber.com) has come to the city, providing a safe and easy way to get from place to place. Download the app before you travel. Taxis are also available. **Taxi B-Seguro** (tel. 664/687-1010) is one of the largest taxi companies, its white and orange taxis found all over the city. Be aware of yellow cabs; they have been linked to acts of violence and are not deemed safe.

Tecate

The small border town of Tecate is a far cry from nearby Tijuana to the west. Rather than a congested metropolis, here you'll find a tranquil town nestled into the foothills of the Sierra de Juárez. The Kumiai (Kumeyaay) were the original inhabitants of this area, and their presence is still felt strongly today through the various museums and rock art sites in the region. In the late 19th century, ranchers came in to settle the land, and the area is still dominated by those large ranches.

In 2012, Tecate was designated as a *Pueblo Mágico,* a "magic town," and the government is working on beautifying the town and improving infrastructure. (*Pueblo Mágico* is a designation given by Mexico's Secretary of Tourism to towns throughout the country believed to

Highlights

Look for ★ to find recommended sights, activities, dining, and lodging.

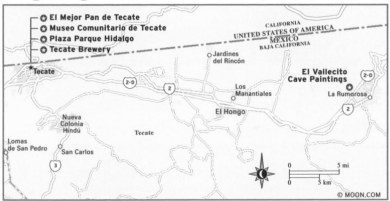

★ **Sit in the shade** of the tall trees at **Plaza Parque Hidalgo** while listening to **mariachi bands** and taking in the daily bustle of Tecate (page 55).

★ **Satiate your sweet tooth** with a visit to **El Mejor Pan de Tecate,** Baja California's most famous bakery (page 55).

★ **Learn about the history** of the region and the local Kumeyaay peoples at the community museum, **Museo Comunitario de Tecate** (page 55).

★ **Visit the Tecate Brewery** and enjoy a free beer in the beer garden (page 56).

★ **Take an easy half-day trip** from Tecate to see the nearby **El Vallecito Cave Paintings** (page 66).

Tecate

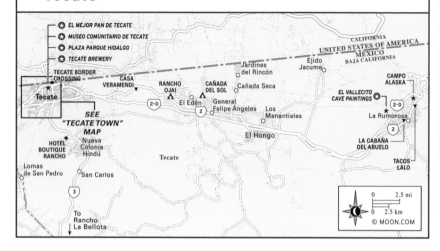

- EL MEJOR PAN DE TECATE
- MUSEO COMUNITARIO DE TECATE
- PLAZA PARQUE HIDALGO
- TECATE BREWERY

TECATE BORDER CROSSING

CASA VERAMENDI

RANCHO OJAI

CAÑADA DEL SOL

Cañada Seca

Tecate

SEE "TECATE TOWN" MAP

HOTEL BOUTIQUE RANCHO

Nueva Colonia Hindú

Lomas de San Pedro

San Carlos

Tecate

To Rancho La Bellota

Jardines del Rincón

Ejido Jacume

El Edén

General Felipe Ángeles

Los Manantiales

El Hongo

CALIFORNIA
UNITED STATES OF AMERICA
MEXICO
BAJA CALIFORNIA

CAMPO ALASKA

EL VALLECITO CAVE PAINTINGS

La Rumorosa

LA CABAÑA DEL ABUELO

TACOS LALO

0   2.5 mi
0   2.5 km
© MOON.COM

offer travelers a "magical" experience whether through natural beauty, cultural riches, or historical importance.) You won't find the immediate colonial charm of many of Mexico's other Pueblos Mágicos, but Tecate is full of hidden gems from the town plaza *zocalo* to the nearby El Vallecito cave paintings. The plaza and Tecate brewery are must-visits for most travelers, as is a stop at El Mejor Pan de Tecate, the famous bakery. Unlike the coastal areas of northern Baja, you won't see as many tourists in Tecate, which makes it even more exciting to explore. With a relatively easy border crossing and very little traffic, many visitors pass through Tecate on their way to or from the Valle de Guadalupe wineries, making it an important gateway to the Ruta del Vino.

PLANNING YOUR TIME

Tecate can easily be explored in a day trip or a weekend. If you're planning on visiting La Rumorosa and El Vallecito cave paintings, it's best to allow for an extra day.

ORIENTATION

Tecate is located right on the U.S. border and is an hour east of Tijuana. The town center is just south of the border and most of the town is sandwiched between the Mexico 2 and Mexico 2D highways. Considered the "Gateway to Valle de Guadalupe," it's an easy and direct drive from Tecate south to the Valle de Guadalupe.

Previous: the organic garden at El Cafecito 3 Estrellas; colorful tile display in Tecate; Museo Comunitario de Tecate.

Sights

★ PLAZA PARQUE HIDALGO

The center of town, **Plaza Parque Hidalgo,** is just a few blocks south of the U.S. border crossing. The lovely plaza has a gazebo in the center surrounded by plenty of benches, mature trees, grass, and flowers. Built in 1952, the plaza is the hub of town life and a lovely spot to sit and relax while getting a good sense of what Tecate is all about. The plaza is lined by small businesses like restaurants, banks, and Michoacan ice cream shops. On the south side of the plaza are a number of tables and chairs, shaded by tall trees, where locals gather in the afternoons and mariachi bands are often heard serenading crowds. A statue of Miguel Hidalgo, who issued the call for Mexican Independence in 1810, welcomes visitors to the northeast corner of the park. Public bathrooms can be found on the south side of the plaza.

★ EL MEJOR PAN DE TECATE

One of Tecate's most famous attractions, **El Mejor Pan de Tecate** (Benito Juárez 331, tel. 665/654-0040, www.elmejorpandetecate.com, open 24 hours daily) is a must-stop for many travelers. The rows full of freshly baked bread, pastries, cookies, and cakes are an impressive sight and will entice anyone with a sweet tooth. The family business has been in operation since 1969 and has been arguably the most famous spot in town for many decades. The bakery is open 24 hours a day, so whenever you find yourself passing through Tecate, grab a tray and tongs to fill up on goodies. There's a parking lot in the back and tables to enjoy your treats out front.

★ MUSEO COMUNITARIO DE TECATE

In the Tecate Cultural Center, **Museo Comunitario de Tecate (Tecate Community Museum)** (Calle Tláloc 400, tel. 665/521-3191, www.carem.org, 10am-5pm Wed.-Sun., US$1.50 adults, US$0.50 children) is a bilingual museum explaining the culture, history, and natural geography of the region. The permanent exhibits feature photographs, murals, artifacts, and informative signs that highlight the three periods of Tecate's history: the prehistoric era, the era of the ranchers, and

Plaza Parque Hidalgo

Best Restaurants and Accommodations

RESTAURANTS

★ **El Lugar de Nos:** Delicious food is served in a welcoming and eclectic setting at this Tecate restaurant (page 60).

★ **Restaurante Amores:** Multicourse tasting menus offer diners a unique and locally sourced meal at one of northern Baja's best restaurants (page 62).

★ **El Cafecito 3 Estrellas:** Enjoy breakfast or lunch on the property of Rancho La Puerta at chef Denise Roa's eatery, with your food coming directly from the ranch's six-acre organic garden (page 62).

ACCOMMODATIONS

★ **Santuario Diegueño:** This high-end hotel offers a relaxing and enjoyable stay with luxury finishes and one of Tecate's top restaurants (page 63).

★ **Rancho La Puerta:** Guests come to this historic ranch in Tecate for a fitness and spa retreat (page 63).

★ **Rancho La Bellota:** The authentic ranch experience at Rancho La Bellota includes horseback riding and an off-the-grid getaway (page 63).

contemporary times. There's also a traditional Kumiai house and a gift shop with traditional indigenous arts for sale. Events and workshops led by local indigenous instructors include basket making, corn processing, music, language, and other arts.

The museum is managed by Corredor Histórico CAREM, a Mexican nonprofit dedicated to the historical and cultural heritage of Baja California. CAREM also offers day trips outside of Tecate to nearby sites like La Rumorosa and El Vallecito.

★ TECATE BREWERY

The **Tecate Brewery** (Dr. Arturo Guerra 70, tel. 656/654-9478 or 665/654-9404, contacto@cuamoc.com, 10am-5pm Mon.-Fri., 10am-2pm Sat.) is hard to ignore. The large white factory with the Tecate sign on top looms over the entire town. The factory is home to a popular beer garden. Light and airy with high ceilings and large windows, the space features a modern design with

sleek furniture. Visitors receive one free beer, which can be enjoyed inside or on the large outdoor patio.

TECATE RAILROAD STATION

Tecate was once part of an important train route from San Diego, California, to Yuma, Arizona. The Tecate railroad station was built in 1915 and today is part of a small historic district adjacent to the Tecate Brewery.

PARQUE LOS ENCINOS

Named for the large oak trees interspersed throughout the park, **Parque los Encinos** (between Encinos, Dr. Arturo Guerra, and Querétaro, 10am-8pm daily, free) is a 10-hectare park where families gather to relax and play. There are picnic areas, playgrounds, soccer fields, skate and bike ramps, and an amphitheater. Many of the town's festivals and events are held at the park. Admission is free.

Tecate Town

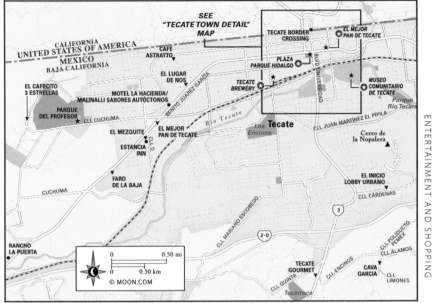

PARQUE DEL PROFESOR

On the western outskirts of town, the **Parque del Profesor** is a 10-hectare park dedicated to Professor Edmond Szekely, the founder of Rancho La Puerta. The sports and cultural complex includes a soccer field and a plaza used for community and private events. Right next to the park and also operated by Rancho La Puerta, **Las Piedras** is an environmental center housed in buildings made to look like giant granite boulders. They have a series of workshops for children.

Entertainment and Shopping

Tecate doesn't have much of a nightlife scene aside from a few quiet bars that generally close early. There are a few Tecate wineries, but most don't have tasting rooms open to the public. The same goes for the local Tecate craft breweries. A few little places serve some of the local wines and beer.

NIGHTLIFE

Since 1957, **Bar Diana** (Cardenas 35, tel. 665/654-0515, 11am-1am daily) has been the local watering hole and gathering spot right on the town plaza. The bar was named after a life-size bronze sculpture of the goddess of hunting that once stood in the courtyard of its patio. The statue was stolen in 1974 and never seen again, but a painting of the sculpture graces the wall behind the large wooden bar. Stop into this Tecate landmark for a cold beer or margarita.

A great way to sample some of the wines from Tecate is by visiting **Tecate Gourmet**

Tecate Town Detail

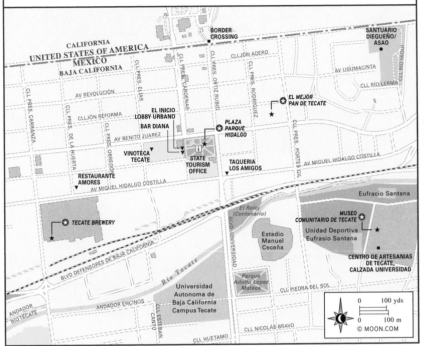

(Carretera Tecate-Ensenada Km. 10, tel. 665/655-6095, noon-9pm Wed.-Mon.). Located south of the central part of town near Rancho Tecate, the wine cave and bistro does tastings of local wines and also serves paninis and salads. They make fresh preserves that are available for purchase.

One of the few Tecate wineries with a tasting room open to the public is **Cava Garcia** (Jacarandas 455 Alfonzo Garzon, tel. 665/103-0014, 10am-10pm Sun.-Wed., 10am-midnight Thurs.-Sat.). The large tasting room is family friendly. Visitors can also tour the farm to see the horses, emus, goats, and donkeys.

Another local winery with a tasting room is **Casa Veramendi** (Carretera Libre Mexicali-Tijuana Km. 117.5, tel. 664/385-2075, www.casaveramendi.com), which opened to the public in 2019. The winery is located on a family ranch 15 kilometers (9.3 miles) east of Tecate, where visitors can see the vineyards, learn a bit about the winemaking process, and try the selection of red and white wines. Tastings and visits are open to the public during the summer (1pm-5pm Sat.-Sun. July-Sept.) and by appointment for the rest of the year.

SHOPPING

The best place to shop for souvenirs is the **Centro de Artesanias de Tecate** (Calzada Universidad in front of Parque Adolfo López Mateos, no tel., 8:30am-6pm Mon.-Fri., 10am-3pm Sat.), where local pottery, tiles, jewelry, and other crafts may be purchased.

1: Parque los Encinos **2:** mariachis playing around Plaza Parque Hidalgo **3:** Museo Comunitario de Tecate **4:** El Mejor Pan de Tecate

Tecate Beer

Mention the word *Tecate* and most people immediately conjure up the image of the red beer can with the stylized eagle on the front. This beer is ubiquitous in Baja California as well as other parts of the world. The exported Tecate has a lower alcohol content than what is available in Mexico.

The beer-making history of Mexico was heavily influenced by 19th-century German immigrants who brought their dark lagers to the region. The influence of these flavors can be seen in beers such as Negra Modelo and Dos Equis Amber. Even today, the commercial beers of Mexico are of a much higher quality than many standard beers from other parts of the world.

Tecate's story began in 1944 when Alberto Aldrete took over an old brick building. He had been operating a malt factory and making beer on the side. With his new factory, he focused on beer full-time and named his brew after the town. The Tecate facility was the first factory in Baja California. Today, Tecate is owned by Heineken and is shipped all around the world for beer drinkers to enjoy.

Food

Tecate has a growing food scene that is beginning to catch up to the gastronomic prowess of neighboring cities such as Tijuana and Ensenada. With new Baja California cuisine joining traditional Mexican restaurants and taco stands, there are a number of solid options for foodies visiting the area.

MEXICAN

At ★ **El Lugar de Nos** (Benito Juárez 384, tel. 665/521-3340, www.ellugardenos.com, 1pm-11pm Wed.-Sat., 1pm-5pm Sun., mains US$11-18), incredibly fresh creations like rib eye pizza, *jamaica* salad, and ahi tuna tostadas are created by chef Mariela Manzano who studied at the Culinary Art School in Tijuana and was formerly a chef at Rancho La Puerta. Mismatched tablecloths, vintage furniture, and funky art create an eclectic, charming, and comfortable atmosphere. There's an intimate and cozy feeling to the restaurant even though the space is large and there are numerous patios and courtyards. In addition to the fresh and creative food, craft cocktails and local artisanal beers round out the menu, and the staff are incredibly friendly and accommodating.

At the high point of the Santuario Diegueño hotel property, **Asao** (Rio Yaqui 798, tel. 665/654-4777, www.santuariodiegueno.com, 1pm-10pm Thurs.-Sat., 9am-8pm Sun., mains US$11-21) offers fine dining with beautiful views. The food is artfully prepared with a delicate presentation. The large and impressive dining room has high ceilings and huge sliding glass doors that look out onto a patio with views of the town and the surrounding hills. On warm days the sliding doors open to create an open-flow concept between the indoor and outdoor spaces. Guests can peer into the kitchen, situated behind a wall of windows on the other side of the dining room, as well as the glassed-in wine cellar full of regional wines.

Open for breakfast and lunch, **Malinalli Sabores Autóctonos** (formerly Polokotlan, Ave. Juarez 861, tel. 665/122-6643, 9am-6pm Tues.-Sat., 8am-4pm Sun., US$7) serves pre-Hispanic Mexican dishes made with traditional methods. They take great pride in making their own mole from scratch and nixtamalizing their own corn for items like house-made tortillas. There is a daily buffet as well as items that can be ordered a la carte.

1: the back patio at El Lugar de Nos restaurant
2: Asao, offering fine dining and a lovely atmosphere

The Estancia Inn's on-site restaurant, **El Mezquite** (Ave. Juárez 1450, tel. 665/521-3066, www.estanciainn.com.mx, 6:30am-8:30pm Tues.-Thurs., 6:30am-10pm Fri., 7am-10pm Sat., 7am-6pm Sun., US$8), serves traditional Mexican dishes and has buffet and a la carte options.

SEAFOOD

For traditional Mexican seafood dishes, head to **Faro de la Baja** (Ave. Juárez 1030, tel. 665/521-2225, 10:30am-5:30pm Tues.-Fri., 9:30am-4:30pm Sat.-Sun., US$8). The friendly service and savory seafood plates make this a popular spot for locals. Don't miss the *albóndigas de pescado* (fish meatball soup).

INTERNATIONAL

There's no written menu at ★ **Restaurante Amores** (Adolfo de la Huerta 42, tel. 665/122-1323, restauranteamores@gmail.com, 1pm-9pm Tues.-Thurs., 1pm-10pm Fri.-Sat., 1pm-7pm Sun., US$15 for three courses), but guests can choose from a three-, five-, or eight-course tasting menu with dishes made from local ingredients. The husband-and-wife team of Marcelo Hisaki and Reyna Vedegas are turning out some of the most delicious and innovative food in the entire region. There are only a few tables at this intimate restaurant, so it's best to email in advance to make a reservation. The restaurant can be difficult to find, but look for the small sign in the window.

Right on the plaza is the hip wine bistro **El Inicio Lobby Urbano** (Calle Cárdenas 45-2, tel. 665/521-2994, 1pm-9pm Mon. and Wed.-Thurs., 1pm-11pm Fri.-Sat., 1pm-5pm Sun., US$6-8). Owner Hector Esparza takes great care in his business and the well-being of customers. The casual eatery has a menu with healthy and well-crafted items like tapas, salads, wraps, and paninis. Baja wines, artisanal beers, and craft cocktails round out the menu.

One block from the plaza, **Vinoteca Tecate** (Ave. Juárez 176, tel. 665/521-3715, 1pm-11pm Tues.-Sat., 1pm-9pm Sun., US$8-10) offers a large selection of Baja wines. The outdoor patio is rustically elegant with brick walls and lights strung from mature trees. The menu ranges from salads and pastas to various seafood and chicken dishes.

STREET FOOD

For the best tacos in town, head to **Taqueria Los Amigos** (Ortiz Rubio and Ave. Hidalgo, tel. 665/521-3851, US$1-2). The stand has been serving up tacos and quesadillas since 1980. The large open-air space has nice wooden tables and chairs. Carne asada is the specialty here, and the flour tacos and quesadillas are large and filling. They have another location just south of town on Avenida Universidad.

CAFÉS

Café **Astratto** (Cerro San Javier 77, tel. 665/851-0747, 1pm-10pm Wed.-Sat., 2pm-9pm Sun., US$4-5) is a favorite spot for hip locals. It serves savory gourmet sandwiches and hamburgers as well as local craft beers. This family-run operation is also known for its artisanal drip and press coffees. Seating is outdoors and there's live music on a regular basis.

Located on the property of Rancho la Puerta and operated by chef Denise Roa and her team from La Cocina Que Canta is ★ **El Cafecito 3 Estrellas** (Prolongación Paseo Cuchuma, tel. 665/654-6200, 9am-6pm Thurs.-Sat., 9am-5pm Sun., US$4-8). The café features farm-to-table organic cuisine with a variety of pescatarian and vegetarian items on the menu. Diners enjoy dishes like chilaquiles and vegetable omelets for breakfast and sandwiches and salads for lunch. All the produce comes from the six-acre organic garden adjacent to the café.

BAKERIES

Baja California's most famous bakery, ★ **El Mejor Pan de Tecate** (Benito Juárez 331, tel. 665/654-0040, www.elmejorpandetecate.com, open 24 hours daily), offers freshly baked bread, pastries, cookies, and cakes. The bakery has a parking lot in the back and tables out front where you can enjoy your goodies.

Accommodations

Tecate is a town of mostly modest accommodations, with a few luxury options for more discerning travelers. There are a handful of hotels in town as well as some ranchos and camping options just outside of town.

HOTELS AND MOTELS

You'll find accommodations that are up to U.S. motel standards at **Estancia Inn** (Benito Juárez 1450, tel. 665/521-3066, www. estanciainn.com.mx, US$60). There are 85 rooms set back from the street with TVs with lots of channels including a decent selection in English. There's a swimming pool, a small gym, secure parking, and a restaurant, El Mezquite, on the property.

For a budget option, **Motel La Hacienda** (Mexico 2 861, tel. 665/654-1250, US$35) has older rooms and bathrooms that are clean and in working order. Beds are comfortable, and there are flat-screen TVs with cable.

Some of the most luxurious accommodations in town are found at ★ **Santuario Diegueño** (Rio Yaqui 798, tel. 665/654-4777, www.santuariodiegueno.com, US$150-229). The hotel's 26 rooms are spacious and well appointed with mini fridges, coffeemakers, wine chillers, flat-screen TVs, fast wireless access, and patios. There's a lovely pool area with a Jacuzzi, and the grounds are landscaped with regional flora. There's an event center, a bar, and two restaurants on the property including the famed restaurant Asao.

RANCHOS

The most famous and recognized name in Tecate lodgings is the historic ★ **Rancho La Puerta** (Mexico 2 Km. 136.5, toll-free U.S. tel. 800/443-7565, www.rancholapuerta.com, US$4,500/week). Guests book a full week here at the famous fitness and spa retreat to relax, detox, renew, and redirect. Activities reflect these principles, and a sample itinerary for the day may include hiking, stretching, yoga, art

class, well-being workshops, or a cooking class at their famous cooking school, **La Cocina Que Canta**. Rates start at $4,500 per week in the high season (Feb.-June) and include all meals, more than 50 options for daily activities, use of the fitness and spa facilities, and transportation to and from the San Diego airport. For those who can't commit to a longer visit, the Rancho La Puerta **Saturdays at the Ranch** are day trips to the ranch from San Diego that include activities like hiking, fitness classes, massages, and cooking demonstrations.

For rustic elegance, **Hotel Boutique Rancho Tecate** (Carretera Tecate-Ensenada Km. 10, tel. 665/654-0011, www.ranchotecate. mx, US$165) is a 650-hectare ranch with 21 rooms. The lobby will give you a true ranch lodge feeling with its large wrought-iron chandeliers, vaulted ceilings with wood beams, and grand fireplace. While the property overall is older, rooms have been recently remodeled and feature modern amenities like flat-screen TVs and slippers and bathrobes. There's a pool and Jacuzzi area, as well as an equestrian center.

For a trip back in time to the days of the Wild West, visit the 1,133-hectare horse ranch of ★ **Rancho La Bellota** (Mexico 3 between Tecate and Valle de Guadalupe, tel. 646/183-0922, www.rancholabellota.com, US$475/ weekend). The rustic cabins fit up to three people and have full bathrooms and wood-burning stoves. There's no electricity (except a small generator used to power the blender for margaritas), cell phone reception, TV, or Internet. Enjoy days of relaxation and trail rides on horseback like the real rancheros.

CAMPING AND RV PARKS

Perfect for families, **Rancho Ojai** (Carretera Mexicali-Tecate Km. 112, tel. 665/655-3014, www.rancho-ojai.com, US$10 pp for tent camping, US$20 for RV, US$75-100 for cabins) offers a range of accommodations from tent camping to RV spaces to cabins that can accommodate up to six people. There's no lack of activities for the family here. Kids will enjoy miniature golf, volleyball, basketball, soccer, bicycles, playgrounds, and a game room with pool and foosball tables. The whole family will enjoy the pool and all of the picnic areas with grills.

With tent camping and cabins, **Cañada del Sol** (Carretera Tijuana-Mexicali Km. 105, tel. 664/129-4242, www.canadadelsol. com, US$10 pp for tent camping, US$75-130 for cabin) is also a popular day destination with myriad activities on offer. There's a pool, horseback riding, ATV riding, basketball, and playgrounds. It's US$5 for a day pass.

Information and Transportation

INFORMATION AND SERVICES

Gas stations, markets, banks, and ATMs are interspersed throughout town. On the south side of Plaza Hidalgo is a **State Tourism Office** (1305 Andador Libertad, tel. 665/654-1095) with brochures and other regional information.

The general hospital, **Hospital General de Tecate** (Calle Quinta 69, tel. 665/654-0806), is open 24 hours a day and is located a few blocks south of Parque los Encinos. They are equipped to handle medical emergencies and minor procedures.

TRANSPORTATION
Getting There
TECATE BORDER CROSSING

The Tecate border is open 5am-11pm daily. This is considered one of the shortest border waits for northbound crossings. Pedestrians often have no wait, and cars will wait considerably less than at Tijuana's San Ysidro border crossing. There are no special expedited lanes for crossing here (Ready Lane or SENTRI). The northbound pedestrian crossing entrance is at Lazaro Cardenas and Callejon Madero (just east of the southbound car crossing). The northbound car crossing is east of this.

CAR

If you will be arriving by car from the United States, CA-188 (accessible from CA-94) leads directly to the Tecate border crossing. It takes about 50 minutes to drive the 40 miles (64 km) from downtown San Diego to the Tecate border, taking CA-94 east to CA-188 south. Tecate is a popular day trip for San Diego residents who enjoy parking their car on the U.S. side of the border (for US$5) and walking across to spend the day.

To get to Tecate from Tijuana, take Mexico 2 east. The fastest and most direct route is to take the Mexico 2D toll road rather than the Mexico 2 free road. It takes just under an hour to drive the 50 kilometers (31 miles) if taking Mexico 2D, but can take well over an hour (and much longer depending on traffic) if taking the Mexico 2 free road.

To get to Tecate from Ensenada or the Valle de Guadalupe, follow the tranquil two-lane Mexico 3 northeast. From Ensenada, the 110-kilometer (68-mile) drive takes about 1.5 hours. From Valle de Guadalupe, the 75-kilometer (47-mile) drive takes just over an hour. To get to Tecate from Mexicali, head west on Mexico 2 for 130 kilometers (81 miles). The trip takes about 1.75 hours and involves tolls.

BUS

The bus station in Tecate is located one block east of the plaza on Avenida Juárez. **Aguila**

1: chef-led garden walk at La Cocina Que Canta
2: La Cabaña del Abuelo restaurant in La Rumorosa
3: La Cocina Que Canta, the cooking school at Rancho La Puerta 4: poolside cabañas at Hotel Boutique Rancho Tecate

(tel. 800/026-8931, www.autobusesaguila. com) has once-daily service to Tecate from Tijuana, Ensenada, and Mexicali. From Tijuana the route takes 1.5 hours and costs US$4. From Ensenada the route takes 3.5 hours and costs US$18. From Mexicali the route takes 2 hours and costs US$13.

Getting Around

Once in Mexico, visitors can walk four blocks south to the plaza and many shops and restaurants. Taxis are readily available for longer rides around town. Travelers who bring a car to Tecate will find the driving to be relatively easy with very little traffic, courteous drivers, and easy street parking.

La Rumorosa and Vicinity

Heading east on Mexico 2 from Tecate leads you to the small, dusty town of La Rumorosa. The main draw for tourists are the cave paintings of El Vallecito, which are just outside of the town. Most travelers visiting the area stay in Tecate and visit La Rumorosa on a day trip. The area is also known for its impressive and picturesque mountains, which are located just east of the town of La Rumorosa, on the way to Mexicali. The windy road through this area has a number of lookouts to take advantage of the views.

SIGHTS
★ El Vallecito Cave Paintings

There are more than 18 rock art sites at El Vallecito (Mexico 2 Km. 72, tel. 686/552-3591, 8am-5pm Wed.-Sun., US$3), although only five may be visited by the public. Of these, El Diablito, a painting of a small red devil, is the most popular. On the winter solstice, a ray of sunlight hits the painting, and his eyes are said to illuminate. There is a three-kilometer (1.9-mile) loop path that visitors can take to visit the five sites that are open to the public. Give yourself about two hours to complete the path and make sure to take drinking water, especially if the weather is warm. El Vallecito is located on the north side of Mexico 2D, five kilometers (3.1 miles) northwest of the town of La Rumorosa.

Campo Alaska

Also of interest in the area is **Campo Alaska** (Mexico 2 Km. 60, 686/552-3591, 9am-5pm Wed.-Sun., US$0.50), located four kilometers (2.5 miles) northeast of the town of La Rumorosa. General Abelardo L. Rodríguez, governor of the state of Baja California, constructed the stone buildings as a seat of government almost 100 years ago. From 1923 to 1929 the Mexicali government offices would move to the site during the months of June to October to escape the summer heat of the city and to enjoy a cooler mountain climate. The buildings were later used as a mental hospital and a tuberculosis hospital until 1955. Today, the historical site is a regional history museum. Call ahead before making the trek out to the site; the museum has recently been closed even during posted opening hours.

FOOD

You can get a great steak or traditional Mexican food in town at **La Cabaña del Abuelo** (Carretera Mexicali-Tecate Km. 75, tel. 686/575-0152, www.cabanadelabuelo. com, 7am-9pm Mon.-Fri., 7am-10pm Sat.-Sun., mains US$8-18). The hearty dishes are served in an inviting mountain cabin atmosphere with friendly and attentive service.

For a more casual meal, **Tacos Lalo** (Carretera Mexicali-Tecate, tel. 686/321-5451, 7am-10pm Tues.-Sun.) is a great place for *tacos al vapor*. They've been serving up the steamed tacos since 1973 and are a must-stop for locals and visitors passing through.

GETTING THERE AND AROUND

La Rumorosa is 60 kilometers (37 miles) east of Tecate, a 45-minute drive on highway Mexico 2.

Heading east from La Rumorosa on highway Mexico 2 winds you down the mountains through scenic rock formations until you reach Mexicali. There are various lookouts along the road to take advantage of the impressive views. The tolls on the roads from Tecate to Mexicali are the most expensive you'll find anywhere on the peninsula.

Rosarito and the Northern Baja Coast

Down the Pacific coast, about a half-hour drive south of the border, is the small beachside town of Rosarito. Weekenders flock here during the summer to enjoy the handsome and expansive beaches that offer visitors the chance to relax or enjoy a wide range of activities.

While Rosarito has only been its own municipality since 1995 (it was previously an extension of Tijuana), the beach town is growing into a destination in its own right with a state center for the arts, an underwater dive park, and a convention center all opening since 2013. Rosarito has traditionally been a summer destination because of the beaches, but there is temperate weather year-round and visitors who come in months other than summer can enjoy the town with cheaper

Look for ★ to find recommended sights, activities, dining, and lodging.

Highlights

★ **Dig into the arts scene** at **CEART State Center for the Arts,** which showcases local talent through exhibits, performances, and festivals (page 73).

★ **Play in the sand** at expansive and beautiful **Rosarito Beach** (page 75).

★ **Ride the waves** in and around Rosarito—home to great surf breaks that draw surfers from both sides of the border (page 75).

★ **Enjoy seafood straight off the fishing boats** in **Popotla** while dining at a casual restaurant right on the sand. Adventurous foodies swear this is the freshest seafood in the region (page 84).

Rosarito and the Northern Baja Coast

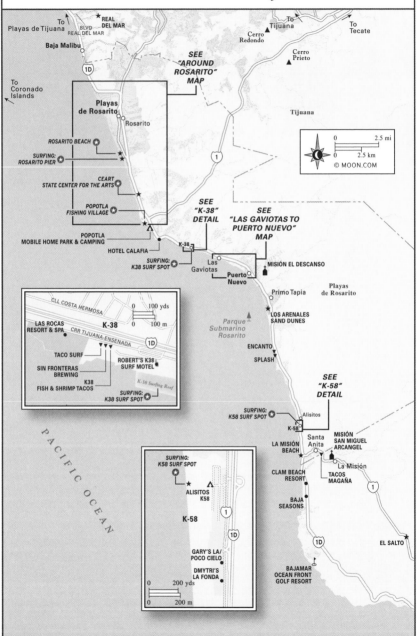

To Playas de Tijuana
REAL DEL MAR
BLVD REAL DEL MAR
Baja Malibu

To Tijuana
To Tecate
Cerro Redondo
Cerro Prieto

SEE "AROUND ROSARITO" MAP

To Coronado Islands

Playas de Rosarito
Rosarito
Tijuana

ROSARITO BEACH
SURFING: ROSARITO PIER

CEART STATE CENTER FOR THE ARTS

POPOTLA FISHING VILLAGE

SEE "K-38" DETAIL

SEE "LAS GAVIOTAS TO PUERTO NUEVO" MAP

POPOTLA MOBILE HOME PARK & CAMPING

HOTEL CALAFIA

K-38
SURFING: K38 SURF SPOT
Las Gaviotas
Puerto Nuevo
MISIÓN EL DESCANSO

Primo Tapia
Playas de Rosarito

LOS ARENALES SAND DUNES

Parque Submarino Rosarito

ENCANTO
SPLASH

K-38 Detail:
CLL COSTA HERMOSA
0   100 yds
0   100 m
K-38
LAS ROCAS RESORT & SPA
CRR TIJUANA-ENSENADA
1D
TACO SURF
SIN FRONTERAS BREWING
ROBERT'S K38 SURF MOTEL
K38 FISH & SHRIMP TACOS
K-38 Surfing Reef
SURFING: K38 SURF SPOT

SEE "K-58" DETAIL

SURFING: K58 SURF SPOT
Alisitos
K-58
Santa Anita
MISIÓN SAN MIGUEL ARCANGEL
LA MISIÓN BEACH
La Misión
TACOS MAGAÑA
CLAM BEACH RESORT
BAJA SEASONS
1
1D
EL SALTO
BAJAMAR OCEAN FRONT GOLF RESORT

K-58 Detail:
SURFING: K58 SURF SPOT
ALISITOS K58
1
K-58
1D
GARY'S LA/ POCO CIELO
DMYTRI'S LA FONDA
0   200 yds
0   200 m

PACIFIC OCEAN

0   2.5 mi
0   2.5 km
© MOON.COM

Best Restaurants and Accommodations

RESTAURANTS

★ **El Nido:** This classic Rosarito restaurant has been serving up hearty traditional Mexican dishes since 1971 (page 77).

★ **Tapanco:** The cozy atmosphere here provides the perfect setting for a savory steak or Mexican dish (page 77).

★ **Tacos El Yaqui:** With delicious Sonoran-style *perrones* tacos, this taco stand is a favorite among locals and foodies (page 79).

★ **El Gaucho Argentino:** This small, family-run operation brings the flavors of Argentina to Rosarito (page 79).

ACCOMMODATIONS

★ **Rosarito Beach Hotel:** This iconic hotel is the most famous landmark in the area and has hosted the rich and famous throughout the decades (page 81).

★ **Las Rocas Resort & Spa:** The stunning pool area at this resort near K38 attracts visitors who come to relax and get away from it all (page 85).

★ **Vista Hermosa Resort & Spa:** With a range of options for accommodations, this charming property near the village of Puerto Nuevo features modern amenities (page 88).

hotel rates and smaller crowds. With its central location, Rosarito is also a great jumping-off spot for exploring Tijuana, Ensenada, and the Valle de Guadalupe.

Rosarito was once a major spring break destination, and while a few of the clubs remain, the city has undergone a transformation in recent years and now attracts a more diverse crowd. This is a popular region for expats (there are an estimated 12,000 living in the area), but it's a friendly mix of locals and nonlocals getting along together. Because tourism is the main draw for the region, many of the employees in the hotels and restaurants speak excellent English. While there are options for hotels in the center of town where most of the action is, many travelers rent a condo or house on the beach somewhere in the greater Rosarito area, which includes regions like K38, La Fonda, Puerto Nuevo, and La Misión to the south.

PLANNING YOUR TIME

Rosarito is a popular weekend destination for people visiting from Southern California or inland areas of Baja, and a few days is a good amount of time to relax and explore the town. Because of Rosarito's central location, it can be a good home base for exploring other areas of northern Baja such as Tijuana, Ensenada, and Valle de Guadalupe. A week will give you enough time to take day trips to explore these surrounding cities and regions.

Around Rosarito

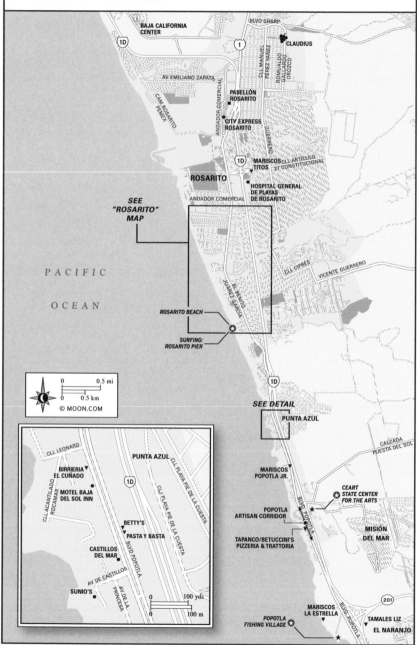

BLVD SHARP

BAJA CALIFORNIA CENTER

CLAUDIUS

1D

1

CLL MANUEL PEREZ YAÑEZ

ROMUALDO GALLARDO OROZCO

AV. EMILIANO ZAPATA

CAM. ROSARITO PEMEX

ANDADOR COMERCIAL

PABELLÓN ROSARITO

CITY EXPRESS ROSARITO

GUERRERO

1D

MARISCOS TITOS

CLL ARTÍCULO 27 CONSTITUCIONAL

ROSARITO

HOSPITAL GENERAL DE PLAYAS DE ROSARITO

ANDADOR COMERCIAL

SEE "ROSARITO" MAP

CLL CIPRÉS

VICENTE GUERRERO

PACIFIC

OCEAN

EL BENITO JUÁREZ GARCÍA

ROSARITO BEACH

SURFING: ROSARITO PIER

0   0.5 mi
0   0.5 km
© MOON.COM

1D

SEE DETAIL

PUNTA AZUL

CALZADA PUESTA DEL SOL

MARISCOS POPOTLA JR.

CEART STATE CENTER FOR THE ARTS

POPOTLA ARTISAN CORRIDOR

BLVD POPOTLA

MISIÓN DEL MAR

TAPANCO/BETUCCINI'S PIZZERIA & TRATTORIA

CLL LEONARD

PUNTA AZUL

CLL PLAYA PIE DE LA CUESTA

BIRRIERIA EL CUÑADO

1D

MOTEL BAJA DEL SOL INN

CLL ACANTILADO

ROCAMAR

BETTY'S

PASTA Y BASTA

CLL PLAYA PIE DE LA CUESTA

CASTILLOS DEL MAR

BLVD POPOTLA

AV DE CASTILLOS

SUNIO'S

AV DE LA PRINCESA

0   100 yds
0   100 m

MARISCOS LA ESTRELLA

BLVD POPOTLA

201

TAMALES LIZ

EL NARANJO

POPOTLA FISHING VILLAGE

Tijuana to Rosarito

As you leave Playas de Tijuana, heading south to Rosarito on toll road Mexico 1D, the buildings fade away and the Pacific Ocean stretches out to your right with views of the Coronado Islands. The scenic drive follows the coast all the way down to Rosarito.

REAL DEL MAR

Along the coast on the way to Rosarito is Real Del Mar (Mexico 1 Km. 19.5, www.realdelmargolfresort.com), an 18-hole golf course (tel. 664/631-3406, US$55) with a 75-room hotel (tel. 664/631-3670, US$79) and a housing community. The hotel's rooms are fairly modern with flat-screen televisions and down comforters. Many of the rooms have ocean views.

BAJA MALIBU

The beach community of Baja Malibu is home to a great surfing spot with a nice beach break.

Baja Farms (Mexico 1 Km. 22.5, tel. 664/368-6081, 10am-5pm Sat.-Sun.) is the closest thing that Rosarito has to a farmers market. It's just one small room, but the produce is fresh and organic and it's a great place to pick up some vegetables on the weekend.

Rosarito

Rosarito has been working hard in recent years to clean up its party-town image. You won't find the beauty of a colonial town here, but there are pockets of charm. Rosarito is home to a number of artists and there are a lot of beautiful street art murals around town.

Boulevard Benito Juárez, the main tourist drag, runs parallel to the beach a few blocks inland. Here you'll find many of the major hotels, shops, and restaurants lining the remodeled street, with palm trees down the middle. Pedestrian-only side streets off of Benito Juárez offer wide pathways for strolling about and enjoying the town center.

SIGHTS
★ CEART State Center for the Arts

Rosarito's Centro Estatal de las Artes or CEART (Paseo La Cascada, tel. 661/100-6338, www.icbc.gob.mx, 9am-5pm Mon.-Fri., free admission) is a large and modern space that's home to galleries, exhibitions, and workshops, as well as a bookstore and cafeteria. The vibrant Rosarito arts scene is highlighted at this state facility through photography, painting, sculpture, dance, music, and theater. Located south of town, the space is also used for large events and festivals. The full calendar of events and exhibitions can be found on its Facebook page at www.facebook.com/CeartRosarito.

The Coronado Islands

The four islands offshore from Rosarito are the Coronado Islands. The islands are uninhabited and mostly undeveloped aside from an abandoned casino turned military base. They attract mostly divers and anglers from both Rosarito and San Diego. Because the islands are just 18 miles from San Diego, they're a popular day trip for anglers who come on fishing charters directly from the United States. H&M Landing (U.S. tel. 619/222-1144, www.hmlanding.com, US$145) operates daily fishing trips to the Coronado Islands from San Diego. If you're looking to visit the islands from Rosarito, Rosarito Ocean Sports (Benito Juárez 890-7,

Rosarito

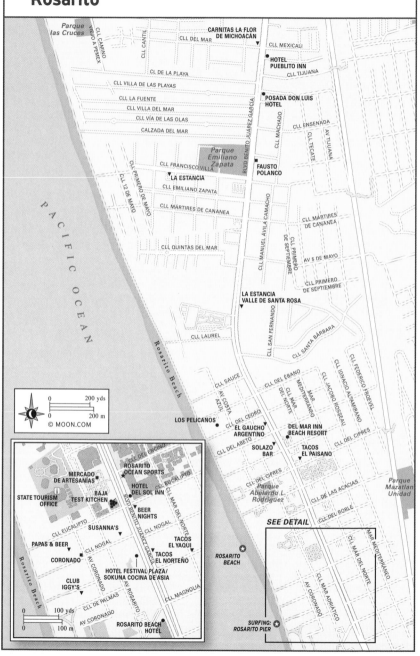

Parque
las Cruces

CLL CAMINO
VIEJO A PEMEX

CLL CANTIL

CLL DEL MAR

CARNITAS LA FLOR
DE MICHOACÁN

CLL MEXICALI

HOTEL
PUEBLITO INN

CL DE LA PLAYA

CLL TIJUANA

CLL VILLA DE LAS PLAYAS

POSADA DON LUIS
HOTEL

CLL LA FUENTE

CLL VILLA DEL MAR

CLL ENSENADA

CLL VÍA DE LAS OLAS

AV TIJUANA

CLL TECATE

CALZADA DEL MAR

CLL MACHADO

BLVD BENITO JUÁREZ GARCÍA

Parque
Emiliano
Zapata

FAUSTO
POLANCO

CLL FRANCISCO VILLA

LA ESTANCIA

CLL EMILIANO ZAPATA

CLL PRIMERO DE MAYO

CLL 12 DE MAYO

CLL MÁRTIRES DE CANANEA

CLL MÁRTIRES
DE CANANEA

CLL MANUEL ÁVILA CAMACHO

CLL PRIMERO
DE SEPTIEMBRE

AV 5 DE MAYO

CLL QUINTAS DEL MAR

CLL PRIMERO
DE SEPTIEMBRE

PACIFIC OCEAN

LA ESTANCIA
VALLE DE SANTA ROSA

CLL LAUREL

CLL SAN FERNANDO

CLL SANTA BÁRBARA

Rosarito Beach

CLL SAUCE

CLL DEL ÉBANO

CLL FEDERICO HOEVEL

0   200 yds

0   200 m

© MOON.COM

CLL COSTA AZUL

LOS PELICANOS

CLL DEL CEDRO

EL GAUCHO
ARGENTINO

CLL DEL ABETO

SOLAZO
BAR

CLL DEL ENCINO

ROSARITO
OCEAN SPORTS

MERCADO
DE ARTESANÍAS

HOTEL
DEL SOL INN

STATE TOURISM
OFFICE

BAJA
TEST KITCHEN

BEER
NIGHTS

BLVD BENITO JUÁREZ GARCÍA

CLL EUCALIPTO

SUSANNA'S

CLL EUCALIPTO

CLL NOGAL

PAPAS & BEER

CLL NOGAL

AV ROSARITO

TACOS
EL YAQUI

CORONADO

TACOS
EL NORTEÑO

Rosarito Beach

CLUB
IGGY'S

HOTEL FESTIVAL PLAZA/
SOKUNA COCINA DE ASIA

CLL DE PALMAS

AV CORONADO

CLL MAGNOLIA

0   100 yds

0   100 m

ROSARITO BEACH
HOTEL

MAR MEDITERRÁNEO

CLL MAR
DEL NORTE

CLL JACOBO ROSSEAU

CLL IGNACIO ALTAMIRANO

DEL MAR INN
BEACH RESORT

CLL DEL CIPRÉS

TACOS
EL PAISANO

CLL DEL CIPRÉS

Parque
Abelardo L.
Rodríguez

CLL DE LAS ACACIAS

CLL DEL ROBLE

SEE DETAIL

ROSARITO
BEACH

Parque
Mazatlán
Unidad

CLL MAR DEL NORTE

MAR MEDITERRÁNEO

AV CORONADO

CLL MAR ADRIÁTICO

CLL MAR DEL NORTE

SURFING:
ROSARITO PIER

tel. 661/100-2196, www.rosaritooceansports. com) can arrange boat tours (US$135) or scuba diving trips (US$150).

BEACHES

Most of the coastline in this area has beaches, but access can be difficult unless you are renting a condo or staying in a hotel along the beach. While all beaches in Mexico allow public access, there are no public parking lots or designated access points to other beaches in the area. For this reason, Rosarito Beach remains the main beach in the area.

★ Rosarito Beach

The expansive **Rosarito Beach** is eight kilometers (5 miles) long and runs parallel to the main street in the center of town. The beach is the center of life in Rosarito when the weather is warm. On summer weekends, it is packed with families who come to spend the day swimming, playing, and relaxing. The beach buzzes with activities like horseback riding, ultralight plane flying, and ATV riding. The **Rosarito Pier,** just in front of the Rosarito Beach Hotel, is great for fishing and is a popular surf spot. Farther north along the beach are Club Iggy's and Papas & Beer, a couple of the town's remaining large clubs. Day and night these are popular spots to enjoy drinks in the sand with ocean views.

There are no official parking lots for the beach, so summer weekends find the streets nearby crowded with beachgoers fighting for spots. If you're staying at one of the hotels in the main area of town, it's a better idea to walk. Access to the beach is gained through any of the many streets that run perpendicular to it.

RECREATION

TOP EXPERIENCE

★ Surfing

There are a number of surf spots in northern Baja that receive the steep-angled swells that skip even most of Southern California. In Rosarito proper, the best break is at the **Rosarito Pier,** next to the Rosarito Beach Hotel. This is a great spot for all levels of surfers, and surf lessons for beginners are available here. South of town at kilometer 38 is the famous **K38** surf spot. This is one of the most popular surf spots in northern Baja. It's a right break, but sometimes lefts can be found here as well. It's best on a mid to low tide. Farther south, at kilometer 58, near the La Fonda

ROSARITO

ROSARITO AND THE NORTHERN BAJA COAST

the pier on the expansive Rosarito Beach

Restaurant and Hotel, is another one of the most popular surf spots in the region, **K58.** The wave here breaks on nearly any swell, but combo swells bring the best shape.

There are board rentals right on the beach at the Rosarito Pier. At K38, the K38 Surf Shop has a selection of board and wetsuit rentals. There are no board rentals at K58.

Diving

In November 2015 the government sank a Mexican navy battleship, the *Uribe121,* to create the **Parque Submarino Rosarito** (www.facebook.com/parquesubmarinorosarito), Rosarito's first artificial reef and underwater park. Just offshore from Puerto Nuevo, the sunken ship is divided into different areas of interest: a sculpture garden, a homage to *Titanic* (the movie was filmed at the nearby Baja Studios), replicas of prehistoric art, and a ship graveyard.

The **Coronado Islands** just offshore are also a popular destination for dive trips. There's a colony of sea lions, rocky reefs, kelp beds, and even the broken wreckage of a yacht to explore. **Rosarito Ocean Sports** (Benito Juárez 890-7, tel. 661/100-2196, www.rosaritooceansports.com) can arrange dive tours to both the Coronado Islands and the Parque Submarino (US$150). They have PADI courses as well as equipment rental. Many of the major hotels arrange dive trips as well.

Parque Metropolitano

There are paths and trails around **Parque Metropolitano** (Lomas de Coronado, entre la Avenida Isla de Coronado y Bulevar Siglo XXI, 7am-7pm daily), a large park located three kilometers (1.9 miles) east of town. This is also a great place for families to spend the day—there are large green spaces, numerous picnic tables and grill areas, and playground equipment for children.

ENTERTAINMENT AND EVENTS
Nightlife

Although Rosarito was a mecca for the spring break crowd, the town has tamed and grown up in recent years. Many of the large clubs have closed, with artisanal restaurants and small cafés and bars taking their place. The nightlife scene in Rosarito is more subdued today, with locals preferring to gather at small bars and restaurants. The larger hotels in town have their own bars where guests can enjoy margaritas and local beers. In a nod to the growing craft beer scene in northern Baja, **Beer Nights** (Benito Juárez 748, tel. 664/114-4270, 4pm-midnight daily) has artisan beers from Mexico and the United States. It's a low-key locals spot with live music on certain nights.

Just outside of the main tourist area is **Solazo Bar** (Abeto, tel. 661/121-8618, 11am-2am Wed.-Sun.). Holding happy hour all day, patrons can enjoy beers and mixed drinks from the covered downstairs area or from the 2nd-floor outdoor patio. The bar doesn't serve food, but there's sometimes a food truck and you can bring in food from outside. The televisions make this a popular spot during football season. Cash only.

Those who are missing the large clubs that used to dominate the nightlife of Rosarito can still get their fix at **Papas & Beer** (Coronado 400, tel. 661/612-0244, www.papasandbeer.com, 10am-1am Mon.-Thurs., 10am-3am Fri.-Sun.) or **Club Iggy's** (11337 Rosarito Centro, www.clubiggys.com, 10am-9pm Mon.-Thurs., 10am-1am Fri., 10am-2am Sat., 10am-10pm Sun.). These spots right on Rosarito Beach are popular with those who want to drink in the sand during the day and party by DJ at night.

Wineries

Because it's only an hour away from the Valle de Guadalupe wine region, many who stay in Rosarito take a day trip to go wine-tasting. **Baja Test Kitchen** (www.bajatestkitchen.com, rates starting at US$199 per person for public tour) offers public group and private gourmet food and wine tours of the Valle de Guadalupe, with door-to-door service for clients from their accommodations in Rosarito.

Rosarito has its own winery in town: **Claudius** (Blvd. Sharp 3722, tel. 661/100-0232), making exceptional wines. They have a tasting room and can accommodate wine-tastings for special occasions or if you call ahead. They also have a wine school where participants attend weekly classes and make 25 cases of their own wine.

Events

Twice a year, in spring and fall, the 80K **Rosarito Ensenada Bike Ride** (www.rosaritoensenada.com) runs from Rosarito to an ending with a big fiesta in Ensenada. It's usually held in May and September.

The annual **Rosarito Art Fest** (www.rosaritoartfest.com), held over a weekend each summer, has become one of the town's most famous events. With the bourgeoning art scene in northern Baja, the festival is a great showcase for local arts in addition to having live music and plenty of food and drinks.

SHOPPING

Just south of town, if you continue on Benito Juárez—the Mexico 1 free road—you'll reach the **Popotla Artisan Corridor,** which has a number of artisan shops where buyers can purchase items like wrought iron pieces, wooden furniture, chimeneas, and colorful Talavera ceramics.

In town just north of El Nido restaurant, the **Mercado de Artesanías** features over 100 stalls carrying Mexican souvenir arts and crafts such as blankets, silver jewelry, ceramics, and glassware. Don't be afraid to bargain for a fair price. If you prefer a more curated shopping experience, don't miss **Fausto Polanco** (Benito Juárez 2400, tel. 661/612-0125, www.faustopolanco.com.mx, 10am-6pm Mon.-Sat.) on the north side of town. A visit to the showroom, featuring hacienda-style Mexican furniture and beautifully re-fined rustic pieces, feels almost like a trip to a museum.

There's also a small mall on the north side of town, **Pabellón Rosarito** (Carretera Libre 300, tel. 661/612-3140, 10am-10pm daily, www.pabellonrosarito.com), that has a Cinemax movie theater, Home Depot, food court, and other small specialty stores.

FOOD

Rosarito doesn't have the hot culinary scene that you'll find in other northern Baja regions such as Tijuana, Ensenada, or the Valle de Guadalupe. But that doesn't mean that there isn't good food here. Rosarito has incredible traditional Mexican restaurants, tasty taco stands, and fresh seafood.

Mexican

For traditional Mexican food or steak, you can't beat any of the restaurants associated with the Perez family. The 13 Perez siblings own many of the best restaurants in town (and the youngest owns the Don Pisto liquor stores). The restaurants all have a similar authentic ranch atmosphere, savory steaks, and rich Mexican food. The original is ★ **El Nido** (Benito Juárez 67, tel. 661/612-1430, 8am-midnight daily, mains US$7-18), which has been a mainstay on the main drag in town since 1971. El Nido features a unique lush setting with abundant trees and plants, caged birds, and flowing fountains. The classic restaurant serves hearty traditional Mexican dishes accompanied by fresh tortillas being made right in the dining room. Just down the street and on the beach is **Los Pelicanos** (Calle del Ebano 113, tel. 661/612-0445, 7am-10pm Sun.-Thurs., 7am-midnight Fri.-Sat., mains US$6-13), which offers the best views of any of the restaurants with the expansive Rosarito Beach just out the window. With their huevos rancheros and *machaca* dishes, this is a popular spot for locals to enjoy brunch on the weekends.

The southernmost of the Perez dynasty in Rosarito is ★ **Tapanco** (Blvd. Popotla Km. 31.5, tel. 661/100-6035, www.tapancorosarito.com, 8am-10pm daily, mains US$5-16), just south of town. The restaurant has expanded over the years to include an outdoor patio and café as well as an upstairs bar called Why Not? Alfredo, the owner, is a welcome presence,

greeting customers and making sure that everyone has an incredible experience. The menu features traditional Mexican dishes as well as fresh seafood, but the specialties are the savory steaks. The house-made soups, salad dressings, and marmalades always add a nice touch to the meal.

Meat lovers will want to head to **La Estancia** (Ave. Francisco Villa 316, tel. 661/613-0695, 8am-10pm Sun.-Thurs., 8am-midnight Fri.-Sat., mains US$6-13) in the northern part of town. Steak, quail, lamb, and rabbit are specialties. The walls are adorned with mounted animals, giving the restaurant a dark, cozy hunting lodge feel. Many locals pop in to have dinner at the large bar, which offers a more casual experience. There is a second location, **La Estancia Valle de Santa Rosa** (Km. 78, 8am-11pm Fri.-Sat., 8am-9pm Sun.), an hour south on the Mexico 1 free road on the way to the Valle de Guadalupe. Situated in a remote location in the Santa Rosa valley, the restaurant offers much of the same menu with stunning views of the countryside.

Carnitas La Flor de Michoacán (Benito Juárez 291, tel. 661/612-1062, 9am-9pm Thurs.-Tues., mains US$5-8) has been serving up *carnitas* to locals in the same location since 1950. The large restaurant is a gathering place for families and groups who come to eat family-style on the cheap. There is a second, smaller location, also on Benito Juárez, closer to the tourist area.

Antojitos and Street Food

The most famous taco stand in town is ★ **Tacos El Yaqui** (Mar del Norte, Esp. La Palma, no tel., 9am-5pm Thurs.-Mon., tacos US$2), a sister taco stand to Tacos Los Perrones in Tijuana. They've been serving traditional Sonoran-style *arrachera* (skirt steak) *perrones* since 1984. *Perrones* are different from the usual Mexican street tacos in that they are served in a flour tortilla with beans

and melted cheese in addition to the usual meat and toppings. Just off the main drag, this spot has become extremely popular with locals and tourists, so expect lines.

For more traditional street tacos, both **Tacos el Paisano** (Blvd. Benito Juarez, US$1-2) and **Tacos el Norteño** (Blvd. Benito Juarez, US$1-2) on the main drag are solid options.

The best deal in town for fish tacos is at **Mariscos Titos** (Blvd. Articulo 27, tel. 661/120-0657, www.mariscostitos.com, 7:30am-5:30pm daily), the large taco stand across from the Soriana grocery store. For under US$1, patrons get a gigantic battered fish taco topped with the works. It's more of a locals' spot because it's out of the tourist area of town, but the affordable and savory tacos make it worth the trek. It has a large menu with a variety of other seafood dishes. Just south of town, **Mariscos Popotla Jr.** (Blvd. Popotla Km. 30.29, tel. 661/100-2598, 9am-7pm daily, tacos US$1-2) is another popular option for fish tacos and *mariscos* such as ceviche, all served in a casual setting.

If you want to eat like the locals, head just south of town to **Birrieria El Cuñado** (Mexico 1 742, no tel., 7am-11pm daily, US$1-5) to enjoy *birria* tacos or a full order of *birria*.

For something different, ★ **El Gaucho Argentino** (Blvd. Benito Juárez #100, tel. 661/613-0853, www.elgauchoargentino rosarito.com, 11am-8pm Wed.-Mon., US$2-6) is an Argentinian spot serving authentic steak and sausage sandwiches (with chimichurri sauce, of course) as well as empanadas. Husband-and-wife owners Gerardo and Flavia are wonderful hosts and make the little shop feel like home. On Saturday they grill a large selection of additional meats for an impressive Argentinian barbecue spread.

Rosarito has its own *colectivo* of outdoor food stalls in front of the Hotel Festival Plaza called **Plaza Food Fest** (Benito Juárez 1207, tel. 661/612-2950, noon-8pm Sun.-Thurs., noon-10pm Fri.-Sat., US$5-9). The Cervecería Tinta Negra stall is one of the best spots in town to try local Baja craft beers. Patrons

---

1: shopping along the Popotla Artisan Corridor, just south of Rosarito 2: fish tacos from Mariscos Titos 3: El Nido restaurant 4: *birria* tacos at Birrieria El Cuñado

order from various stands and can enjoy their food at the outdoor tables as they watch the world go by along Rosarito's main drag.

International

Owned by a California native and a favorite restaurant of many of the expats who live in town, **Susanna's** (Pueblo Plaza, tel. 661/613-1187, www.susannasinrosarito. com, 1pm-9:30pm Wed.-Thurs. and Sun.-Mon., 1pm-10:30pm Fri.-Sat., mains US$14-24) specializes in California cuisine with fresh salads, hearty pastas, savory chicken and fish dishes, and steak. To top it off, the menu features wines from the nearby Valle de Guadalupe.

Located downstairs from the Hotel Festival Plaza is **Sokuna Cocina de Asia** (Benito Juárez 1207, tel. 661/612-5231, noon-10pm Thurs.-Tues., US$8-10), which will satisfy cravings for Asian food. The Asian fusion dishes are made of fresh ingredients and are flavorful and filling. There are a number of vegetarian options. The décor, an eclectic collection of well-curated vintage pieces, is chic as well as comfortable and welcoming.

If you're hungry for a burger, **Betty's** (Blvd. Popotla Km. 28, tel. 661/116-2160, 11am-6pm Tues.-Sun., US$6-9) serves authentic U.S.-style burgers just south of town. The family-run operation has friendly and personal service and uses fresh ingredients to create gourmet burgers. They have great options for vegetarians and vegans as well.

When they're in the mood for Italian, hip locals head to **Betuccini's Pizzeria & Trattoria** (Blvd. Popotla Km. 28.8, tel. 661/100-6148, www.betuccinispizzeria.com, 8am-11pm daily, US$9-13), where the homemade pizzas, pastas, and salads are a welcome change for those tired of Mexican food. When the weather is warm, sit on the outdoor patio where the string lights and lush setting provide a perfect backdrop for a summer meal.

Another option for Italian is **Pasta y Basta** (Blvd. Popotla Km. 28.5, tel. 661/120-0766, www.pastaybastarosarito.com, noon-9:30pm Tues.-Sat., noon-8:30pm Sun., US$14-20). The cozy restaurant is owned by a northern Italian chef and his wife. They also operate a small store a few doors down that carries imported Italian products like pastas and olive oil, in addition to fast Italian cuisine such as panini and lasagna.

ACCOMMODATIONS

Hotels in Rosarito tend to be expensive for the quality of accommodations you get in return. Prices go up on weekends during peak season (summer), especially in August when the town is flooded with residents of Mexicali and other inland areas who come to the coast to escape the heat. While there are no luxury hotel accommodations in Rosarito, there are a number of very nice condo and house rentals, a popular option for visitors. A few campsites and RV parks can be found south of town on the beach in the stretch between Rosarito and Ensenada.

Under US$50

The budget **Posada Don Luis Hotel** (Benito Juárez 272, tel. 661/612-1166, donluisprofile@gmail.com, US$42) has very basic rooms but offers a small outdoor pool and off-street parking. Another budget option, **Motel Baja Del Sol Inn** (Carretera Libre Km. 26.8, tel. 661/612-0401, US$25), is just south of town and has a pink and purple exterior that's hard to miss. Rooms are outdated but have all of the basic amenities.

US$50-100

The 60 rooms at **Del Mar Inn Beach Resort** (formerly Brisas del Mar, Benito Juárez 22, tel. 661/612-2549, www.delmarinn.com.mx, US$95) have air-conditioning and heating, cable TV, wireless Internet, balconies, and room service. There's a pool and Jacuzzi in addition to a restaurant and bar. The hotel is only two blocks from the beach, and has parking in the courtyard.

Los Pelicanos (Calle del Ebano 113, tel. 661/612-0445, US$60-95) is a cozy little hotel right on the beach with a lush pool and Jacuzzi area. Rooms are spacious but older and in need of an update. There's a great Mexican restaurant by the same name on-site.

With 47 rooms, **Hotel Pueblito Inn** (Benito Juárez 286, tel. 661/612-2516, www.hotelpueblitoinn.com, US$80-90) offers basic accommodations with cable TV, air-conditioning, and heating. It's in the northern part of town, so you'll likely need to take a cab to the central tourist area where many of the restaurants, shops, and other hotels are located.

With a good location right in town, **Hotel Del Sol Inn** (Benito Juárez No. 32, tel. 661/612-2552, www.del-sol-inn.com, US$85) is walking distance to lots of restaurants and shops as well as the beach. There's a friendly staff and working wireless Internet.

City Express Rosarito (364 Col. Reforma, tel. 661/614-4141, www.cityexpress.com, US$110) in the Pabellón mall caters to business travelers attending conventions at the Baja California Center. The 113-room hotel offers modern accommodations with Internet and air-conditioning. There is a swimming pool and a fitness room.

US$100-150

The iconic ★ **Rosarito Beach Hotel** (Benito Juárez 31, tel. 661/612-1111, toll-free U.S. tel. 866/767-2748, www.rosaritobeachhotel.com, US$100) is the most prominent landmark in Rosarito and also one of the most recognized hotels in Baja. It first opened to the public in 1925 and has been the hub of action in Rosarito ever since. The traditional Mexican ambience, old-world charm, and history of the hotel continue to attract most of the visitors who come to Rosarito today, whether they stay as guests or come to eat or drink in any of the restaurants or bars. Past guests have included Orson Welles, Gregory Peck, Spencer Tracy, and such ladies as Marilyn Monroe, Lana Turner, Kim Novak, and Rita Hayworth, prompting the declaration painted over the lobby entrance: "through this door pass the most beautiful women in the world." The founder's nephew, Hugo Torres, who runs the hotel today with his family, was the first mayor of Rosarito. He was integral in growing the town of Rosarito and turning it into a tourist destination. His entire family is involved in local politics and promotion.

Today, the Rosarito Beach Hotel has 500 rooms, including a 17-story luxury condo-hotel tower built in 2008, with units available to rent as hotel rooms. These accommodations are newer and more modern than rooms in the older section of the hotel. The hotel often features special packages and deals, so check their website before booking.

With its location in the heart of Rosarito, imposing size, and brightly colored carnival-themed architecture, it's hard to ignore **Hotel Festival Plaza** (Benito Juárez 1207, tel. 661/612-2950, toll-free U.S. tel. 800/453-8606, www.hotelfestivalplaza.com, US$85-115). Just look for the large building with the faux roller coaster on the facade. The hotel, once buzzing with people and energy, feels somewhat neglected these days. There are plans for much-needed renovations and improvements. Rooms are basic and offer wireless access and cable TV. A small pool and Ferris wheel (no longer operational) are in the courtyard. There are a number of restaurants that rotate in and out of business on the property. With its interior courtyard and central location, the hotel is host to many of the city's art and food festivals.

Just south of town, **Castillos del Mar** (Carretera Libre Km. 29.5, tel. 661/612-1088, www.castillosdelmar.com, US$135) offers basic accommodations right on the water. Many guests feel that the price is high for what they get in return, with rooms and a property that could use an updating. There's a beach-side bar, **Sunio's,** that has fresh architecture and decor and beautiful beach and ocean views. It offers beers and small bites such as tacos and tostadas.

Vacation Rentals

The abundance of new high-rise condominiums and classic Mexican houses on the beach makes renting a condo or house for the weekend a popular choice in Rosarito.

The Oceana Rosarito Inn (Benito Juárez 907-24, tel. 888/849-4500, www.rosaritoinn.com, US$250-550) is an option right in town that can accommodate up to 10 people in its four-bedroom units. The condominium resort La Paloma (tel. 664/609-5555, www.rosaritolapaloma.com) is just south of town, set on a beautiful property right on the water with multiple swimming pools and Jacuzzis. They have units with up to three bedrooms.

South of Rosarito, Las Gaviotas (www.las-gaviotas.com) is a popular choice for U.S. travelers coming down for the weekend to rent a house. You may be able to find private rentals in La Jolla Del Mar/La Jolla Real or Club Marena (www.clubmarenarentals.com), which comprise the most luxurious accommodations in the area.

INFORMATION AND SERVICES

Rosarito has major services like large grocery stores, banks, ATMs, and gas stations. The large structure just north of town is the Baja California Center (tel. 664/609-7900, www.bccenter.mx), a convention center that attracts international conferences.

Tourist Information

There is a State Tourism Office (Benito Juárez 907, tel. 661/612-5127, 8am-6pm Mon.-Fri., 9am-1pm Sat.) on the main drag downtown providing brochures and information about Rosarito.

Medical Services

Rosarito has a number of hospitals and clinics. The Hospital General de Playas de Rosarito (Galilea Este 2200, tel. 661/612-6164) is right across from city hall. The modern building has an emergency room, state-of-the-art facilities, and a skilled staff. They provide services at very affordable prices.

1: Los Pelicanos restaurant, popular for oceanview dining 2: the beach at Castillos del Mar, a resort just south of Rosarito

TRANSPORTATION
Getting There

Most visitors coming to Rosarito arrive by car because the town is about a 30-minute, 25-kilometer (15.5-mile) drive south from the San Ysidro border crossing in Tijuana. For those coming south over the Otay Mesa border crossing, the Boulevard 2000/Mexico 201 highway connects to Mexico 1 just south of Rosarito near the fishing village of Popotla. The 65-kilometer (40-mile) drive from the Otay Mesa border crossing to Rosarito takes one hour.

Taxis and shuttle vans (called colectivos or calafias) make the trip from Rosarito to the San Ysidro border crossing and vice versa. Expect to pay around US$30.

THE TOLL ROAD AND THE FREE ROAD

There are two options for driving to Rosarito from the San Ysidro border crossing: the Mexico 1 free road and the Mexico 1D toll road. Most tourists take the toll road to avoid the traffic and confusion of navigating Tijuana streets and to enjoy the scenic ocean views. The toll is US$2 at each toll station. There is a station in Playas de Tijuana and another just south of Rosarito. Once you are in Rosarito, the free road (carretera libre) and the toll road run parallel to each other until La Fonda, where the free road turns inland and the toll road follows the coast south. The roads converge again just north of Ensenada in San Miguel where the third and final toll station is located. It's possible to get on and off of the toll road between stations around the Rosarito area without having to pay the toll if you are driving on stretches between the stations.

Getting Around

It's easy to walk around the downtown tourist area of Rosarito. Taxis are also easy to hail along Benito Juárez in downtown. Uber, based in Tijuana, serves Rosarito as well, but allow for extra time as there may not be one immediately in the area.

Rosarito is a fairly easy city to drive in, especially considering that most of the tourist-oriented businesses are along Benito Juárez. Street parking is usually relatively easy to procure and hotels as well as some restaurants will have their own parking lots.

Rosarito to Ensenada

Many travelers who come to the Rosarito area opt to stay somewhere south of town itself. The stretch between Rosarito and Ensenada is full of little villages and communities with plenty of options for accommodations, dining, and activities. The addresses for establishments along the **Mexico 1 free road** *(carretera libre)* will be referenced by the kilometer marking. The numbers for the kilometer markings get larger as you head farther south.

★ POPOTLA FISHING VILLAGE

Those unfamiliar with the fishing village of Popotla, a 10-minute drive south of Rosarito via the Mexico 1 *carretera libre,* may be initially deterred by the grimy appearance, fishy smell, and derelict buildings. Restaurant employees aggressively call out to passersby to come into their establishments, which are not much more than ramshackle buildings perched on the rocks. The weekends here are especially overwhelming: Hundreds of local families converge on the small beach-front village, causing traffic to back up all the way to the highway. But herein lies the secret to Popotla, because underneath its repellent appearance, adventurous foodies swear that this is the best place for the freshest seafood in the region.

Food

There are plenty of restaurants lining the few streets that comprise the village. **Mariscos La Estrella** (Blvd. Popotla, tel. 661/116-7005) is a solid choice with fresh seafood dishes, friendly service, and a pleasant atmosphere. Be sure to make it down to the beach where the fishers bring in their fresh seafood to sell. There are a few more restaurants directly on the beach where customers can sit in the sand to enjoy a meal while they watch the day's catch coming in. Popotla specialties include the giant spider crab and *pescado zarandeado,* where the fish is butterflied, lathered with mayonnaise and ancho chile, and then grilled.

Just outside the entrance to Popotla at the corner of Boulevard 2000 and the free road is the popular **Tamales Liz** (Carretera Libre Km. 33, tel. 661/850-8697, 9am-5pm daily, US$2). The fresh-made tamales are a local favorite and come in a variety of flavors such as chicken, pork, and chili with cheese.

Accommodations

Just south of the fishing village, the **Popotla Mobile Home Park Camping & RV** (Carretera Libre Km. 34, tel. 661/612-1502, www.popotla.mx) is a trailer park with spaces for camping (US$25) and for RVs with full hookups (US$35). The ocean views are stunning from around the property and also at the restaurant and bar. There's beach access and also a small pool.

Getting There

Most visitors coming to Popotla arrive by car. The town is about a 10-minute, 9-kilometer (5.6-mile) drive south of Rosarito on the free road. Taxis from Rosarito cost about US$5.

CALAFIA POINT

Anyone who frequented this region in the 1980s and '90s has likely stayed or eaten at the legendary **Hotel Calafia** (Carretera Libre Km. 35.5). Perched on a dramatic point right on the Pacific, the restaurant here comprised a series of terraces with stunning views. Calafia claims to be a historic mission site (it wasn't), and there are buildings in the parking lot set up to mimic an old colonial town and mission. The property today is a shadow of its glory days. While the stunning views from the point remain the same, the restaurant goes in and out of operation, and the hotel rooms are tired and outdated. The only signs of life are the residential towers just to the north.

K38

One of northern Baja's most famous surf spots is **K38,** recognized as much for the surf as for the giant statue of Jesus up on the hill with arms outstretched toward the ocean. There's a right surf break here, but sometimes lefts can be found as well. The spot is best on a mid- to low tide. Watch out for sea urchins, especially at the mouth of the river. There's another break just south at kilometer 38.5 in front of the Club Marena condo buildings.

Food

For a quick and tasty bite, **K38 Fish & Shrimp Tacos** (Carretera Libre Km. 38, US$1.50) is at the south end of a strip of buildings alongside the highway and serves delicious traditional seafood tacos. The casual taco stand also serves a chipotle shrimp taco that's a unique treat. Just a few doors up, **Taco Surf** (Carretera Libre Km. 38, 10am-7pm daily, US$1.50) is the place to go for carne asada and *al pastor* tacos and tortas.

For live music and a cold beer, **Sin Fronteras Brewing** (Carretera Libre Km. 38, tel. 552/219-4624, www.sinfronterasbrewery. com, noon-8pm Mon.-Thurs., noon-10pm Fri.-Sat., 10am-8pm Sun.) offers a variety of regional Baja craft beers on tap. There's a large outdoor space where patrons can enjoy impressive ocean views. Pets are allowed on leashes and children under 18 are allowed before sunset.

Accommodations

Just north of K38 is the large ★ **Las Rocas Resort & Spa** (Carretera Libre Km. 38.5, tel. 661/614-9850, U.S. toll-free tel. 866/445-8909, US$80). While the property is older and

in need of a remodel, it's still a popular option for weekenders visiting from Southern California. There's a small spa on the property as well as a restaurant and two bars. The pool and Jacuzzi area boasts beautiful views overlooking the Pacific. Most surfers stay at **Robert's K38 Surf Motel** (Carretera Libre Km. 38, U.S. tel. 310/613-4263, www. robertsk38.com, US$65). It has clean, comfortable rooms and secure gated parking. Surfboards, kayaks, booties, and wetsuits are available to rent.

Getting There

Most visitors coming to K38 arrive by car. It's a 12-minute, 11-kilometer (6.8-mile) drive south from Rosarito. A taxi from Rosarito should cost about US$8.

PUERTO NUEVO LOBSTER VILLAGE

For years, the famous "lobster village" of northern Baja was a draw for tourists coming across the border to eat lobster served "Puerto Nuevo style": split in half, fried, and served with flour tortillas, rice, and beans.

Those who have frequented Puerto Nuevo for decades remember when they would buy platters heaped with lobsters for just a few dollars each. Today, the prices have gone up considerably as the village panders to tourists, but you can still get a lobster meal with ocean views for cheaper than you would in the United States. Many visitors to the region make it to Puerto Nuevo for a meal during their trip, as it's located just a 15-minute drive south of Rosarito.

Sights

Just south of Puerto Nuevo, **Misión el Descanso** (also sometimes called San Miguel la Nueva) was established in 1810 by Padre Tomás de Ahumada after floods had destroyed the mission site in nearby La Misión. In 1830, new buildings were constructed by Padre Felix Caballero but were abandoned in 1834 for the new Nuestra Señora de Guadalupe church in what is the

Las Gaviotas to Puerto Nuevo

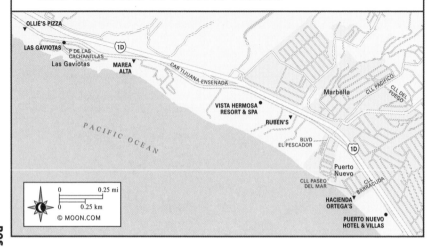

current-day Valle de Guadalupe. An archaeological dig in 1997 revealed stone foundation ruins and a few adobe walls from the 1830 structure. Today they are preserved by INAH and partially covered by a steel awning. The ruins are located east of the Mexico 1 free road about 1 kilometer (0.6 mile) south of Puerto Nuevo.

Food

Within the few square blocks that comprise the village are a number of restaurants, all with generally the same menu and prices. They will also all have an employee out on the street trying to lure you into the restaurant. The large **Ortega's** (www.ortegas.com), along the water on the south side of town, is popular with tourists. It has both indoor and outdoor seating and, of course, plenty of lobsters and margaritas to keep the crowds happy. The family owns multiple restaurants in town, so chances are even if you don't eat at this location, you'll still end up at one of the Ortega restaurants. Their other popular restaurant, **Hacienda Ortega's,** has a more intimate atmosphere and a lovely upstairs patio. It's on the north street in town.

There are also a number of artisan stalls in town, so shoppers can get their fill of silver jewelry, Mexican knickknacks, and locally made flavored tequilas.

Outside of town on the free road just north of the housing community of Las Gaviotas, **Ollie's Pizza** (Carretera Libre Km. 40.4, tel. 664/231-7946, www.olliesbrickovenpizza.com, 4pm-10pm Wed.-Sun., pizza US$9-14) is serving up some of the best artisanal brick-oven pizza in the area. Kids (of all ages) can ask to go behind the counter to don a chef's hat and put the toppings on their pizza before it goes into the oven. Don't miss drizzling the homemade chili oil on your pizza.

Just south of Las Gaviotas is **Marea Alta** (Carretera Libre Km. 41.5, tel. 686/243-3348, 11:30am-8pm Thurs.-Tues., US$8-12), serving up incredibly fresh seafood in the form of gourmet ceviches, tuna tostadas, and sandwiches. They also serve local craft beers and wine. There's some seating indoors and a small patio with outdoor seating as well.

1: the Pacific fishing village of Popotla 2: fresh-caught crab 3: the daily catch being sold on the shores of Popotla 4: Las Rocas Resort & Spa

Baja Studios

Just north of Popotla is the famous **Baja Studios** (formerly Fox Studios) where big blockbuster hits like *Titanic, Master and Commander, All is Lost,* and the James Bond flick *Tomorrow Never Dies* have been filmed. The studio is home to the world's largest water tank, covering more than three hectares. Unfortunately, the studios are not open to the public for tours as they were when owned by Fox. They are still actively used for filming, and it's not uncommon to see big Hollywood stars around town who are shooting at the studios and have made Rosarito their temporary home for a few months. Many of the local expats are regular extras for TV shows and movies that are filmed at the studios.

Accommodations

Right next door to the village is the large **Puerto Nuevo Hotel & Villas** (Carretera Libre Km. 44.5, tel. 661/614-1488, www.puertonuevohotelyvillas.com, US$108-120). With a beautiful oceanfront location, the hotel boasts 300 rooms, indoor and outdoor pools, a spa, and restaurant.

North of the village a few kilometers, there are a few more options for accommodations. At kilometer 43, ★ **Vista Hermosa Resort & Spa** (formerly Bobby's by the Sea, Carretera Libre Km. 43, tel. 661/614-1135, www.vistahermosaresort.com) has daily, weekly, or monthly condo and casita rentals. The charming property offers modern amenities and a restaurant and bar on the property that's popular with local expats. The housing community of **Las Gaviotas** (Carretera Libre Km. 41.5, www.las-gaviotas.com) is a classic community for expat homes and weekend rentals for tourists.

Getting There

Most visitors coming to Puerto Nuevo arrive by car. It's a 15-minute, 18-kilometer (11.2-mile) drive south from Rosarito. A taxi from Rosarito should cost about US$12.

PRIMO TAPIA

A 20-minute drive south of Rosarito, the small town of Primo Tapia is mostly known to expats and tourists as the home of the housing community of Cantamar and a few restaurants that are popular with local expats.

Sights

One kilometer (0.6 mile) south of town, **Los Arenales sand dunes** are right on the ocean and attract motocross and 4x4 riders. The land is owned by the local *ejido,* which charges US$5 to enter. You can rent an ATV for US$35 an hour.

Food

Ruben's (Carretera Libre Km. 46.5, tel. 661/613-2369, www.rubenspalmgrill.mx, 11am-9pm Mon.-Thurs., 11am-11pm Fri.-Sat., 9am-9pm Sun., mains US$8-13) is a popular spot for expats and tourists, especially for its Sunday brunch (US$17 per person) with live music, Mexican folk dancing, and bottomless mimosas. Another popular expat spot is **Splash** (Carretera Libre Km. 52, tel. 661/614-0095, www.splashcantina.com, 9am-10pm daily, US$12-18), which is in a large two-story building right on the coast. The ocean views from the 2nd floor are superb. The menu ranges from traditional Mexican dishes and local seafood to American classics like burgers and steaks. Happy hour is 4pm-7pm Monday-Thursday, with fish tacos and draft beer for US$1.25 each. Right next door to Splash, **Encanto** (Carretera Libre Km. 52.5, tel. 661/688-0126, 9am-9pm, US$10-16) has the same great views, which can be enjoyed from the quaint indoor space or the outdoor patio. Patrons enjoy lobster and other seafood dishes with a beer or margarita.

Getting There

Most visitors coming to Primo Tapia arrive by car. The town is located 20 kilometers (12.4 miles) south of Rosarito along the free road and the drive takes 20 minutes. A taxi from Rosarito costs about US$10.

LA FONDA/K58

Home to the famous **K58 surf spot,** the area along the ocean here is often referred to by tourists as "La Fonda" because of the namesake hotel/restaurant that has been around since the 1970s.

Food and Accommodations

The place to camp here is **Alisitos K58** (Carretera Libre Km. 58, no tel., US$15). The only things offered in terms of facilities are bathrooms (bring your own toilet paper) and outdoor showers. But the tranquil oceanfront spot and access to the waves are what keep the surfers coming back.

The restaurant at **Poco Cielo** (Carretera Libre Km. 59, tel. 646/155-0606, www. pococielo.com, US$8-12) serves a selection of Mexican food in its large indoor dining room and on its outdoor patio looking over the Pacific. They also have hotel rooms

available (US$95-120), each decorated in a different theme.

Due to owner disputes, the famous La Fonda property is currently split into two separate businesses—**Gary's La Fonda** (Carretera Libre Km. 59, tel. 646/155-0308, www.garyslafondabaja.com, US$100) and **Dmytri's La Fonda** (Km. 59, tel. 646/155-0872, dmytrislafonda@gmail.com, US$100). You can't miss the competing signs out front that seem to grow louder and more outrageous every month. Both properties offer hotel rooms, restaurants, bars, and a popular Sunday brunch with a large buffet and bottomless Bloody Marys or margaritas.

Getting There

K58 is located 33 kilometers (20 miles) and 25 minutes south of Rosarito. Most visitors arrive by car. A taxi from Rosarito costs about US$13.

LA MISIÓN

The town of La Misión is where the free road and the toll road split. The Mexico 1 free road heads inland here, through the small ranching town of La Misión and into the country toward the northern entrance to the Valle de

sunset at La Fonda

Guadalupe wine region. The Mexico 1D toll road follows the coast south on a scenic route to Ensenada. There are no hotels here, but there is a large expat community and vacation houses available for rent.

Sights and Recreation

La Misión Beach is best reached by staying on the toll road. The large and expansive beach is a popular spot for families on summer weekends, but remains empty most of the week. There are a few *palapas* for shade as well as a number of food stalls. The waves and riptides can be fierce here, so this is a good beach for relaxing, sunbathing, and taking walks, but not a good one for swimming.

The adobe Misión San Miguel Arcangel was constructed from 1793 to 1800 under Dominican padre Luis Sales. After severe flooding in 1809, the operation was moved to another mission in Descanso in 1810. Today, the adobe ruins are in a fenced-off area in town next to the school, just off of the free road.

Just 11 kilometers (6.8 miles) south of La Misión is El Salto (Carretera Libre Km. 76, tel. 664/407-7751, www.elsaltoensenada.com, 7am-5pm daily), a nice spot for hiking, camping, and picnicking. It's a popular area for hiking because of the striking large granite rock formations and water that forms natural pools and waterfalls depending on the time of year. There are grill and picnic areas to enjoy. There's a daily use fee of US$3 per person. Camping overnight costs US$5.

Food

If you're taking the free road through town, Tacos Magaña (Carretera Libre Km. 65, tel. 646/155-0586, 6:30am-11:30pm daily, US$4-8) is a good stop for a bite to eat or a bathroom break before driving into the countryside. Their tacos are tasty, and the huge burritos are large enough for two people to share.

Getting There

Many visitors coming to La Misión arrive by car. The town is about a 27-minute, 37-kilometer (23-mile) drive south from Rosarito.

Both Autobuses de la Baja California (ABC, tel. 664/104-7400, www.abc.com.mx) and Aguila (toll-free Mex. tel. 800/026-8931, www.autobusesaguila.com) have bus service from Rosarito to La Misión multiple times a day for about US$2. The ride takes 35 minutes and the bus will drop you off at the bridge over the estuary in the center of La Misión.

SOUTH TO ENSENADA

Visitors who take the scenic toll road to Ensenada will be treated to dramatic ocean views that some people liken to the drive along Big Sur. There are a handful of camping and RV parks in the area that take advantage of the vast beaches and dramatic cliff views.

Sights and Recreation

There's a popular lookout, El Mirador, just off of the toll road at Kilometer 84 that is accessible to southbound traffic (the lookout is not accessible to northbound traffic). Stop to take photos of the breathtaking views from the top of the cliffs overlooking the Pacific Ocean. There are usually a few vendors selling fruits and other snacks.

Golfers who are looking for a relaxing day filled with scenic views head to Bajamar (Mexico 1D Km. 77, U.S. tel. 619/425-0081, www.bajamar.com, golf US$94). Set along five kilometers (3.1 miles) of stunning coastline, there are 27 holes divided into three courses (lakes, ocean, views) with nine holes each. Greens fees are for 18 holes, so golfers get to choose which two courses to golf. There are also a driving range and a putting green.

Food and Accommodations

On a beautiful stretch of beach, Clam Beach Resort (Mexico 1D Km. 70, tel. 646/155-0976, www.clambeachresort.com, US$30-65) comprises an RV park with 82 sites with 50-amp full hookups. The property is newer and in good condition. Wireless Internet is available around the property, and there are bathrooms with hot showers as well as coin laundry.

Just south of Clam Beach, another RV park, **Baja Seasons** (formerly Baja Oasis, Mexico 1D Km. 72.5, tel. 646/484-5561, www. bajaseasonsresort.com, US$35-60) is an older property that has fallen into slight disrepair in recent years, but still offers a stunning beach location. There's a pool and wireless Internet in the clubhouse. The restaurant is open during summer weekends.

In addition to its three nine-hole golf courses, **Bajamar** (Mexico 1D Km. 77, U.S. tel. 619/425-0081, www.bajamar.com, US$150) has a beautiful hacienda-style hotel with 81 rooms set around a courtyard. Accommodations are modern with duvet covers and plasma TVs, but retain Mexican colonial charm with Saltillo tile floors and Juliet balconies. There's a heated pool and Jacuzzi as well as a spa. The restaurant on the property serves breakfast, lunch, and dinner, and the bar is a popular spot for a blended margarita after a day on the golf course. Don't miss taking a venture up to the small tower lookout. Drinks are sometimes served at the bar up on "El Mirador," but even if they aren't serving, it's worth it to see the spectacular 360-degree views.

For camping with views, **Playa Saldamando** (Mexico 1D Km. 94, tel. 646/118-5974, U.S. tel. 619/857-9242, www. playasaldamando.com, tent camping US$17 per vehicle, US$19 motor home, US$45-85 trailer rental) has a mile of coastal property with campsites on the beach and up on the cliffs. Tent camping and motor home camping (there are no hookups) are allowed, and trailer rentals are available.

Getting There

This region must be accessed by private vehicle. A taxi from Rosarito will cost about US$15-20, depending on your exact destination.

Ensenada

Ensenada, the third-largest city in Baja, hosts tourists from the cruise ships that dock here, weekenders who come down from Southern California, and road-trippers passing through. But locals know that Ensenada still retains a small Mexican pueblo feel. While it's a popular weekend destination, there are enough attractions to keep a family occupied for a week or more.

The downtown and harbor area of Ensenada is easily explored on foot, and many of Ensenada's best sights can be visited in a day just walking around this area. The *malecón* and *mercado de mariscos* are along the harbor, and just a block away is Avenida López Mateos, the main street in town, with souvenir shops and plenty of restaurants and bars.

There's a significant culinary scene in Ensenada that draws

Look for ★ to find recommended sights, activities, dining, and lodging.

Highlights

★ **Taste a fish taco at Mercado de Mariscos,** Ensenada's bustling fish market (page 95).

★ **Go for a stroll on Avenida López Mateos,** bursting with shops, restaurants, and bars (page 96).

★ **Admire the elegant architecture** (and enjoy a margarita) at the beautiful and historic **Riviera del Pacifico,** home to Ensenada's cultural center (page 97).

★ **Marvel at La Bufadora,** the natural sea geyser that shoots water up to 30 meters into the air (page 99).

★ **Catch a wave** at the birthplace of Mexican surfing—there's something for everyone here, from big-wave aficionados to beginners (page 101).

Best Restaurants and Accommodations

RESTAURANTS

★ **Cocina Madre:** The chic and simple atmosphere provides the perfect setting for carefully crafted food with traditional Mexican dishes at heart (page 104).

★ **Muelle 3:** This small restaurant serves deliciously crafted ceviches and seafood dishes (page 104).

★ **Tacos El Fenix:** Visit this street cart for some of the most famous fish and shrimp tacos in Baja (page 106).

★ **La Guerrerense:** Anthony Bourdain once called this seafood spot "the best street cart in the world" (page 106).

★ **Manzanilla:** Enjoy inventive cocktails and savory dishes from one of Mexico's top chefs, Benito Molina, at one of Baja's top restaurants (page 106).

ACCOMMODATIONS

★ **Torre Lucerna:** This luxury hotel features modern rooms with ocean views and an impressive breakfast buffet (page 110).

★ **Las Rosas:** Take in the stunning view of waves crashing onto the shore right in front of this charming hotel (page 110).

★ **Hotel Coral & Marina:** This sleek hotel features upscale accommodations and its own marina (page 111).

ENSENADA

foodies with its famous street carts, high-end restaurants, and everything in between. Don't miss eating fish tacos or *mariscos* (seafood) that come right out of the Pacific. There's a growing craft beer scene in Ensenada, and the Valle de Guadalupe, Mexico's wine region, is just a half-hour drive inland.

PLANNING YOUR TIME

Located a two-hour drive south of the U.S. border, Ensenada is a perfect weekend destination. A couple of days allows visitors sufficient time to see the sights. Visitors who want to spend some time also exploring the nearby Valle de Guadalupe wine country should add an extra day to their itinerary.

ORIENTATION

Downtown Ensenada is located just a block inland from the coast, where the *malecón* stretches along the harbor. Many of Ensenada's restaurants and shops are located in the downtown area. North of town, El Sauzal is home to some of the best surfing in Baja as well as a number of craft breweries and restaurants, which are all located right along highway Mexico 1. South of town, La Bufadora is located on the coast in a fairly remote area about an hour from downtown Ensenada.

Previous: the coastline south of Ensenada; Sabina Restaurante; the Riviera del Pacifico, once a grand hotel and now a cultural center for the city.

Ensenada and South

Sights

★ MERCADO DE MARISCOS

Fishing has always been one of Ensenada's primary industries. To get an idea of the diversity of seafood caught in the waters off Ensenada, take a walk through the fish market. Down along the harbor, the **Mercado de Mariscos** (Miramar 16, 8am-8pm daily) hosts a number of stalls full of shrimp, tuna, mussels, abalone, and odd-looking geoduck clams. You may hear locals refer to the market as the Mercado Negro, or black market, as it used to be called (the name supposedly comes from the fact that the market used to be very dirty, not because they were selling illicit goods). Try one of Ensenada's famous fish tacos at one of the many stands right outside the market.

MALECÓN

The best way to take in Ensenada's harbor area is to go for a walk along the *malecón,* which stretches along the water from Miramar to Castillo streets. The pedestrian walkway is a nice spot for checking out the fishing boats and cruise ships while doing some souvenir shopping at the stalls along the way. At the north end of the *malecón* is the fish market and at the south end is access to the cruise ship pier. Also near the south end is Parque de la Bandera, a plaza with a large Mexican flag, a water feature, and a new stage and pavilion. The plaza is often used for local festivals and events and popular with families for weekend gatherings. Just around the corner, **Plaza Cívica** features large gold busts of three prominent historical figures: Benito Juárez (the first president of Mexico), Padre Miguel Hidalgo (who began the Mexican Revolution), and Venustiano Carranza (the first president after the revolution).

ENSENADA
SIGHTS

Ensenada

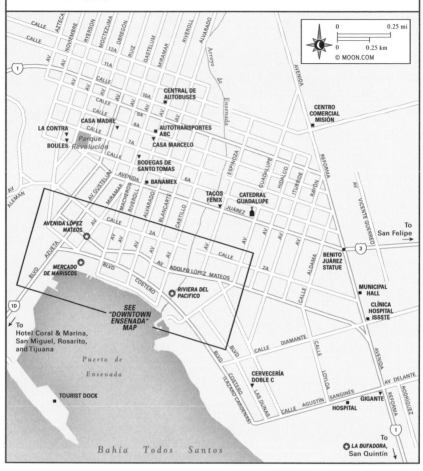

★ AVENIDA LÓPEZ MATEOS

The heart of the action in downtown Ensenada is **Avenida López Mateos** (Calle Primera). Along with souvenir stalls, shoppers will find a variety of brick-and-mortar stores selling silver jewelry, home decor items, and handicrafts from mainland Mexico. Interspersed with the shops are restaurants and bars where tourists will be beckoned in to enjoy a margarita or tequila shot. Many of the restaurants have sidewalk seating or an open-air concept, so this can be a nice spot to relax and take in the city while enjoying a bite to eat or drink. This is a great place to get a general feel for Ensenada; locals and travelers all congregate in this area to enjoy some of the best shopping, food, and drink that Ensenada offers.

★ RIVIERA DEL PACIFICO

With its elegant Spanish architecture, the **Riviera del Pacifico** (Blvd. Lázaro Cárdenas 1421, tel. 646/176-4310, www.rivieradeensenada.com.mx) has been one of Ensenada's crown jewels since 1930. The white building, surrounded by gardens, was one of Ensenada's grandest hotels when it was opened by famed boxer Jack Dempsey. Many of Hollywood's elite, including Bing Crosby and Rita Hayworth, spent time here during Prohibition. Today, the space operates as a local cultural center and event center, with an open-air theater and a number of rooms used for workshops and classes. Much of the original tile and paintings have been preserved throughout the structure.

Visitors who want to see the architecture and learn more about the history of the building can go to **Bar Andaluz** (5pm-11pm Mon., 10am-11pm Tues.-Sat., 10am-8pm Sun.) in the main building at street level. The mural behind the bar was painted by Alfredo Ramos Martínez and is original to the building. Both Bar Andaluz and Hussong's Cantina claim to be the original home of Mexico's iconic beverage, the margarita. Bar Andaluz has a well-known 2-for-1 margarita night on Wednesday where you can enjoy the famous cocktail inside at the bar or outside in the courtyard if the weather is nice. Inquire at the bar about tours of the entire property.

MUSEO CARACOL

Just across the street from the Riviera del Pacifico is the **Caracol Museo de Ciencias y Acuario** (Calle Club Rotario No. 3, tel. 646/117-0897, www.caracol.org.mx, 9am-5pm Tues.-Fri., 10am-5pm Sat.-Sun., US$3 adults, US$2 students). This family-friendly museum focuses on a hands-on approach to science. The museum is still being constructed, but there are a number of open exhibits—all related to the science and history behind elements relating to the sky, land, or sea. The large and impressive space will eventually be home to a rooftop café, cafeteria, and gift shop.

HUSSONG'S CANTINA

As the oldest and most famous cantina in Baja California, **Hussong's Cantina** (Ave. Ruiz 113, tel. 646/178-3210, 9am-2am Tues.-Sun.) is more than just a bar—it's an institution. Founded in 1892 by a German immigrant named John Hussong, more than 100 years and three generations later Hussong's is still

the *malecón* in downtown Ensenada

Downtown Ensenada

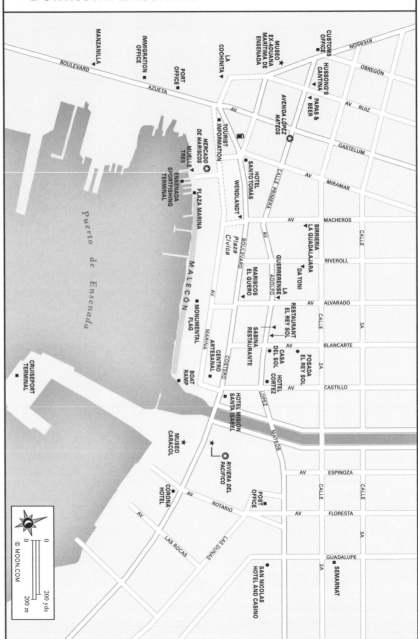

a family-run operation. The bar has remained much the same over the years and has been visited by the likes of Marilyn Monroe, Steve McQueen, and John Wayne. This is one of the places that vies for being the birthplace of the margarita, so don't miss ordering one of the classic cocktails. Saddle up at the long bar or grab a seat at one of the tables. Don't mind the peanut shells on the floor.

CHAPULTEPEC HILL MIRADOR

For the best views of Ensenada, head up to the *mirador* on **Chapultepec Hill** (GPS: 31.862557, -116.633984). From this spot northwest of the harbor, you'll get scenic overviews of the harbor and the bay, the Todos Santos islands, and the town. There's not much else aside from a crumbling pony wall here, but it's a nice spot to take some photos and sit and enjoy the views for a bit. You can drive by following Calle Segunda to Miguel Alemán (park on the street in the neighborhood; there's no official parking lot) or make the 10-minute hike from the base of the hill.

OUTSIDE ENSENADA
★ **La Bufadora**

One of Ensenada's most famous attractions is about an hour south of town on the Punta Banda peninsula. At the end of a long and winding coastal road is **La Bufadora,** a natural geyser that shoots water up to 30 meters in the air. The ocean swells come into a sea cave here, and when the water recedes, the air and water spout upward along with a thunderous noise. The blowhole shoots off about every minute or so, to the delight of bystanders who gather along viewing areas next to it.

A number of shops selling Mexican souvenirs and food have lined up along the walkway that leads out to La Bufadora and the viewing areas. Don't miss the *almejas gratinadas* (au gratin clams) at one of the stalls near the blowhole if you're looking for a bite to eat. You'll need to pay about US$2 for parking and then walk about 700 meters along the walkway to get to La Bufadora. There's no charge to see La Bufadora, but be prepared to pay a few pesos to use the bathrooms.

Ojos Negros

A drive east on the southern branch of Mexico 3 (heading toward San Felipe) will bring travelers to the small, dusty town of **Ojos Negros.** This agricultural region was named "black eyes" for all of the wells in the area that look like black eyes when viewed from above. The town of Ojos Negros itself doesn't have much to offer tourists, but there are a few small ranches in the area that serve food and drink. Just east of the town is Rancho la Campana, better known these days as the home of Ramonetti cheeses and **La Cava de Marcelo** (Mexico 3 Km. 43, 646/117-0293, 1pm-6pm Thurs.-Sun., tour and cheese tasting US$10). Since 1911, the Ramonetti family has been making cheese on their large dairy farm. Visitors can take an interesting tour of the farm to see the cows and learn about the cheese-making process. At the end of the tour, visitors go underground to have a wine and cheese tasting and to see the cheese cave, which can hold up to 10,000 wheels of cheese. They've opened a restaurant on the property, so visitors can enjoy farm-fresh food at the tables under the trees.

Beaches and Recreation

BEACHES

Ensenada has a number of picturesque Pacific beaches, great for relaxing, swimming, surfing, and snorkeling. (Plan to bring your own gear or make arrangements in advance.)

North of town in the area of the tollbooths is the famous surf spot of **San Miguel.** In town, the large, sandy **Playa Hermosa** is great for families and is buzzing with people on the weekends. Twelve kilometers (7.5 miles) south of town, the Río San Carlos meets the bay to create an estuary. Out here, **Estero Beach** has a more relaxing scene where visitors can enjoy horseback riding or take it easy with fewer crowds. Near La Bufadora, **Arbolitos** is a great spot for diving, snorkeling, and kayaking among the natural caves.

TOP EXPERIENCE

★ SURFING

Ensenada is largely regarded as the birthplace of Mexican surfing, and everyone from big-wave aficionados to beginners will find a place to catch a wave. Off the coast, the **Isla Todos Santos** is a challenging spot where waves can reach heights of up to 60 feet. There are five breaks on the island, and the Big Wave Surf contest has taken place here a number of years. Along the coastline back on the peninsula, there are a series of point and beach breaks. Experienced surfers can also head to **San Miguel,** north of town in El Sauzal, where they'll find one of the most famous right point breaks in Baja. Beaches like **Playa Hermosa** are perfect for beginners thanks to a sandy bottom and gentle waves.

For those of all levels seeking surf lessons, **Surf Ensenada** (tel. 646/194-0846, www.surfensenada.com) offers private and group instruction for all ages. Owner Miguel Arroyo

is a fun and enthusiastic instructor as well as a great ambassador for Ensenada. He has a great team of knowledgeable and friendly instructors working with him.

The Todos Santos islands and the coastline from Salsipuedes to El Sauzal (the area collectively known as Bahía Todos Santos) were designated the sixth world surf reserve in 2014. The world surf reserves are a designation to help identify and preserve the world's most important surf zones and the surrounding habitats. Under the surf reserve program, conservation groups work with local officials to help preserve the region.

FISHING

The glory days of Ensenada as a sportfishing mecca have diminished over the years due to the commercial fishing in the area, but sport anglers can still catch lingcod, calico bass, barracuda, bottom fish, bonito, and, every once in a while, yellowtail. It's easy to hire an outfitter for fishing at the north end of the harbor near the fish market. **Sergio's Sportfishing Center** (tel. 646/178-2185, U.S. tel. 619/399-7224, www.sergiosfishing.com) has a variety of vessels and welcomes anglers of any experience level. They offer private deep-sea tours as well as open party trips. Their large fleet ranges from *pangas* to an 85-foot yacht.

BOATING

Ensenada is an official Mexico port of entry, so boaters arriving from U.S. waters must check in with the port captain's office on Boulevard Azueta to get their FMM tourist permits and temporary importation permit for their vessel to clear customs. Most marinas in Ensenada can help you with customs clearance if you contact them in advance.

Conveniently located downtown, **Ensenada Cruiseport Village Marina** (tel. 646/178-8801, www.ecpvmarina.com)

1: La Bufadora, a natural geyser **2:** the picturesque coastline on the way out to La Bufadora

Playa Hermosa

has 200 slips and can accommodate oversize boats. They provide 24-hour security as well as showers, restrooms, and a laundry. They can help you with customs clearance for no additional charge. **Baja Naval** (tel. 646/174-0020, www.bajanaval.com) will also help you with all of the required customs and importation paperwork and has 50 slips that can accommodate boats up to 100 feet. **Marina Coral** (tel. 646/175-0050, www.hotelcoral.com) at the Hotel Coral & Marina has 350 slips and offers a range of services including a fuel dock, maintenance services, pump-out service, free wireless Internet, and use of hotel facilities like the swimming pool and spa.

Entertainment and Shopping

ENTERTAINMENT AND EVENTS
Nightlife

Most of Ensenada's nightlife centers on the downtown area. Despite its fame with tourists, **Hussong's Cantina** (Ave. Ruiz 113, tel. 646/178-3210, 11am-2am Tues.-Sun.) remains a popular spot for the locals, who go for the 2-for-1 drink specials (beer on Tuesday and margaritas on Saturday).

Down the block from Hussong's is **Papas & Beer** (Calle Primera, tel. 646/174-0145, www.papasandbeer.com), where people can get a taste of the club scene that used to dominate Ensenada's spring break vibe. **Ultramarino Oyster Bar** (Calle Ruiz 57, tel. 646/178-1195) is the spot to go for DJs and live music on the weekends.

For a hipper and more clandestine bar, check out **Santos en el Pacifico** (Paseo Hidalgo 6, tel. 646/175-9583, 7pm-2am Tues.-Sun.), on the hillside just above the downtown area. They make a variety of specialty cocktails and serve food like hamburgers and ceviche. They often have live music on the weekends. Watch for the sign of a heart and the neon "BAR" sign outside.

Mezcal lovers will want to head to **Mezcalería La Penca** (Avenida Miramar 666, tel. 646/174-0300, 6pm-midnight Wed.-Sat.), where the dimly lit setting provides a cozy atmosphere for sipping various mezcals.

The Margarita

One of Mexico's most iconic commodities is the margarita. There are variations on the drink, but it most commonly consists of fresh lime juice, tequila, and Controy (Mexico's orange liqueur), served with ice. When you order a margarita, you can have it blended (*liquada*) or on the rocks (*en las rocas*), with salt on the rim of the glass (*con sal*) or without (*sin sal*).

There are a number of reputed stories about where the margarita was invented. In Ensenada, both Hussong's and the Riviera del Pacifico claim to be the birthplace of the margarita.

If you're new to mezcal drinking, the friendly staff can guide you through your experience.

With a number of locations throughout town, Lucky Irish Pub (Calle Cuarta, tel. 646/175-9169, 3pm-2am daily) is a favorite for its draft beers and pub food. Locals flock there Sunday through Wednesday nights for their specials on wings and beer. Lucky Irish 4 (Mexico 1 Km. 106.8, tel. 646/977-8055, 1pm-2am daily) is a beer garden north of town in El Sauzal with a large outdoor patio and ocean views.

For wine lovers who don't want to make the trek out to Valle de Guadalupe, the oldest winery in the region, Bodegas de Santo Tomás (Avenida Miramar 666, tel. 646/178-3333, www.santo-tomas.com, 10am-9pm Mon.-Sat., 10am-5pm Sun.), has a tasting room in downtown Ensenada. They offer tastings daily and with advance reservations can arrange for an impressive tour of the facility for groups of four or more.

TOP EXPERIENCE

Breweries

For tasty craft beers and views of the Pacific, head north of town to Agua Mala (Mexico 1 Km. 104, tel. 646/175-8853, www.aguamala. com.mx, 2pm-6pm Tues., 2pm-midnight Wed.-Sat., 1pm-9pm Sun.). The brewery is constructed of shipping containers and the 2nd-story bar looks directly out at the ocean for fantastic sunset views. There are a variety of beers made in-house, such as the Sirena Pilsner and Astillero IPA. They serve food and often collaborate with famous chefs

and restaurants in the region to create special menus offered for a limited time.

In town is the brewpub location of Wendlandt (Blvd. Costero, tel. 646/178-2938, www.wendlandt.com.mx, 6pm-midnight Tues.-Sat.). Hip locals and beer-loving tourists go here to sip on beers like Hann Zomer Saison and the Harry Polanco Red Ale and enjoy gourmet pub food like artisanal pizzas. The actual brewery (Calle 10 385-B, tel. 646/174-7060, 1pm-9pm Wed.-Thurs., noon-11pm Fri.-Sat., noon-8pm Sun.) is in a warehouse just north of town in El Sauzal. They have a large patio space and on Saturdays offer food from invited chefs.

South of town, looking out at Playa Hermosa, is craft brewery Cervecería Doble C (Blvd. Lázaro Cárdenas, tel. 664/338-4951, 4pm-11pm Tues.-Fri., 3pm-11pm Sat.-Sun.). The industrial space features exposed brick, corrugated metal, and communal wooden bar tables that share space with the beer tanks at the end of the room. Beer lovers will enjoy the Session IPA and hoppy pale ale while looking out the large picture windows at the ocean.

Events

Ensenada hosts a number of events each year including a Carnaval celebration in February, the Rosarito Ensenada Bike Ride (www. rosaritoensenada.com) twice a year (spring and fall), and a large beer fest (www. ensenadabeerfest.com) in March. The state tourism site, www.bajanorte.com, has a thorough calendar of events. Perhaps Ensenada's largest event each year is the kickoff celebration and race start (and sometimes the finish as well, depending on the course) of the famous **Baja 1000** (www.score-international.com) off-road race each November.

SHOPPING

Ensenada has some great artisanal and souvenir shopping along **Avenida López Mateos** (Calle Primera), where there's a good mix of touristy stands selling shot glasses and blankets and brick-and-mortar shops selling higher-end artisanal items from mainland Mexico. There are a number of souvenir stands along the harbor near the Mercado de Mariscos as well.

Los Globos (Calle Nueve and Cinco de Mayo, open daily) is a huge market where visitors can find everything from produce to meat to books to clothing to secondhand items. The market spans multiple blocks and is partially indoors, but has expanded so that additional vendors can set up tents nearby. The market is open every day, but the extra stalls are there only on weekends.

Food

From street food to fine dining, Ensenada is a town with dining options that will satisfy even the most discerning foodie. While the focus is primarily on fresh seafood, the dining scene here has an international feel and it's possible to find a variety of foods across all price points.

MEXICAN

For artisanal breakfast made with fresh local ingredients, head to **Casa Marcelo** (Ave. Riveroll between Calles 7 and 8, tel. 646/187-3158, 8am-6pm Wed.-Mon., mains US$5-7). The restaurant is related to Rancho La Campana (home to Ramonetti cheeses and the cheese cave La Cava de Marcelo) in Ojos Negros; many of the restaurant's dishes are made with the cheeses and butter from the ranch. Egg dishes are handcrafted and paired with fresh produce and local meats, topped with cheeses and butter from the ranch. They also have the cheese and butter available for sale.

The heart of Baja Californian cuisine, which takes traditional Mexican dishes and adds a modern twist with fresh local ingredients, is on display at ★ **Cocina Madre** (Calle Octava 444, tel. 646/977-5608, 2pm-10pm Mon.-Tues. and Thurs., 2pm-midnight Fri.-Sat., 2pm-6pm Sun., US$10-15). Chef Miguel Bahena is one of the region's rising new chefs and he takes deep-rooted dishes from mainland Mexico and adds a Baja Californian twist. The chic but casual setting features wood tables, brick wall accents, industrial light fixtures, and well-curated artwork.

La Hoguera (Ave. Blancarte 172, tel. 646/244-5150, 1pm-10pm Tues.-Sat., 1pm-8pm Sun., mains US$11-16) is where locals head for meats grilled over a wood fire and served in a casual setting. There's indoor and outdoor seating on the large patio. Enjoy grilled meats, fish, and pork, served alongside cold beers, tequila, and wine.

SEAFOOD

Seafood lovers and foodies won't want to miss ★ **Muelle 3** (Blvd. Teniente Azueta, tel. 646/174-0318, noon-6:30pm Tues. and Thurs.-Sat., US$6-10) down on the pier just north of the fish market. Don't let the simple and unassuming interior fool you—this is some of the most sophisticated seafood coming out of Ensenada. Chef David Martinez takes fresh Ensenada seafood and gives it a kick of Baja and Asian flavors. The *ceviche de la casa* is a delectable mix of octopus, clams, fish, and avocado.

1: Agua Mala, one of Ensenada's top craft breweries
2: souvenir shopping in Ensenada's downtown area

Popular with cruise ship passengers, **Mahi Mahi** (Paseo Hidalgo 33, tel. 646/178-3494, www.mahimahi.com.mx, noon-10pm daily, mains US$8-12) is a large casual restaurant in town. It is conveniently located at the end of López Mateos, the prices are reasonable, and they offer an extensive seafood menu.

ANTOJITOS AND STREET FOOD

Many locals claim that the best fish tacos in town come from the ★ **Tacos El Fenix** (Ave. Espinoza, 8am-8pm Mon.-Sat.) food cart. They've been serving up both fish and shrimp tacos since 1970. There's no seating here; locals and foodies gather on the sidewalk to enjoy a quick and savory bite from the cart. There are also a number of fish taco stands outside the Mercado de Mariscos, including **Tacos Lily,** the stand where Anthony Bourdain went in his TV show *No Reservations*. Another option for fish tacos farther east in town is **El Chopipo** (Diamante 449, tel. 646/177-0202, 7am-8pm daily), a small stand with some tables and chairs for seating. In addition to fish and shrimp tacos, they serve ceviche tostadas.

It was called "the best street cart in the world" by Anthony Bourdain, and ★ **La Guerrerense** (López Mateos and Alvarado, www.laguerrerense.com, 10am-5pm Wed.-Mon.) lives up to its reputation. With sophisticated flavors, Sabina Bandera serves up ceviches and unique seafood combinations on tostadas out of her street cart in downtown Ensenada. Don't miss the award-winning *ceviche de erizo con almeja* (sea urchin with clams), or the signature *La Guerrerense ceviche,* made with orange juice. Because the street cart has garnered so much popularity, the family opened a sit-down restaurant down the street, **Sabina Restaurante** (López Mateos 917, tel. 646/174-0006, 10am-6pm Tues.-Sun.), serving the same favorites as the cart in addition to pozole, dessert, and beer and wine.

Just a block west of La Guerrerense is another seafood cart, **Mariscos El Guero** (Blvd. Costero and Alvarado, tel. 646/277-1941,

10:15am-5:30pm daily), serving up *cocteles de mariscos* (seafood cocktails) consisting of various types of seafood in a tomato-based broth. Served chilled, this is a perfectly refreshing and delicious meal for any seafood lover. Near Playa Hermosa, **Mariscos Yiyo's** (Blvd. Costero and Calle Floresta, tel. 646/116-4214, 10am-6pm Thurs.-Mon.) serves fresh seafood cocktails, tostadas, *molcajetes,* and clams from the casual seafood cart. Don't miss the *pulpo enamorado*, with shrimp and octopus bathed in garlic and butter and served with a house-made sauce.

For *birria* (a traditional meat stew often served as a taco using just the meat), locals have been heading to **Birrieria La Guadalajara** (Calle Macheros, tel. 646/174-0392, www.birrieriaguadalajara.com, 7am-8pm daily, mains US$4-6) since it opened in 1972. The tender and savory *birria* is available in lamb, goat, beef, and pork. The large sit-down restaurant is known for quick service, affordable prices, and good food.

For those looking for a taco fix at any hour, **El Trailero** (Ave. J, tel. 646/204-7678, open 24 hours) should be your destination. Located north of town in El Sauzal along Mexico 1, this mega taco stand has multiple stations serving all types of tacos—fish, *al pastor,* carne asada, *cabeza*—as well as tortas and *birria*.

Local hipsters get their taco fix at **Criollo Taqueria** (Mexico 1 Km. 103, tel. 646/153-0822, 1pm-10pm Wed.-Fri., 9am-10pm Sat.-Sun., US$3-4), where the menu offers an assortment of tacos as well as tortas, tostadas, and chilaquiles. This place north of town in El Sauzal offers an outdoor seating area with unobstructed ocean views. They serve brunch on the weekends.

INTERNATIONAL

Chef Benito Molina, one of the most well-known chefs in Mexico, created ★ **Manzanilla** (Recinto Portuario,

1: the *trompo* (vertical rotisserie) at El Trailero taco stand **2:** La Guerrerense street cart **3:** fish taco stands outside the Mercado de Mariscos **4:** dishes at Sabina Restaurante

The Birthplace of the Fish Taco

While fish tacos can be found all over the Baja peninsula, they are especially prevalent in Ensenada, a city that claims to be the original home of the delicious dish. Strips of whitefish or shark are battered, fried, and served in a corn tortilla, topped off with cabbage, *crema*, salsa, and a squirt of fresh lime.

The history of the fish taco is a bit murky, and both San Felipe and Ensenada claim the title as home of the first fish taco. Ensenada asserts that the fish taco was influenced by the Japanese immigrants that came to the area in the 1920s. The fish batter for the fish taco is similar to a tempura, and the *disca*, which is used to fry the fish taco, is similar to a wok.

Fish tacos are a breakfast/lunch specialty in Baja. For the most part, you won't find fish tacos available after about 5pm.

Teniente Azueta 139, tel. 646/175-7073, www.rmanzanilla.com, 1pm-11pm Wed.-Sat., 1pm-6pm Sun., mains US$12-17) alongside his wife and fellow chef, Solange. As one of Ensenada's top restaurants, it boasts a chic setting and a menu with items like oysters, steaks, abalone, and quail ravioli. The restaurant is right next to the port, and the industrial feel of the area is reflected in the eclectic decor. The large converted warehouse features a large, traditional wooden bar and funky chandeliers set against a concrete background. The dining room looks out onto a small patio garden.

Hip locals and foodie travelers head to **Boules** (Moctezuma 623, tel. 646/175-8769, 2pm-10pm Tues.-Thurs., 2pm-midnight Fri.-Sat., mains US$9-16), where Javier Martinez (brother of chef David Martinez at Muelle 3) serves up dishes like *queso fundido de mar* (seafood in melted cheese), crab ravioli, and *tuetano* (bone marrow) served in a gigantic bone, accompanied by mini corn tortillas, limes, and red onions. Most seating is on the patio under the trees and string lights. Local wines and beers round out the menu. And yes, there's boules for those who want to play an after-meal game.

Located inside Lucky Irish Beer Garden is a culinary hidden gem in the form of **Krausen Cocina de la Baja** (Mexico 1 Km. 106.8, no tel., 1pm-10pm Sun.-Thurs., 1pm-midnight Fri.-Sat.). Chef Ryan Steyn is originally from South Africa but has been one of the Baja's top chefs for many years. From ceviche and tacos to burgers and ribs, the food is hearty and flavorful and pairs perfectly with the beer on tap and the stunning ocean views.

The French cuisine at **El Rey Sol** (López Mateos 1000, tel. 646/178-1733, www.elreysol.com, 7am-11pm daily, mains US$13-20) has been a staple of fine dining in Ensenada since 1947. Weekend brunch is a classy affair where patrons can order off the menu or feast at the buffet and listen to live piano music in the formal dining room. Don't miss the decadent pastries and baked goods they're famous for.

Italian restaurant **Da Toni** (Ave. Riveroll 143, tel. 646/113-4338, 2pm-10pm Thurs.-Sat., 2pm-9pm Sun.-Mon., US$10-15) is a local favorite. Owner Toni is often present and he and his staff carefully prepare all of the food by hand. The intimate spot has a diverse selection of pasta and appetizers as well as a chalkboard full of daily specials. They carry a curated assortment of Valle de Guadalupe wines to accompany your meal. They don't accept reservations, but you can call a little bit in advance to secure one of their few tables. Cash only.

For rib eye or filet mignon, **Sano's Steak House** (Mexico 1 Km. 108, tel. 646/174-5145, www.sanos.com.mx, 1pm-midnight Thurs.-Tues., US$18-27) is a classy spot with cocktails, a swanky atmosphere, friendly staff, and great steaks. For non-steak eaters, they also have a selection of pastas, fish, and chicken on the menu.

The fine-dining restaurant at **Punta Morro** (Mexico 1 Km. 106, tel. 646/178-3507, www.hotelpuntamorro.com, 8am-10pm Mon.-Thurs., 8am-11pm Fri., 9am-11pm Sat., 9am-10pm Sun., mains US$17-34) is as famous for its dramatic views as for the food. Built out over the edge of the water, the bountiful windows allow for dramatic sea vistas with waves crashing onto the rocks below. Diners enjoy items like lobster enchiladas, ribs, grilled octopus, and *arrachera* steak.

CAFÉS

North of town on the highway, **La Flor de la Calabaza** (Mexico 1 Km. 107, tel. 646/174-4092, flordelacalabaza@gmail.com, 8am-5pm Mon.-Sat., 8am-3pm Sun.) is not only a café serving up healthy, organic breakfasts and lunches, but also a local organic market.

Also serving healthy lunches and coffee is **Casa Antigua Café** (Calle Obregón 110, tel. 646/205-1433, 8am-10:30pm Mon.-Sat., 2pm-10pm Sun.), located in a historical house in a convenient spot in town. Around the corner, the tiny **Breve Café** (Calle Segunda 380, tel. 646/174-0049, 7am-10pm Mon.-Fri., 8am-11pm Sat.) is a chic espresso bar that opens right onto the sidewalk. There are a few stools for patrons, or it's perfect for a macchiato on the go.

Accommodations

Peak season in Ensenada is summer, especially during the Valle de Guadalupe Vendimia season in August, when hotels fill up with those attending the wine harvest festival. Prices are the most expensive on summer weekends. Most hotels are significantly cheaper during the week than on the weekends. Reservations should be made in advance when possible as the many festivals and events that Ensenada hosts can quickly deplete hotel inventory.

If you're planning on visiting the Valle de Guadalupe during your time in Ensenada, it's best to book a hotel in town or north of town for easier access.

UNDER US$100

The 118-room **San Nicolas Hotel and Casino** (Ave. Guadalupe, tel. 646/176-1901, www.snhotelcasino.com, US$80-90) enjoys a central location and has a large parking lot. Rooms need updating, but the central pool and Jacuzzi area is lovely and the poolside bar serves up good margaritas. The attached casino is a draw for those who like playing the slot machines.

It's hard to miss **Hotel Santo Tomas** (Blvd. Costero 609, tel. 646/178-3311, US$40), the brightly painted hotel in the heart of the action of Ensenada. Rooms are basic and clean and there's secure, off-street parking. Another in-town option is **Hotel Casa Del Sol** (López Mateos and Blancarte 1001, tel. 646/178-1570, www.casadelsolmexico.net, US$65). Rooms are basic, but there's a pool area and a café attached to the hotel.

Hotel Mision Santa Isabel (formerly La Pinta, Blvd. Lázao Cárdenas and Ave. Costillo, tel. 646/178-3616, www.hotelmisionsantaisabel.com, US$80) has rooms built around a courtyard with a small pool and seating areas. The Spanish hacienda architecture features tile floors and wood-beam ceilings.

North of town, **Quintas Papagayo** (Mexico 1 Km. 108, tel. 646/174-4575, www.quintaspapagayo.com, US$80) offers accommodations right on the ocean. Rooms vary among cabins, suites, studios, and chalets, with the price varying accordingly as well. The property has been around since 1947; the rooms are clean but older and could use an update.

US$100-200

With a great in-town location, **Posada El Rey Sol** (Ave. Blancarte 130, tel.

646/178-1601, www.posadaelreysol.com, US$125) has 52 rooms, all comfortable and decorated with Mexican charm. There's a friendly staff, pool and Jacuzzi area, and free breakfast. The famous El Rey Sol restaurant is across the street, known for its French cuisine and delicious pastries.

On the harbor, the 92-room **Corona Hotel & Spa** (Blvd. Lázaro Cárdenas 1442, tel. 646/176-0901, www.hotelcorona.com.mx, US$160) is walking distance to the downtown area. Rooms all have wireless Internet, air-conditioning and heating, and flat-screen TVs, and many have harbor views. There's a pool and Jacuzzi, and the on-site Marina Spa offers full spa services and has a hair salon and sauna. They have a nice remodeled bar and Los Veleros restaurant on-site.

The Ensenada location of ★ **Torre Lucerna** (Mexico 1 Km. 108, tel. 646/222-2400, www.hoteleslucerna.com, US$160) has 146 beautiful, modern rooms offering Wi-Fi, air-conditioning, cable TV, and down comforters. Oceanview rooms have vistas of the Pacific and Todos Santos Island. The staff is attentive and friendly, and the property has an outdoor pool, a fitness center, and a restaurant on-site.

In town, **Hotel El Cid Best Western** (López Mateos 993, tel. 646/178-2401, U.S. toll-free tel. 800/352-4305, www.hotelelcid.com.mx, US$145) has 52 rooms, decorated in Mediterranean style with Spanish charm. Rooms feature flat-screen TVs, mini refrigerators, air-conditioning, and patios. There's no elevator, so ask for a room on a lower level if you aren't able to take stairs.

The beautiful oceanfront location draws travelers to stay north of town at ★ **Las Rosas** (Mexico 1 Km. 105.5, tel. 646/174-4310, www.lasrosas.com, US$170). The property is nicely kept and has a fabulous pool area perched right on the ocean. The infinity edge appears to drop right into the Pacific. Rooms are well appointed, and there's a spa on the property providing a range of services. Even people who aren't staying at the hotel come to

have a margarita at sunset to enjoy the views, or go to Sunday brunch at the restaurant.

Also north of town is the new **City Express Plus** (Mexico 1 Km. 104, tel. 646/152-8450, www.cityexpress.com, US$150). Unlike most other City Express hotels, which are geared toward business travelers, this hotel has more of a resort feel with a lovely rooftop swimming pool, luxury finishes throughout, and prime ocean views. There is also a regular City Express hotel in town.

On Playa Estero south of town, the **Estero Beach Hotel and Resort** (Playas del Estero, tel. 646/176-6225, www.hotelesterobeach.com, US$180) has been a favorite of travelers since the 1950s. Rooms are tasteful with cable TV and private patios. The lovely pool area is set against the background of the ocean and beach. A restaurant and bar on-site are convenient since the hotel is situated far from the center of town.

Out of town, about 10 kilometers (6 miles) east on the Mexico 3 to San Felipe, is **Horsepower Ranch** (Mexico 3 Km. 9, tel. 646/151-2896, U.S. tel. 949/656-1088, www.hprbaja.com, US$100), a classic spot for off-roaders. The 40-hectare ranch has 49 rooms and is home to many pre-race parties throughout the year. Room rates include breakfast and dinner.

OVER US$200

The intimate hotel at **Punta Morro** (Mexico 1 Km. 106, tel. 646/178-3507, www.hotelpuntamorro.com, US$235) is smaller than most of the other higher-end hotels in Ensenada. Rooms are nicely appointed, and they have a range of units from studios to three-bedroom suites, making it a great spot for families or groups. The entire property has beautiful ocean views, and the restaurant attracts diners from both sides of the border who come to watch the waves crash onto the rocks as they enjoy a gourmet meal.

Some of the nicest accommodations in Ensenada can be found north of town at ★ **Hotel Coral & Marina** (Mexico 1 Km. 103 #4321, tel. 646/175-0000, www. hotelcoral.com, US$205). With the black leather couches, modern light fixtures, and sleek design, the swanky vibe is something you would be more likely to find in Las Vegas or Cabo rather than Ensenada. The hotel has its own marina, indoor and outdoor pools, a covered parking area, and a grill and bar.

The **Hotel Marea Vista** (Ave. Acapulco 177, tel. 646/173-5323, www.mareavistahotel. com.mx, US$209) is located near Playa Hermosa and features sleek, modern rooms. There's a spa on the property in addition to a bar, steak house, and sushi restaurant.

Information and Services

Ensenada is a large city by Baja standards, and there are a number of banks, ATMs, markets, and stores. There are plenty of gas stations and service shops.

TOURIST INFORMATION

There's an office for **Proturismo de Ensenada** (Blvd. Lázaro Cárdenas 540, tel. 646/178-2411, 8am-8pm Mon.-Fri., 8am-6pm Sat.-Sun.) conveniently located near the fish market. It has a number of brochures about the area and a helpful staff that speaks English.

MEDICAL SERVICES

Hospital Velmar (De Las Arenas 151, tel. 646/173-4500, www.hospitalvelmar.com) is open 24 hours and can handle emergency services. There are plenty of pharmacies that can be found along Avenida López Mateos.

ORGANIZED TOURS

Foodies won't want to visit Ensenada without taking a culinary tour of the city. **Baja Test Kitchen** (www.bajatestkitchen.com) offers an "Ensenada Eats" tour, visiting some of the city's best street food carts and breweries. They can also arrange for wine-tasting tours of the Valle de Guadalupe departing from Ensenada.

Transportation

GETTING THERE

Outside of the cruise ship passengers, most visitors arriving on their own in Ensenada come by private car. Ensenada is just two hours and 150 kilometers (93 miles) south of San Diego and is a popular weekend destination. From San Diego, take Mexico 1 along the coast for two hours until arriving in town.

There is bus service from other large cities in Baja through companies such as **Autobuses de la Baja California** (ABC, tel. 664/104-7400, www.abc.com.mx) and **Aguila** (toll-free Mex. tel. 800/026-8931, www.autobusesaguila.com). The **Central de Autobuses bus station** is on Calle 11 and Avenida Riveroll.

GETTING AROUND

Most everything in downtown Ensenada can be easily explored on foot. A car is necessary to visit La Bufadora or some of the restaurants and breweries north of town. It's fairly easy to drive around Ensenada, and free street parking is not hard to find. Taxis can be found along López Mateos or at the bus station on Calle 11 and Avenida Riveroll. It should cost less than US$7 to get around town. Negotiate the fare before getting in.

ENSENADA
TRANSPORTATION

Isla Guadalupe

Isla Guadalupe is a volcanic island 350 kilometers (215 miles) southwest of Ensenada. It is home to one of the largest populations of great white sharks on the planet. Complementing the large number of sharks are clear waters with up to 45-meter visibility, which make this remote island one of the world's best destinations for shark viewing and diving. Multiday live-aboard cage diving tours take place July through November and generally cost around US$4,000.

Islander Charters (tel. 619/224-4388, www.islander-charters.com) has vessels that depart directly from San Diego. They've been featured on National Geographic, The History Channel, and Shark Week on the Discovery Channel. **Great White Adventures** (www.greatwhiteadventures. com) and **Nautilus Explorer** (www. guadalupegreatwhitesharks.com) bus clients down to Ensenada, where their boats depart for Isla Guadalupe.

Northern Mexico Wine Country

Just a few hours south of the U.S. border is
one of the world's fastest-growing wine regions. Here the noise and
clutter of big cities melts away to fields of vineyards and picturesque
tasting rooms. Outdoor restaurants speckle the landscape and boutique hotels and B&Bs boast unique architecture and personal service. This is Mexico's premier wine region, producing 90 percent
of the country's domestic wine. Grapes were first brought here by
the Spanish missionaries hundreds of years ago, and the tradition
of winemaking in this region has only grown stronger in the past
few decades. The rest of the world is taking note, making this a top
travel destination attracting people from all corners of the globe.

Look for ★ to find recommended sights, activities, dining, and lodging.

Highlights

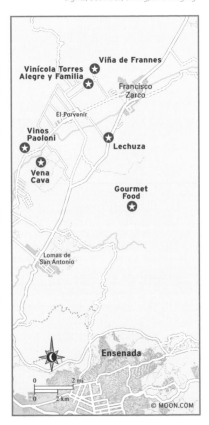

★ **Sample sophisticated wines** at the family winery **Vinícola Torres Alegre y Familia** while taking in bird's-eye views from its modern tasting room (page 119).

★ **Enjoy your wines with impressive views** from the back deck of the small winery **Viña de Frannes** (page 120).

★ **Go wine-tasting in a wine cave** made from upside-down vintage fishing boats at the unique micro winery **Vena Cava** (page 122).

★ **Try "Mexican wines with an Italian heart"** at the boutique winery **Vinos Paoloni** (page 123).

★ **Taste some of the best wines in Mexico** and enjoy the personal service at the family-run winery **Lechuza** (page 123).

★ **Feast on gourmet farm-to-table food,** prepared by the best chefs in the country, at **outdoor** *campestre* **restaurants** while looking out at the vineyards (page 129).

Best Restaurants and Accommodations

RESTAURANTS

★ **Fauna:** One of the hottest restaurants in all of Mexico attracts diners with inventive and savory dishes in a gorgeous setting (page 129).

★ **Corazón de Tierra:** Chef Diego Hernandez brings farm-to-table foods to a heightened sophistication in this beautiful restaurant in the Valle de Guadalupe (page 129).

★ **La Cocina de Doña Esthela:** Locals and foodies from around the world flock to this restaurant for some of the best breakfast on the peninsula (page 131).

★ **Finca Altozano:** Chef Javier Plascencia's *campestre* restaurant features flavorful food and alfresco dining overlooking the vineyards in Valle de Guadalupe (page 131).

★ **Malva:** Delicate dishes are served in a lush open-air setting at this superb restaurant from chef Roberto Alcocer (page 132).

ACCOMMODATIONS

★ **Casa Mayoral:** Airy cabins and casitas offer comfortable accommodations at this pet- and child-friendly property (page 135).

★ **Bruma:** A serene setting and dramatically natural architecture make this boutique hotel one of the best places to stay in the region (page 135).

★ **La Villa del Valle:** This Tuscan-style villa nestled into the Valle the Guadalupe gives guests a dose of luxury in Baja's rustic wine region (page 135).

★ **Cuatrocuatros:** Chic glamping and dramatic Pacific views draw guests to this spot just outside of the Valle de Guadalupe (page 137).

A large majority of the more than 150 Baja California wineries are located along the Ruta del Vino in the Valle de Guadalupe, but if you're looking to escape the crowds, take a trip down to the Antigua Ruta del Vino in Valle de la Grulla and Valle de Santo Tomás to check out the handful of wineries in that area. Whichever region you choose, you won't be disappointed.

PLANNING YOUR TIME

Valle de Guadalupe can be easily visited in a day trip from Ensenada, Rosarito, Tijuana, or Tecate. It's also a popular weekend destination, and a few days is plenty of time to leisurely enjoy a number of wineries and fantastic restaurants of the valley. Valle de la Grulla and Valle de Santo Tomás are best visited together in a single day trip from Ensenada.

Previous: the outdoor setting of Deckman's en el Mogor restaurant; large patio at Bodegas F. Rubio winery; sipping wine under the shade of oak trees at Casa Magoni winery.

Northern Mexico Wine Country

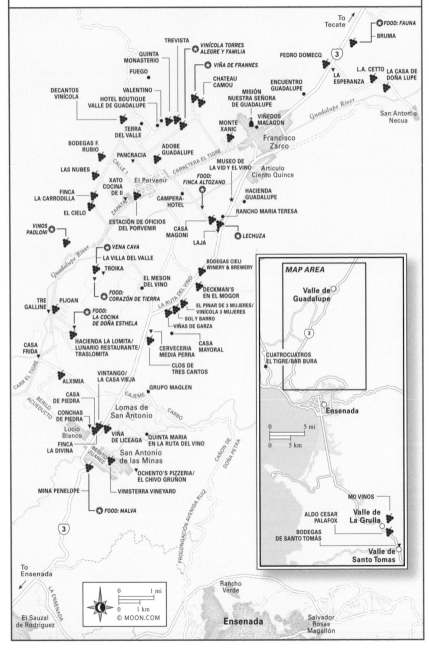

To Tecate

FOOD: FAUNA
BRUMA

TREVISTA

VINÍCOLA TORRES ALEGRE Y FAMILIA

QUINTA MONASTERIO

PEDRO DOMECQ

Viña de Frannes

LA ESPERANZA

L.A. CETTO

LA CASA DE DOÑA LUPE

FUEGO

CHATEAU CAMOU

ENCUENTRO GUADALUPE

VALENTINO

MISIÓN NUESTRA SEÑORA DE GUADALUPE

DECANTOS VINÍCOLA

HOTEL BOUTIQUE VALLE DE GUADALUPE

VIÑEDOS MALAGÓN

San Antonio Necua

TERRA DEL VALLE

MONTE XANIC

Guadalupe River

Francisco Zarco

BODEGAS F. RUBIO

PANCRACIA

ADOBE GUADALUPE

LAS NUBES

CALLE 1

XATO COCINA DE II

El Porvenir

CARRETERA EL TIGRE

MUSEO DE LA VID Y EL VINO

Artículo Ciento Quince

FINCA LA CARRODILLA

FOOD: FINCA ALTOZANO

HACIENDA GUADALUPE

EL CIELO

ZAPATA

CAMPERA HOTEL

RANCHO MARIA TERESA

ESTACIÓN DE OFICIOS DEL PORVENIR

CASA MAGONI

VINOS PAOLONI

VENA CAVA

LAJA

LECHUZA

LA VILLA DEL VALLE

Guadalupe River

TROIKA

BODEGAS CIELI WINERY & BREWERY

EL MESON DEL VINO

DECKMAN'S EN EL MOGOR

TRE GALLINE

PIJOAN

FOOD: CORAZÓN DE TIERRA

LA RUTA DEL VINO

EL PINAR DE 3 MUJERES/ VINÍCOLA 3 MUJERES

FOOD: LA COCINA DE DOÑA ESTHELA

SOL Y BARRO

VIÑAS DE GARZA

CASA FRIDA

HACIENDA LA LOMITA/ LUNARIO RESTAURANTE/ TRASLOMITA

CERVECERIA MEDIA PERRA

CASA MAYORAL

CARR EL TIGRE

ALXIMIA

VINTANGO/ LA CASA VIEJA

CLOS DE TRES CANTOS

BERILO

CASA DE PIEDRA

CAJEME

GRUPO MAGLEN

ACUEDUCTO

CONCHAS DE PIEDRA

Lomas de San Antonio

CARBO

Lucio Blanco

VIÑA DE LICEAGA

QUINTA MARIA EN LA RUTA DEL VINO

CAÑON DE DOÑA PETRA

FINCA LA DIVINA

BENITO JUAREZ

San Antonio de las Minas

MINA PENELOPE

OCHENTO'S PIZZERIA/ EL CHIVO GRUÑON

VINISTERRA VINEYARD

PROLONGACIÓN AVENIDA RUIZ

FOOD: MALVA

3

To Ensenada

LA ENSENADA

El Sauzal de Rodríguez

Rancho Verde

Ensenada

Salvador Rosas Magallón

0   1 mi
0   1 km
© MOON.COM

MAP AREA

Valle de Guadalupe

3

CUATROCUATROS EL TIGRE/BAR BURA

0   5 mi
0   5 km

Ensenada

MD VINOS

Valle de La Grulla

ALDO CESAR PALAFOX

BODEGAS DE SANTO TOMÁS

Valle de Santo Tomas

Valle de Guadalupe

East of Ensenada, La Ruta del Vino takes travelers into Baja's rapidly growing wine region, the Valle de Guadalupe. Here, dirt roads wind through the arid valley and bring travelers to beautiful boutique wineries serving award-winning wines. Outdoor *campestre* restaurants allow diners to look out at the vineyards while enjoying gourmet farm-to-table food prepared by the best chefs in the country. Luxury B&Bs give travelers time to truly absorb the intimate tranquility and beauty of the region.

This is an area unparalleled on the rest of the peninsula, and the whole world is taking notice. In the past few years, the region has gained attention through the likes of the *New York Times, Wall Street Journal, Vogue,* and *Condé Nast Traveler,* as well as from renowned chefs like Anthony Bourdain and Rick Bayless. It's been referred to as the "Napa of Baja" and the "Tuscany of Mexico," but anyone intimate with the Valle de Guadalupe will tell you that this is a unique place with its own rustic charm, friendly spirit, and an essence that is distinctively Mexican.

Wine has been made in this region for well over 100 years, but it's just been since the turn of the millennium that the new wine movement has brought so much attention to the valley. Characterized by boutique wineries producing small batches of high-quality wines, this new wine movement paved the way for a foodie movement as well. Chefs came to the valley to open *campestre* restaurants—open-air venues serving regional seafood and meats cooked over wood fires, fresh vegetables from the garden, and locally made cheeses and olive oil. What makes Valle de Guadalupe attractive is the great wine, but what makes the region extraordinary is the incredible food.

There are now over 150 wineries here. Weekends are the best for finding them all open—they are also the busiest time for tourists to visit and people from Southern California to come down. If you have flexibility with your schedule, Thursday and Friday are days when most wineries and restaurants will be open and you won't have to deal with the weekend crowds. Many restaurants and wineries are closed on Monday.

Summer has traditionally been considered the peak season for the valley, because the vineyards are full of grapes and the harvest begins in August. Coinciding with the beginning of harvest season is the Fiestas de la Vendimia, the annual wine harvest festival. For three weeks, crowds converge on the region to enjoy festivals, parties, dinners, and lots of wine. This is by far the busiest time to visit the valley, and reservations for hotels must be made nearly a year in advance. If you're unable to get a hotel in the valley, check accommodations in nearby Ensenada or Rosarito. In addition to the crowds, summer can also bring temperatures of well over 100 degrees. Now that the valley is becoming better known and restaurants and wineries are open year-round, it's more pleasant to avoid the heat and the crowds and visit in the fall or spring.

Orientation

The Valle de Guadalupe runs diagonally from southwest to northeast. There are **two paved roads, Mexico 3** and **Carretera El Tigre,** that follow this same direction and come to a point in the northeast corner of the valley. Mexico 3 runs along the southern/eastern edge of the valley, and Carretera El Tigre runs along the northern/western edge of the valley.

There are **three main towns** in the valley: **Francisco Zarco, El Porvenir,** and **San Antonio de las Minas.** Francisco Zarco is located in the northeast corner of the valley where Mexico 3 and Carretera El Tigre meet. El Porvenir is located on Carretera El Tigre near the center of the valley, and San Antonio

Mexican Wines

Ninety percent of the wines from Mexico come from this region, and a majority of the wines that are produced here go to one place—Mexico City. There's such a demand for wines from Valle de Guadalupe in the restaurants in Mexico City that wineries have a difficult time producing enough to fulfill orders. That means there isn't much left for distribution anywhere else, which is why Mexican wines haven't received much exposure outside of the country.

Most visitors are surprised to learn that Mexico has such a vibrant wine industry. While many of the varietals from this area will be familiar, other grapes that thrive in the region, such as the Spanish tempranillo and the Italian nebbiolo, may be new to some wine drinkers. In addition, many of the wines coming out of this region are blends (as opposed to monovarietals), which means that the winemakers are creating unique taste profiles that you won't find anywhere else.

The one factor that keeps Mexican wine production limited is the lack of water in the region. All the water in the Valle de Guadalupe comes from private wells and underground rivers and aquifers, which have been at very low levels due to recent years of drought. Even those with a well on their property may not be able to use it if they don't have the water rights.

Most of the wineries in the Valle de Guadalupe are small producers, making only a few thousand cases every year. U.S. citizens crossing at the California border may only bring back one liter of alcohol per adult into the U.S. every 30 days (a wine bottle is 750 ml).

de las Minas is located on Mexico 3 in the southwest corner of the valley.

TOP EXPERIENCE

LA RUTA DEL VINO

La Ruta del Vino, The Wine Route, is the name given to the collection of wineries and restaurants in the Valle de Guadalupe that are now drawing visitors from all over the world. There are over 150 wineries in the Valle de Guadalupe, ranging in size from small micro wineries to large commercial wineries. Many visitors to the Valle will agree that the charm and soul of the region lies in the small and medium boutique wineries where the winemakers are often found around the property, and visitors will get a more distinctive and personal experience in the tasting room. Wine tastings range US$10-20. The region is heavy on red wines, but most wineries make at least a few white or rosé wines.

There are only a handful of paved roads in the Valle de Guadalupe; the rest of the valley is a network of unnamed dirt roads. A day wine-tasting in the Valle often requires winding along dirt roads (seemingly lost) before arriving at a stunning boutique

winery or *campestre* restaurant with gourmet food. There are a series of blue signs on the main roads through the valley designating the turnoffs from the paved roads for various wineries and restaurants. From here, you'll need to keep an eye out for any private signs that the business has put up along the road directing you to the property. Some of the individual establishments that are more difficult to find will have maps and more precise directions on their website or Facebook page. Because many of the best wineries and restaurants are tucked away out of sight from the paved roads, it's a good idea to have picked out a few wineries ahead of time that you know you'd like to visit. Calling ahead to make a reservation or to at least make sure that the winery will be able to receive you on the day that you desire is a good idea as well. Those who simply drive around the valley in hope of stumbling across good wineries may find themselves frustrated and disappointed.

Francisco Zarco
BRUMA

It's not just about the looks at the gorgeous tasting room at **Bruma** (Mexico 3 Km.

73.5, tel. 646/194-8239, www.bruma.mx, 11am-5pm daily). Local architect Alejandro D'Acosta used a 300-year-old oak tree in the construction of the tasting room and the results are stunning. And as beautiful as the tasting room is, the wines are right up to par. Winemaker Lourdes Martinez Ojeda is one of the rising stars in Valle de Guadalupe and her wines are truly exceptional. There's a hotel and the award-winning Fauna restaurant on the same property.

PEDRO DOMECQ

One of the oldest wineries in the region, **Pedro Domecq** (Mexico 3 Km. 73, tel. 646/155-2249, www.pedrodomecq.com, 10am-6pm daily), has received a facelift that includes a tasting room that's open to the public. The modern tasting room features a nice indoor area as well as an expansive outdoor space. The winery started in 1972 and has also operated as a distillery. Brandy is still made on the property in addition to wine. They offer a tour of their museum and wine cave.

LA CETTO

For a larger, more commercial experience, **LA Cetto** (Mexico 3 Km. 73.5, tel. 646/155-2179, www.lacetto.mx, 10am-5pm daily) has been around since 1928 and is one of the oldest and biggest wineries in the region. You can take a tour of the facility to learn about the winemaking process and then do a tasting afterward.

MONTE XANIC

Monte Xanic (Francisco Zarco, tel. 646/155-2080, www.montexanic.com.mx, 10am-5pm daily) is another large winery experience, with beautiful views from a remodeled tasting room.

SOLAR FORTÚN

Tucked into its own corner of the valley is family winery **Solar Fortún** (Cañada de Guadalupe, tel. 646/116-7235, www.solarfortun.com, 11am-5pm Sat.-Sun.).

Wine-tastings take place at tables on the large patio; guests can also order food from the on-site restaurant, which features items such as ceviches and its famous smoked marlin tacos. The comfortable and serene setting is family friendly and the perfect spot for spending a lazy afternoon.

Along Carretera El Tigre: El Porvenir
DECANTOS VINÍCOLA

With a large and impressive facility, **Decantos Vinícola** (Rancho San Miguel Fraccion A, tel. 646/688-1019, www.decantosvinicola.com, 11am-7pm daily) is a popular choice among the millennial crowd. The sleek tasting room features expansive floor-to-ceiling windows as well as an outdoor deck, all with beautiful views. The property hosts a number of large events and festivals throughout the year.

ADOBE GUADALUPE

The tasting room at **Adobe Guadalupe** (Parcela A-1, tel. 646/155-2093, www.adobeguadalupe.com, 10am-5pm daily) is open daily. There's a food truck outside the tasting room and a patio with tables for enjoying the weather on a nice day.

★ VINÍCOLA TORRES ALEGRE Y FAMILIA

The family-run **Vinícola Torres Alegre y Familia** (Parcela 52, tel. 646/688-1033, 11am-5pm daily) takes great care in making wines, from de-stemming the grapes to ensuring the flavors are perfectly balanced without adding chemicals. The results are superb, with the winery creating some of the most respected wines coming out of the valley. The white wines are particularly complex and exceptional. Family patriarch Victor Torres Alegre studied winemaking in Bordeaux, France, before returning to Mexico to help revitalize the Mexican wine industry. The winery boasts a beautiful tasting room with 360-degree views of the surrounding vineyards.

QUINTA MONASTERIO

The beautiful stone archway will lead you to the cute and cozy tasting room at **Quinta Monasterio** (Parcela 12, tel. 646/156-8023, www.quintamonasterio.com.mx, 11am-6pm daily). The family operation has been run by multiple generations, and entering the tasting room is almost like being welcomed into the family's living room. There's also a popular spa on the property as well as cabins for rent.

TREVISTA

The personal attention and gracious hospitality are what keep visitors coming back to **Trevista** (Parcela 18, tel. 646/156-8027, www.trevistavineyards.com, tastings Saturdays at noon and 3:30pm). Owners Hilda and James take great care in growing their grapes, making their wines, and sharing their creations with visitors. Their tempranillo is a favorite of those familiar with Valle de Guadalupe wines and their tasting comprises a vertical tasting of tempranillo with paired tapas.

CASA EMILIANA

You'll feel right at home at **Casa Emiliana** (Parcela 107, tel. 646/688-1013, 11am-5pm daily) thanks to its friendly service and personal attention. This hidden gem offers a peaceful and cozy setting, making it the perfect place to escape the crowds and truly relax. There's a small B&B (tel. 646/155-2240) that they run, located off the property out on the paved road.

CHATEAU CAMOU

Nestled into its own little corner of the valley, **Chateau Camou** (Domicilio Conocido, tel. 646/177-3303, www.chateau-camou.com.mx, 10am-4:30pm daily) uses all French grapes and French winemaking techniques. The winery has been in operation for 20 years, and it's worth it to take a tour of the facilities, which include the large barrel room where classical music is played according to a weekly schedule in order to help with the stabilization process of the wine, getting the molecules of the wine and barrel to vibrate together. Make sure you get to see the impressive bottle room, home to almost 300,000 vessels arranged in fun designs on the walls.

★ VIÑA DE FRANNES

Right next to Chateau Camou, **Viña de Frannes** (Cañada del Trigo, tel. 646/688-1955, www.vfrannes.com, 10am-6pm daily) has a beautiful, modern tasting room with impressive vineyard views. Situated on more than 3,000 acres, the property was once owned by Mexican president Abelardo Rodríguez in the 1930s. He planted the sauvignon blanc grapes that the winery still makes its sauvignon blanc from today. The signature wine is a cabernet franc that is excellent and a unique treat for the region. There's also a small restaurant on the property and the outdoor patio is a wonderful place to spend the afternoon enjoying crisp wines with fresh seafood dishes. This is a great place to buy olive oil; they produce a high-quality version made from olives that they grow on the property.

LAS NUBES

First-time travelers, frequent visitors, and locals all find themselves enjoying the fantastic views and good wine at **Las Nubes** (Callejon Emiliano Zapata, tel. 646/156-8037, www.vinoslasnubesbc.com, 11am-5pm daily). Owner and winemaker Victor Segura not only creates easy-to-drink wines, but has established a welcoming environment for all guests. Perched on the northern hillside of the valley, the beautiful stone winery (all of the stones used to build it were mined from the property) offers sweeping views from the large outdoor terrace and the chic indoor tasting room. It's easy to understand where the name Las Nubes, meaning "The Clouds," came from when you're standing out on the terrace looking at the scenic vista of the valley and feeling the gentle breeze. The friendly staff, affordable tastings, large space, and good wines make this spot a favorite for many valley visitors.

1: Las Nubes winery **2:** views from the back patio of Viña de Frannes winery **3:** Chateau Camou winery

BODEGAS F. RUBIO

Just east of Las Nubes, family-operated **Bodegas F. Rubio** (Callejon de la Liebre Parcela 70, tel. 646/156-8046, www. bodegasfrubio.com, noon-7pm Thurs.-Mon.) has a nice indoor facility as well as a large outdoor patio for wine-tasting. Try their montepulciano wine, an Italian red grape that is a rarity in the valley. Restaurant **Parcela 70** (www.parcela70.com, noon-7pm Thurs.-Mon.) serves up delicious and inventive dishes. Because the winery and restaurant open later in the day and stay open until 7pm on the weekends, this is one of the few places in the valley to visit past 5pm once most of the other wineries have closed.

FINCA LA CARRODILLA

The rooftop garden at **Finca La Carrodilla** (Parcela 99 Z1 P14, tel. 646/156-8052, www. fincalacarrodilla.mx, 10am-5pm Wed.-Sun.) looks out onto the gardens and vineyards on the property. It's the perfect setting for enjoying their organic biodynamic wines.

EL CIELO

El Cielo (Carretera El Tigre Km. 7.5, tel. 646/151-6515, www.vinoselcielo.com, 10am-8pm Mon.-Fri., 9am-9pm Sat., 9am-8pm Sun.) offers tastings and has the restaurant **Latitud 32** on the property as well as a large store selling wine and other regional products. In 2019, a large hotel opened on the property offering accommodations in private luxury villas.

Along Carretera El Tigre: Central Valley
★ VENA CAVA

The unique architecture is part of the allure for **Vena Cava** (Rancho San Marcos Toros Pintos, tel. 646/156-8053, www. venacavawine.com, 11am-5pm daily, tastings on the hour). The wine cave is dug out of the hillside and topped with decommissioned wooden fishing boats from Ensenada. Winemaker Phil Gregory is often around the winery regaling guests with stories and talking about his winemaking process. He and his wife, Eileen, are also the owners of La Villa del Valle B&B and Troika food truck, both on the same property as the winery. Favorite wines at Vena Cava are the tempranillo, the "Big Blend" red, and the special espumoso brut rosé (one of only a handful of sparkling wines produced in the Valle de Guadalupe). Also on the property is famed restaurant Corazón de Tierra.

Vena Cava is a winery constructed of old fishing boats from Ensenada.

VINOS PIJOAN

Visitors will feel comfortably at home at the intimate winery at **Vinos Pijoan** (Carretera El Tigre Km. 13.5, tel. 646/127-1251, www.vinospijoan.com, 11am-5pm Wed.-Mon.). The inviting outdoor patio creates a serene setting for enjoying wine while looking out onto the vineyards. Pau Pijoan, the owner-winemaker, is often around, and you'll get personal attention from the tasting room employees. If they aren't too busy, ask them for a behind-the-scenes tour of their unique wine cave.

★ VINOS PAOLONI

With an Italian winemaker and varietals, **Vinos Paoloni** (formerly Villa Montefiori, Camino el Porvenir Parcela 26-1, tel. 646/156-8020, www.villamontefiori.mx, 11am-5pm Mon.-Thurs., 10am-6pm Fri.-Sun.) creates "Mexican wines with an Italian heart." Winemaker Paolo Paoloni started growing grapes in the Valle de Guadalupe in 1997 and today uses the most modern technology available for his production. The new tasting room is expansive and features indoor and outdoor space with sweeping vineyard views.

HACIENDA LA LOMITA

The sister winery to Finca La Carrodilla, **Hacienda La Lomita** (Fraccionamiento San Marcos, tel. 646/156-8466, www.lomita.mx, 10am-5pm Wed.-Sun.) is known for its bright young wines and the hip vibe in the tasting room. The winery also has an outdoor restaurant, TrasLomita, on the property that's perfect for lunch, and an indoor restaurant, Lunario Restaurante, that's open in the evenings for dinner.

Along Carretera El Tigre: West Valley

ALXIMIA

Looking somewhat like an adobe spaceship, **Alximia** (Camino Vecinal al Tigre Km. 3, tel. 646/127-1453, www.alximia.com, 11am-6pm daily) is a winery that comes from a family of scientists. Winemaker Alvaro Alvarez is a former mathematician, his father was an astronomer at the national observatory in San Pedro Mártir, and his mother was a schoolteacher. *Alximia* means chemist, and the main wines produced here are named after the four classical elements (earth, water, air, and fire) and created by drawing on Alvaro's background in chemistry. There is a restaurant, LaX, located on the outdoor patio of the winery.

RELIEVE

Family-run winery **Relieve** (Calle Berilo, tel. 646/178-6650, 11am-6pm Wed.-Mon.) is producing some of the top wines in the region such as their tempranillo. The large, modern tasting room has both indoor and outdoor seating. They have a chic seasonal restaurant, Mixtura, on the property that serves delicious Baja California cuisine from April to November.

Along Mexico 3: Central Valley
★ LECHUZA

Family-operated **Lechuza** (Mexico 3 Km. 82.5, tel. 646/256-4437, www.vinoslechuza.com, 11am-5pm Wed.-Mon.) offers a tranquil setting for enjoying some of the best wines coming out of the Valle de Guadalupe. This boutique winery takes great care in making its wines, which have become insider favorites. Their stainless steel chardonnay and bold nebbiolo are standouts. The tasting room staff is friendly and knowledgeable and members of the family are often around to chat about the wines and the winemaking process.

CASA MAGONI

One of the godfathers of the Valle de Guadalupe is Camile Magoni, who has been making wine in the region for over 50 years. For 49 of those years, he was the winemaker for LA Cetto, but he now has his own winery, **Casa Magoni** (Mexico 3 Km. 83, tel. 646/187-0483, www.casamagoni.com, 11am-5pm Wed.-Sun.). Guests enjoy their wine under the shade of giant oak trees, which is the quintessential way to spend an afternoon in Valle.

VIÑAS DE GARZA

Serving up wine and beautiful vineyard views from a covered deck, **Viñas de Garza** (Mexico 3 Km. 87, tel. 646/175-8883, www.vinosdegarza.com, 11am-4:30pm Fri.-Sun.) offers an intimate and picturesque wine-tasting experience.

VINÍCOLA 3 MUJERES

Vinícola 3 Mujeres (Mexico 3 Km. 87, tel. 646/171-5674, 11am-5pm Fri.-Sun.) was started in 2005 by three friends who met while studying winemaking at La Escuelita. Ivette Vaillard, Eva Cotero Altamirano, and Laura McGregor Garcia were the first women winemakers in the region, and today they serve their wines in a rustic and intimate cave.

SOL Y BARRO

Affectionately known as the "hobbit house," **Sol y Barro** (Mexico 3 Km. 87, tel. 646/268-7244, 11am-6pm daily) features a distinctly unique architecture that's like something out of a fairytale. Swiss owner Aimé built the structures himself from clay dug on the property ("sol y barro" translates to "sun and clay"). The winery produces only a small amount of wine, so a trip to the tasting room is a special experience to see the unique property, try some of the limited-production wines, and chat with the friendly staff.

CLOS DE TRES CANTOS

The unique, pyramid-like architecture at **Clos de Tres Cantos** (Mexico 3 Km. 89, tel. 558/568-9240, 10am-5pm Wed.-Sun.) continues underground into the wine caves below. If you're looking for a one-of-a-kind experience, pay to take the tour (all tour profits go to charity) to see the cave and underground "cathedral." They have two rooms available to rent for overnight stays on the property.

BODEGAS CIELI WINERY & BREWERY

For sweeping valley views and a fun atmosphere, head to **Bodegas Cieli Winery & Brewery** (Mexico 3 Km. 84.7, tel. 646/185-4478, www.cieliwinery.com, 11am-9pm Thurs.-Sat., 11am-6pm Sun.), where owner Ron McCabe creates both boutique wine and a "chamvier" product that beer lovers will enjoy. Perched on the hill, the comfortable and relaxed environment offers beautiful views of the valley from the outdoor deck. This is one of the best spots in the valley to sit and relax during sunset while enjoying a drink in the company of friends. Ron owned an Italian restaurant in the United States, and he regularly hosts special dinners and events at the bodega.

MOGOR BADAN

With tastings in the wine cave on the weekends, **Mogor Badan** (Mexico 3 Km. 86.5, tel. 646/156-8156, 11am-5pm Sat.-Sun.) is a family project. The Badan family has been in the region for decades and matriarch Natalia Badan is one of the leading figures in the region today. The entire property is organic, from the wine grapes to Natalia's famous produce garden. The popular Deckman's en el Mogor restaurant is on the same property.

Along Mexico 3: San Antonio de las Minas

MINA PENELOPE

Open on the weekends, **Mina Penelope** (Mexico 3 Km. 96, tel. 646/155-3085, www.minapenelope.com, 11am-6pm Sat.-Sun.) offers crisp white wines and bold reds that are found on the wine lists of some of Mexico's top restaurants. Guests enjoy tastings in the wine cave and enjoy warm hospitality at this family winery. Restaurant Malva is on the property, so if the winery isn't open, you can enjoy a glass of wine at the restaurant.

CASA DE PIEDRA

Winemaker Hugo D'Acosta is largely considered one of the pioneers in the Mexican wine industry, and a trip to his winery, **Casa de**

1: Vinos Paoloni winery 2: patio at Lechuza winery
3: Alximia winery 4: El Chivo Gruñon beer cave

"La Escuelita": School of Wine

One of the most important factors in the recent rise of the Valle de Guadalupe is the wine school, **Estación de Oficios del Porvenir,** known affectionately as **"La Escuelita."** Highly respected winemaker Hugo D'Acosta started the nonprofit school in 2004 to promote the production of boutique wine and to educate locals about winemaking traditions. The idea was to create a place where the local farmers—who, at the time, were growing grapes for the few large wineries that existed—could learn how to cultivate grapes that were good for making wine and learn how to make wine themselves. La Escuelita offered them classes at an affordable price and access to winemaking machinery. The school was pivotal in creating quality Mexican wines in the valley and opening the door for new winemakers. Today, a majority of the boutique wineries in the valley have winemakers who attended La Escuelita. The school still thrives and may be found in the town of El Porvenir. You'll recognize it by the eclectic architecture that makes use of reclaimed materials.

Piedra (Mexico 3 Km. 93.5, tel. 646/156-5267, www.vinoscasadepiedra.com, 11am-5pm Fri.-Sun.), will give you a chance to try some of his wines and learn more about him as a person. D'Acosta also started La Escuelita, the wine school in Valle de Guadalupe that is credited with teaching many of the local winemakers and creating the boutique winery boom in the region.

VINTANGO

Vintango (Mexico 3 Km. 93, tel. 646/193-0072, 9am-5pm Sat.-Sun.) has a tasting room and art gallery in La Casa Vieja, one of the oldest buildings in Valle de Guadalupe. Red wine lovers will appreciate the focus on red varietals and will love the bold wines that winemaker Jo Ann Knox has created.

WINE TOURS

Most of the Valle de Guadalupe is unmarked dirt roads without signs, so it can be challenging for first-time visitors to navigate the valley on their own. If it's your first time to the Valle de Guadalupe and you want to make the most of your experience, it's best to take an organized wine tour. This also alleviates the problem of needing a designated driver for a day of wine-tasting. **Baja Test Kitchen** (www.bajatestkitchen.com, rates starting at US$199 per person for public tour) operates single- or multiday tours that can originate in either San Diego or anywhere in northern

Baja for groups of 2 to 25 people. Public group tours run on a weekly basis and private custom tours are also available. The owners are residents of the region and have close relationships with many of the winemakers and restaurateurs in the valley, so guests get a very personal and unique experience.

SIGHTS
Museo de la Vid y el Vino

To learn a bit about the history of wine and the Valle de Guadalupe, stop in at the **Museo de la Vid y el Vino** (Mexico 3 Km. 81.3, tel. 646/156-8165, www.museodelvinobc.com, 9am-5pm Tues.-Sun., US$3). The large facility also features an art gallery, garden, and outdoor amphitheater. All of the information is in Spanish, but the museum usually has a tour guide available who can walk you through the museum (for free) in English.

Misión Nuestra Señora de Guadalupe del Norte

The last mission founded in both Alta and Baja California was the **Misión Nuestra Señora de Guadalupe,** founded in 1834. Dominican padre Felix Caballero oversaw the mission until his death (a possible poisoning) in 1840. The last of the missions on the peninsula closed down by 1849. Not much is left of this one, aside from the ruins of the foundation walls, which have been developed into a historical park. There's also a small but well-done and informative museum run by INAH on the property. The museum touches on the history of the region and the influence of the native Kumeyaay, the Russian Molokans, the Mexican ranchers, and the Spanish missionaries. Displays are in both Spanish and English. The park and museum are open 9am-5pm Wednesday-Sunday; admission is free. They are just off of the northern paved road in the town of Francisco Zarco.

Museo Ruso

Not many people know that the Valle de Guadalupe was heavily influenced by a group of Russian Molokans who settled in the region in the early 1900s after fleeing the Bolshevik revolution. The descendants of these settlers are still in the region today, and there's a small Russian museum in Francisco Zarco, **Museo Ruso** (Calle El Tigre #276, tel. 646/155-2030, 10am-4:30pm Wed.-Mon., US$2), where visitors can get a guided tour of one of the old Russian adobe houses and learn more about the history and lives of these people. For a tour of the museum in English or Spanish, inquire at restaurant Familia Samarín, which is located on the same property; it offers some traditional Russian dishes on its menu and has a small gift shop with some local and Russian items.

ENTERTAINMENT AND EVENTS

There's no nightlife in the valley; once most of the wineries close at 5pm, you'll be hard-pressed to find much open aside from restaurants. There are a few wineries that stay open until 7pm or 8pm, but that's the extent of the nightlife. Visitors staying overnight in the Valle de Guadalupe will find that a peaceful quiet falls upon the valley in the evenings after the last wineries have shut their doors. Most visitors will buy a bottle of wine during the day to enjoy back at their hotel room in the evening.

For stunning sunset views over the Pacific, head to **Bar Bura** (Carretera Libre Tijuana-Ensenada Km. 89, www.

cuatrocuatros.mx, noon-9pm daily), located on the **Cuatrocuatros** property, just outside of the valley. Perched on the cliffs looking down at the ocean, the completely open-air bar features breathtaking views. There are some tables and covered hay bales for seating, arranged under canopies. They don't have a full menu at the bar (there's a full restaurant on another part of the property), but they do serve some appetizers such as ceviche. They make their own wines on the property, which they serve along with other local wines and beverages. You'll need to pay an entrance fee (US$8 per person) as well as a minimum consumption (US$30 per person). To get to the bar, you'll park below on the property and be driven in one of their vehicles up to the bar. It's best to make a reservation; they stop letting people up to the bar once they've hit capacity.

There are a few options for beer drinkers in Valle de Guadalupe. Located on the property of pizzeria Ochento's in San Antonio de las Minas is the beer cave **El Chivo Gruñon** (Rancho Cimarrón, tel. 646/210-1761, elchivogrunon@gmail.com, noon-8pm Sun.-Thurs., noon-10pm Fri.-Sat.), serving up its own craft beer in a clandestine tasting room fitted out like a retro clubhouse. Beer maker Juan is a genial and knowledgeable host regaling guests with stories over his delicious beers. Another option for craft beer is **Cerveceria Media Perra** (Camino a Casa Mayoral, tel. 646/181-4631, www.mediaperra. com, 1pm-7pm Thurs.-Sun.), in the Central Valley off of Mexico 3, with a stunning, uniquely modern tasting room and a variety of house-made beers.

The famous **Fiestas de la Vendimia** wine harvest festival (www.provinobc.mx) takes place over three weeks every July and August. Coinciding with the beginning of the harvest season, the festival is a series of private parties and dinners held at the wineries and restaurants in the valley. There are two large events that bring together most of the wineries and draw huge crowds: the **Muestra del Vino** (wine-tasting), at the beginning of

the festival, and the famous **Concurso de Paella** (paella contest), which closes the festival. Tickets for these events are generally around US$50. Tickets for private events and parties are sold at a premium (starting around US$100). The Vendimia is considered one of Ensenada's most high-society events.

★ FOOD

When the Valle de Guadalupe started garnering international recognition for its wine in recent years, Baja chefs began flocking to the region to open restaurants. Many of these were built in the *campestre* (country) style, characterized by outdoor seating and local ingredients cooked over fire grills. Some restaurants that have entirely outdoor seating close for the winter or have reduced hours, so inquire ahead of time if visiting at that time of year.

Francisco Zarco

The hottest restaurant in Valle de Guadalupe is ★ **Fauna** (Mexico 3 Km. 75, tel. 646/103-6403, www.faunarestaurante.mx, 1pm-9pm Sun.-Wed., 1pm-10pm Thurs.-Sat., US$18-27), located on the property of Bruma. Chef David Castro Hussong worked around the world at Noma, Blue Hill, and Eleven Madison Park before returning to his hometown of Ensenada. He prepares simple and traditional Mexican dishes but often with an unexpected twist. The indoor dining room features floor-to-ceiling windows that look out to the outdoor dining room, with views beyond of the valley. The multicourse tasting menu features dishes that are served family-style at the large wooden communal tables.

Tijuana chef Miguel Angel Guerrero brings his "BajaMed" style of food to the valley with **La Esperanza** (Mexico 3 Km. 73.5, tel. 664/155-2785, 1pm-10pm Wed.-Sat., 1pm-7pm Sun., mains US$9-15). The rustic, industrial setting looks out over the vineyards and offers both indoor and outdoor seating. Because the restaurant is located on the L.A. Cetto property, it serves only L.A. Cetto wines.

Along Carretera El Tigre: El Porvenir

The architecture is stunning at **Pancracia** (Parcela 69 Ejido el Porvenir, tel. 646/977-7517, 8am-8pm Mon.-Tues., 8am-10pm Wed.-Thurs., 8am-11pm Fri.-Sat., 8am-9pm Sun., US$16-20), where a large and modern open-air structure is surrounded by water features. The two-story restaurant also has a nice bar and plenty of areas for lounging and relaxing. The dynamic menu features modern Mexican dishes with Mediterranean and Asian influences. Hotel Agua de Vid is on the same property.

All the cool kids and the foodies are heading to **Xato Cocina de II** (Parcela 103 Ejido el Porvenir, tel. 646/688-1018, 11am-7pm Thurs.-Mon., US$9-12), where the incredibly fresh food is delicately crafted and packed with flavor. Expect classic Baja Californian dishes such as tacos, tostadas, fish, and ribs, elevated to new levels. This is gourmet dining in a casual setting without the pretentiousness. The restaurant is located on the property of the winery Bodegas del Paraíso.

Along Carretera El Tigre: Central Valley

Chef Diego Hernandez creates exquisite local food at his restaurant ★ **Corazón de Tierra** (Rancho San Marcos Toros Pintos, tel. 646/977-5538, www.corazondetierra. com, 6pm-8:30pm Wed.-Thurs., 1:30pm-9:30pm Fri.-Sat., 11am-4pm Sun., 1:30pm-8:30pm Mon., US$85). Vegetables and herbs come from the garden on the property and meats and fish are locally sourced. There's no menu—the six courses change daily depending on what's fresh and in season. Don't skip doing the wine pairing with the meal. The pairings perfectly complement the food for a completely unforgettable experience. Even

---

1: Bar Bura on the Cuatrocuatros property
2: striking architecture at Pancracia restaurant
3: Museo Ruso 4: Misión Nuestra Señora de Guadalupe del Norte

though this is upscale dining, the restaurant feels comfortable with bright mismatched chairs and wooden tables. The floor-to-ceiling windows open when the weather is warm for a complete open-air experience looking out onto the beautiful garden where much of the food for the meal comes from. Reservations should be made in advance on the website and require a prepayment.

On the same property is the food truck of Diego Hernandez, **Troika** (tel. 646/246-4123, 11am-6pm daily, mains US$6-10). The project is a collaboration between Hernandez, Vena Cava winery (on the same property), and Wendlandt brewery. The food truck is right outside of Vena Cava winery and serves gastropub fare like sliders with bacon marmalade and beer-battered tomatillos, suckling pig tacos, and octopus tostadas. The *campestre* setting features picnic tables set under a canopy of woven repurposed irrigation tubing.

Located on the property of the winery Hacienda La Lomita, outdoor *campestre* restaurant **TrasLomita** (Parcela 71 San Marcos, tel. 646/156-8469, noon-5:30pm Wed.-Thurs., noon-6:30pm Fri.-Sun., US$8-12) features creative and delicious dishes from one of the valley's top female chefs, Sheyla Alvarado. Food is cooked over a wood-fired oven or grill and served in a serene garden setting. The menu boasts fresh ceviches and *aguachiles* as well as marinated ribs and grilled lamb and steak. Chef Alvarado is also at the helm of the indoor restaurant that opened in 2019 on the same property, **Lunario Restaurante** (tel. 646/156-8469, 7pm-10:30pm Wed.-Sun., US$10-15), offering Baja Californian cuisine such as elevated softshell crab tacos and artfully prepared *lengua*. Only open in the evenings for dinner, the restaurant features a glass ceiling and large glass windows—perfect for stargazing while you eat. Diners can choose from a fixed menu that changes seasonally or order items a la carte.

Locals and foodies head to ★ **La Cocina**

de Doña Esthela (Carretera El Tigre a Guadalupe, tel. 646/156-8453, 8am-5pm Tues.-Sun., mains US$5-9) for one of the best breakfasts on the peninsula. The signature *machaca con huevos* and the corn pancakes are dishes that shouldn't be missed. Everything served here is made in house, from the savory meat dishes to the fresh tortillas. They're also open for lunch. Don't expect a fancy setting—the operation started with Blanca Esthela Martínez Bueno, known to the world now as Doña Esthela, making cookies and eventually serving food out of her personal kitchen to local patrons. They've expanded to multiple dining rooms and a large outdoor patio space, but it still features the same warm hospitality and homemade cooking. Doña Esthela is there herself most of the time, checking on customers to make sure they have everything they need. If visiting on the weekend, go early—this has become a popular spot, so long waits can now be expected on Saturday and Sunday mornings.

For some of the best Italian food outside of Italy, head to **Tre Galline** (Carr. Emiliano Zapata Km. 12.5, tel. 612/119-9718, 1pm-7pm Tues.-Sun. Apr.-Oct., US$13-17). Chef Angelo Dal Bon serves up deliciously inventive Italian dishes made from local Baja ingredients. The restaurant is seasonal—in the winter the operation moves to its sister location in Todos Santos.

Along Carretera El Tigre: West Valley

Millennials flock to **Casa Frida Asador Campestre** (Rancho San Marcos, tel. 646/113-4836, www.casafridavalle.com, 11am-8pm Fri.-Sun., US$10-15), where the setting is picturesque and the food is delicious. Chef Christian Herrera prepares fresh seafood and other dishes in typical Baja California *campestre* style. There's also a winery and B&B on-site.

Along Mexico 3: Central Valley

The *campestre* restaurant of Tijuana chef Javier Plascencia is ★ **Finca Altozano**

1: dish at TrasLomita 2: dining outdoors at Troika
3: the rustic, industrial setting of La Esperanza

(Mexico 3 Km. 83, tel. 646/156-8045, www.fincaltozano.com, 1pm-9pm Tues.-Thurs., 1pm-10pm Fri.-Sat., noon-8pm Sun., mains US$9-14), where locals and visitors go for incredible food and a casual but chic atmosphere. The open-air restaurant features tables that look out onto the vineyards. Food is cooked over a wood-fired grill that produces unforgettable flavors. Don't miss the *pulpo del pacifico*, an octopus dish made with citrus sauce and peanuts. Other standouts are the brussels sprouts grilled with aioli and parmesan cheese, and the lamb *birria*. They've turned large wine barrels into lookouts with benches that are scattered around the property. Grab a glass of wine and climb the stairs to enjoy your after-meal *vino* with views of the valley. In summer, Plascencia sets up a pop-up restaurant, **Animalón** (tel. 646/688-1973, www.animalonbaja.com, 5pm-10pm Wed.-Thurs., 2pm-10pm Fri.-Sun. Apr.-Nov., tasting menu US$50-95), under a 200-year-old oak tree on the property, where diners can order a three-, five-, or eight-course set menu. The setting is romantically beautiful and the food is delectable. A vegetarian menu is also available.

The original haute dining experience in the valley was chef Jair Tellez's **Laja** (Mexico 3 Km. 83, tel. 646/155-2556, www.lajamexico.com, 1:30pm-8:30pm Wed.-Sat., 1:30pm-5:30pm Sun., US$40-60). Opened in 1999, Laja was the original farm-to-table restaurant here and for decades was the only option for gourmet dining in the region. Because of this, Laja was often referenced as the "French Laundry" of the Valle de Guadalupe. Today, it remains on the San Pellegrino list as one of the top 50 restaurants in Latin America. The fixed menu changes daily depending on what's in season and growing in the garden. The intimate restaurant is simple but elegant and sets the mood for the fresh food and local wines.

On the property of Mogor Badan winery, **Deckman's en el Mogor** (Mexico 3 Km. 85.5, tel. 646/188-3960, www.deckmans.com, 1pm-7pm Wed.-Thurs., 1pm-8pm Fri.-Mon., US$15-25) is an outdoor *campestre*

experience, set under the trees and looking out over the vineyards. Chef Drew Deckman serves sustainable local ingredients including fresh seafoods like oysters, octopus, and king crab.

A wonderful option for *campestre* dining under the trees is **El Pinar de 3 Mujeres** (Mexico 3 Km. 87, tel. 646/101-5268, ismene.venegas@gmail.com, 1pm-6pm Fri.-Sun. Apr.-Oct., winter by appointment only, US$17-22) on the property of Tres Mujeres winery. Patrons sit under a canopy of pines and dine on six courses (with a choice of fish, meat, or vegetarian for the main course) from Chef Ismene.

Along Mexico 3: San Antonio de las Minas

Diners may choose from a three-, six- or nine-course experience at ★ **Malva** (Mexico 3 Km. 96, tel. 646/155-3085, 1pm-9pm Wed.-Sun., 1pm-7pm Mon., US$35-75). Chef Roberto Alcocer has an impressive background and brings his experience and creativity to all of the detailed dishes on the menu. The beautiful outdoor deck with a tall palapa roof is nestled into a grove of trees overlooking the valley, and gives the sensation of being in an exclusive tree house. They have local wines on the menu, including some from Mina Penélope, the winery on the same property.

Anyone who loves seafood and sparkling wine should head directly to Deckman's sister restaurant, **Conchas de Piedra** (Mexico 3 Km. 93.5, tel. 646/162-8306, 9am-5pm Mon., 11am-6pm Thurs.-Sun., US$5-10). Located on the property of winery Casa de Piedra, the casual outdoor restaurant serves their bubbly alongside fresh oysters and inventive ceviches.

If you want to dine like the locals, head for pizza night at **Ochento's Pizzeria** (Rancho Cimarrón, tel. 646/130-0651, www.ochentospizza.com, 1pm-7pm Wed., 1pm-10pm Thurs.-Sun., US$12-15). This

1: *campestre* dining at Finca Altozano 2: breakfast at La Cocina de Doña Esthela 3: sparkling wine and oysters at Conchas de Piedra 4: the outdoor setting of Deckman's en el Mogor

family-style pizza spot has a fun and lively atmosphere with live music most nights and is a great place to watch the sun setting over the valley from the back deck.

ACCOMMODATIONS

In keeping with the intimate feeling of the area, most accommodations in Valle de Guadalupe are small (fewer than 10 rooms), so they tend to book up quickly, especially during summer weekends and holidays. Visitors used to traveling in other parts of Baja may also be surprised to find the expensive prices. Rates are higher on weekends, so you'll be able to find cheaper rooms Sunday-Thursday. Prices peak during the Fiestas de la Vendimia in July and August. Be aware that many of the nice hotels require a two-night minimum stay during peak season. Even the nicest will not have televisions, and wireless Internet is often unreliable.

Under US$100
ALONG CARRETERA EL TIGRE: CENTRAL VALLEY

For a unique experience, **Glamping Ruta de Arte y Vino** (Tecate Km. 13, tel. 646/185-3352, rutadearteyvino@gmail.com, US$85) has five Airstreams that guests stay in for a fun, rustic experience. Camping is also allowed on the property for US$20 per night.

ALONG MEXICO 3: CENTRAL VALLEY

With a central location that's easy to find just off the highway, **Rancho Maria Teresa** (Mexico 3 Km. 82.5, tel. 646/688-1020, US$90) has 27 rooms and two villas. The grounds are extremely lush for the area, with palms and citrus trees all around. The large property includes mountain bike trails, two pools and Jacuzzis, and plenty of picnic areas with barbecues. Be aware that during the summer the ranch doubles as a *balneario,* where families can come for the day between 9am and 6pm to enjoy the pools and picnic areas.

One of the most popular budget options in the valley is **El Meson del Vino**

(Mexico 3 Km. 88, tel. 646/151-2137, www. mesondelvino.net, US$70). There are 12 basic rooms as well as a small swimming pool and a restaurant that's open for breakfast. This is one of the few properties in the valley that allows pets.

US$100-200
FRANCISCO ZARCO

In the town of Francisco Zarco, **Viñedos Malagon** (Calle Sexta 75, tel. 646/155-2102, www.vinedosmalagon.com, US$125) has a four-room bed-and-breakfast that serves some of the best breakfast in the valley. The 100-year-old ranch sits on 400 acres where they have their own vineyards and make their own wine.

ALONG CARRETERA EL TIGRE: EL PORVENIR

There are five rooms at boutique hotel **Terra del Valle** (San José de la Zorra Road, tel. 646/117-3645, www.terradelvalle.com, US$195). The peaceful property has wireless access throughout, and bikes are available for guests to use to visit nearby wineries and restaurants. Breakfast includes freshly squeezed orange juice made from oranges grown on the property. There's a communal grill and refrigerator for those who want to prepare their own food. The personal attention of the owners Ana and Nacho is what keeps guests returning.

Hotel Boutique Valle de Guadalupe (Camino de los Ranchos 1, tel. 646/155-2164, www.hotelboutiquevalledeguadalupe. com, US$190-240) is a newer property, but is not necessarily well maintained. The ample grounds include a pool, large lawns, and plenty of areas for sitting and lounging. There are free bikes that guests can use, as well as stables with horses on the grounds. The open-air **Fuego** restaurant on the 2nd floor has views of the valley. Many people prefer to stay just across the road at its sister property, **Valentino** (tel. 664/804-2682, www.hbvalentino.com, US$170). The property features six individual modern and well-appointed cabins perched on the hillside, each with its own deck.

ALONG MEXICO 3: CENTRAL VALLEY

There are six sustainable *cabañas* and two houses with a light and airy design at ★ **Casa Mayoral** (Mexico 3 Km. 88.5, tel. 664/257-2410, www.casamayoral.com, US$100-150). All units have air-conditioning, large bathrooms, plenty of windows, high ceilings, and patios. Breakfast is included in your stay. There are plenty of tables and seating under the shade of tall eucalyptus trees where you can enjoy the serene setting, or grab a bike to spend some time riding around the 10-hectare grounds. The property welcomes pets and children.

ALONG MEXICO 3: SAN ANTONIO DE LAS MINAS

If you're looking to get away from it all, **Quinta Maria en la Ruta del Vino** (Calle Grenache 1, tel. 646/185-1513, US$115) is a hidden gem in the middle of the valley. The artfully eclectic house and surrounding outbuildings are beautifully and comfortably decorated. Breakfast is provided each morning on the outdoor patio looking over the peaceful valley. The secluded property is wonderfully serene with only three rooms. Rooms are equipped with air-conditioning, hair dryers, and mini fridges.

Over US$200

FRANCISCO ZARCO

The chic five-room ★ **Bruma** (Mexico 3 Km. 75, tel. 646/116-8031, www.bruma.mx, US$290) is situated on the east side of the valley on 80 hectares. The beautiful eco-architecture features stone construction and large windows to take advantage of the natural setting. Breakfast for two is included in the room rate. There's a pool and Jacuzzi, common areas, and bicycles to use. Also on the property are a beautiful winery of the same name and the highly acclaimed restaurant Fauna.

The eco-lofts at **Encuentro Guadalupe** (Mexico 3 Km. 75, tel. 646/155-2935, www.grupoencuentro.com.mx, recepcion encuentro@gmail.com, US$385) are individual cabins perched on the hillside, each with their own terrace and fire pit. The units are simple, mixing rustic and contemporary style. Because the units are located on a steep hillside, many guests find it challenging to get from the rooms down to the reception and bar area. Some customers enjoy the rustic nature of the hotel, while others feel the price is too high for what they get in return.

ALONG CARRETERA EL TIGRE: EL PORVENIR

Another option that's been around in the Valle de Guadalupe for a number of years is **Adobe Guadalupe** (Parcela A-1, tel. 646/155-2094, www.adobeguadalupe.com, US$275). The bed-and-breakfast also has a winery, restaurant, and food truck on the property.

ALONG CARRETERA EL TIGRE: CENTRAL VALLEY

The wonderfully serene ★ **La Villa del Valle** (Rancho San Marcos Toros Pintos, tel. 646/156-8007, www.lavilladelvalle.com, US$295) will make you feel like you've been transported to a residence in Tuscany. The well-curated six-room B&B is on the same property as Corazón de Tierra restaurant, Vena Cava winery, and Troika food truck. Owners Phil and Eileen Gregory have created a relaxing sanctuary where guests can sip on a glass of wine while overlooking the valley or enjoy a refreshing dip in the swimming pool. Guests start their mornings with a full breakfast and spend their evenings enjoying a *botana* and a glass of wine. A complimentary wine-tasting at Vena Cava winery is included with a stay at the villa.

Opened in 2019, **El Cielo Winery & Resort by Karisma** (Carretera El Tigre Km. 7.5, U.S. toll-free tel. 866/527-4762, www.karismahotels.com, US$975) features individual villas that are spacious and fully equipped with luxury finishes throughout.

El Cielo winery and Latitud 32 restaurant are on the property.

For a unique experience, **Campera Hotel** (Calle Emiliano Zapata, tel. 646/116-7006, www.camperahotel.com, US$226) gives guests the opportunity to sleep in a bubble in the middle of the vineyards. The 12 individual plastic bubble rooms each have their own private bathroom, queen-size bed, and luxury amenities. Stargaze from bed at night in these quirky accommodations. A curtain draws around the bed for a touch of privacy.

ALONG MEXICO 3: CENTRAL VALLEY

The Spanish-style **Hacienda Guadalupe** (Mexico 3 Km. 81.5, tel. 646/155-2859, www. haciendaguadalupe.com, US$250) has 16 rooms that all have king-size beds with new down comforters, air-conditioning and heating, in-room safes, and Saltillo-tiled floors. There's a pool and Jacuzzi on the property as well as a good restaurant that serves breakfast, lunch, and dinner. The winery on the property, Melchum, offers wine-tastings.

ALONG MEXICO 3: SAN ANTONIO DE LAS MINAS

Chef Javier Plascencia, who owns Finca Altozano restaurant in the valley, brings guests **Finca la Divina** (Mexico 3 Km. 93.5, tel. 646/155-3238, www.fincaladivina.com, US$235-250), a three-bedroom home turned into a beautiful bed-and-breakfast. Common areas include a kitchen, large living room with fireplace, and an outdoor area with a pool, Jacuzzi, and barbecue. Breakfast is available in the morning for an additional US$12.

Grupo Maglen (Mexico 3 Km. 90.8, tel. 646/120-5372, www.grupomaglen. com, US$200-250) operates three boutique properties in the valley: **Villas Maglen, El Encinal,** and **Tesela.** Each has only a handful of accommodations, but features modern and well-appointed rooms with wireless

1: Bruma hotel 2: Terra del Valle hotel 3: La Villa del Valle, a popular B&B 4: cabins at the hotel Valentino

Internet, minibars, safes, coffeemakers, and room service.

EL TIGRE

Just outside of the valley, near the town of El Tigre, ★ **Cuatrocuatros** (El Tigre, Carretera Libre Km. 89, tel. 646/174-6789, www. cabanascuatrocuatros.com.mx, US$200-215) offers glamping in 12 platform cabana tents. The *cabañas* have air-conditioning, minibars, fireplaces, and private terraces. The impressive property offers stunning views from its bar on the cliffs overlooking the Pacific.

INFORMATION AND SERVICES

There are no ATMs in the valley. Many of the wineries do not accept credit cards, so be sure to get cash in Ensenada or Rosarito before arriving in the Valle de Guadalupe. There is a gas station located in the town of San Antonio de las Minas and another in Francisco Zarco.

GETTING THERE AND AROUND

You will need to drive or take a private vehicle to get to the wineries and restaurants in the valley. Ensenada is the closest city to Valle de Guadalupe, about 30 kilometers (19 miles) away. Visitors from Ensenada can take Mexico 1 north and then take Mexico 3 northeast to reach Valle de Guadalupe. The drive takes 30-45 minutes, depending on the destination in Valle de Guadalupe. From Tijuana, the 100-kilometer (62-mile) drive takes 1.5 hours by driving south on Mexico 1D to Ensenada and then taking Mexico 3 northeast. From Rosarito, the 85-kilometer (53-mile) drive takes 1 hour by driving south on Mexico 1D to Ensenada and then taking Mexico 3 northeast. From Tecate, drive 75 kilometers (47 miles) south on Mexico 3 for an hour to reach Valle de Guadalupe.

There are only a handful of paved roads in the Valle de Guadalupe—otherwise the entire valley consists of unmarked dirt roads. The government has been better about marking wineries and restaurants: Look for blue signs around the valley marking establishments. Four-wheel drive is not normally necessary, but after heavy rains some of the dirt roads can be in rough condition and flooded, so inquire with the specific establishment you are visiting if you have any concerns.

Valle de la Grulla and Valle de Santo Tomás

While the Valle de Guadalupe takes most of the spotlight when it comes to Baja wines, there are actually five valleys in the region where wine grapes are grown. Though most of these valleys remain purely agricultural, two of them farther south have a few wineries where the wines are good and visitors can get off the beaten path.

Much smaller and lesser known compared with the Valle de Guadalupe, **Valle de la Grulla** (located in Ejido Uruapan) is quickly making a name for itself. There are currently only a handful of wineries here, but the wines they produce are excellent, the valley is lush and beautiful, and you won't have to battle the crowds of the Valle de Guadalupe. Most of the wineries are family-run operations and offer an intimate and special experience for all who visit. There are no accommodations out here and almost no options for food unless arrangements have been made in advance, but the wineries are exceptional and shouldn't be missed. Most travelers stay in Ensenada and explore Valle de la Grulla on a day trip. The turnoff for Valle de la Grulla is at kilometer 42 on Mexico 1. All wineries are marked with signs that are clear and easy to follow once turning off the highway.

Just 5 kilometers (3.1 miles) south of Valle de la Grulla, travelers will encounter another wine region, **Valle de Santo Tomás,** with the oldest winery in Baja California. The agricultural valley is beautifully picturesque and green and lush after rains. The Valle de Santo Tomás is usually visited in combination with Valle de la Grulla for a full day of wine-tasting.

LA ANTIGUA RUTA DEL VINO

Valle de la Grulla and Valle de Santo Tomás are part of the **La Antigua Ruta del Vino,** or the old wine route. This is where the missionaries first introduced wine production in the late 19th century and where the northern Baja wine industry began. Tastings range US$7-15.

Valle de la Grulla
MD VINOS

With an impressive facility and beautiful property on an expansive 41 hectares, **MD Vinos** (Ejido Uruapan, tel. 646/116-6397, www.mdvinos.com, 10am-5pm Tues.-Sun.) is well situated with vineyards, crops, stables, and areas to relax and enjoy the beautiful views. Wine-tastings take place in the main building where the wine cave is located and consist of five wines. On another part of the property is a picturesque picnic area where guests can rent *palapas* for the day to eat, drink, and relax. Food such as *carnitas,* carne asada, fresh fish, and other grilled specialties is available on the weekends with advance notice.

ALDO CESAR PALAFOX
Aldo Cesar Palafox (Mexico 1 Km. 42, tel. 646/174-5035, www.aldopalafox.mx, 11am-5pm Sat.-Sun.) has a beautiful and modern tasting room and winemaking facility. Tastings consist of four exquisite wines that

1: vineyard tractor tour at Bodegas de Santo Tomás
2: the picnic area at MD Vinos

are bold and complex but easy to drink. All of their grapes are grown on their property, and the views from the tasting room are of the beautiful vineyards and valley. They also have a quixotic outdoor space with shady oak trees and a small stage for events. They are only open to the public on weekends, but advance reservations can be made during the week for groups larger than 6. Meals can be arranged for groups larger than 10.

VINICOLA SANTO DOMINGO

At the entrance to the Valle de la Grulla just off of Mexico 1 is **Vinicola Santo Domingo** (Mexico 1 Km. 42, tel. 646/153-9156, 10am-6pm daily). Housed in a brick building, this family-run operation has been in business for just over 10 years. They aren't always available for tastings, so contact them ahead of time if you want to do a wine-tasting and get a tour of the facility.

Valle de Santo Tomás
BODEGAS DE SANTO TOMÁS

The Valle de Santo Tomás is one of the five wine-producing valleys in this part of Baja California and home to the oldest winery in Baja California: the **Bodegas de Santo Tomás** (Mexico 1 Km. 49, tel. 646/127-1686, www.santo-tomas.com, 10am-5pm daily), established in 1888. They have 350 hectares where they grow 21 varietals of grapes. They have a nice tasting room set in a grove of eucalyptus trees. The wine tour consists of a tasting on a tractor ride through the vineyards and is a uniquely special experience. Regular wine-tasting in the tasting room doesn't require a reservation, but it's necessary to make advance reservations for the vineyard tractor tour. Bodegas de Santo Tomás also has tasting rooms in Ensenada and the Valle de Guadalupe.

WINE TOURS

Baja Test Kitchen (www.bajatestkitchen. com) operates wine tours to La Antigua Ruta del Vino that can originate in either San Diego or in northern Baja for groups of 2 to 25 people. They have a popular multiday tour that spends one day in Valle de Guadalupe and one day along La Antigua Ruta del Vino.

SIGHTS
Misión Santo Tomás de Aquino

Misión Santo Tomás de Aquino was founded in 1791 by Dominican padre José Loriente. The mission was relocated in 1794 and again in 1799. It was the last operating mission in California. It was finally abandoned in 1849 when the military took over, using it as a base and governmental seat for northern Baja California. The third (and final) site of the mission is just east of Mexico 1 as you enter Santo Tomás near the palm trees just north of El Palomar campground.

Ruins of the first two mission sites can be seen on the graded road out to La Bocana/Puerto Santo Tomás. The 1791 site has just a small section of wall remaining. Five and a half kilometers (3.4 miles) after turning onto the dirt road to La Bocana, take a road to the left and go nearly one kilometer (0.6 mile) to a clearing near the picnic area. The 1794 site is now a planted field (just a few pieces of melted adobe and rocks remain) about 1.5 kilometers (0.9 mile) east of the 1791 site, on the graded road to La Bocana.

FOOD AND ACCOMMODATIONS
Valle de la Grulla

There are no accommodations in Valle de la Grulla and no food available without having made previous arrangements. Both MD Vinos and Aldo Cesar Palafox wineries can arrange for food for larger groups with advance notice.

Valle de Santo Tomás

El Palomar (Mexico 1 Km. 51, tel. 646/153-8002, vivepalomar@gmail.com, 7am-10pm daily, camping US$18, hotel US$35-45) has been a popular campsite, *balneario,* and picnic area for decades. *Balnearios* are swimming resorts where families can use swimming pools and picnic areas for the day or camp for the night. There are two swimming pools as well as a small lake (swimming areas are open only in summer). In addition, El Palomar has 10 hotel rooms and a restaurant, bar, and store directly on the highway. The store carries curios, souvenirs, and wine from Santo Tomás, as well as basic provisions and supplies.

GETTING THERE AND AROUND

You must use a private vehicle to get to and around this area. From Ensenada, head south on Mexico 1 for 40 kilometers (25 miles) to arrive at Valle de la Grulla at Kilometer 42. The drive will take about an hour depending on traffic. To get to Valle de Santo Tomás from Valle de la Grulla, head south on Mexico 1 for 5 minutes and 5 kilometers (3.1 miles).

Background

The Landscape

GEOGRAPHY

The Baja peninsula stretches 1,300 kilometers (810 miles) from Tijuana in the north to Cabo San Lucas at its southern tip. As the northwestern region of Mexico, the Baja peninsula is separated from mainland Mexico by the Golfo de California (Gulf of California), more commonly referred to as the Mar de Cortés (Sea of Cortez). The Pacific Ocean borders the western side of the Baja peninsula.

There are four main desert areas that make up 65 percent of the peninsula—the San Felipe Desert, the Central Coast Desert, the Vizcaíno

Desert, and the Magdalena Plain Desert. There are 23 mountain ranges on the peninsula with the highest peak being Picacho del Diablo at 3,095 meters (10,154 feet) in the Sierra de San Pedro Mártir.

CLIMATE

While the climate varies by region and season, what attracts most travelers to Baja California is the warm, sunny weather. In northern Baja, the areas along the Pacific coast are temperate year-round, while temperatures inland can be extremely hot in the summer.

ENVIRONMENTAL ISSUES

Most of the Baja peninsula remains undeveloped due to the desert and mountain terrain and a lack of freshwater. The lack of water is especially prominent in Valle de Guadalupe, where rapid development has been occurring as the wine region has been growing in popularity. Wildcoast (www.wildcoast.net) is an active nonprofit working to preserve the environment along the Pacific in Baja California (Norte).

PLANTS

There are over 4,000 plant species and subspecies on the peninsula with over 600 species endemic to Baja. For the most descriptive information on the flora of Baja California, pick up a copy of the *Baja California Plant Field Guide* by Jon P. Rebman and Norman C. Roberts. Northern Baja is home to the chaparral biome, with shrubs and other drought-tolerant plants covering the landscape.

Cacti

There are 120 species of cactus in Baja, and many of them flower after rains, which can paint the desert with a vibrant splash of color for a few weeks. The most dominant, and perhaps most recognizable, cactus of the Baja landscape is the *cardón* or elephant cactus. It's also the largest cactus and can reach heights

of up to 20 meters (66 feet) and can weigh up to 10 tons. Some of the older plants are believed to be over 200 years old. Other common types of cacti found on the peninsula include varieties of the barrel cactus, cholla, and *nopal* (prickly pear). The *nopal* is an edible cactus and commonly found on menus around the region.

Agaves

There are over 20 species of agave growing on the peninsula. Many are edible, so the agaves have always been a source of food, drink, and fiber. Agaves live many decades before they flower, earning them the name "century plant" (although flowering actually happens between years 30 and 60). The flower stalk emerges from the cluster of basal stems.

Trees

Trees found along the peninsula are often very specific to their regions. Many Baja travelers consider it a surprise to see conifers such as cypress, cedar, Sierra lodgepole pines, and white fir in the mountain ranges on the northern part of the peninsula.

ANIMALS

The animal life is just as diverse as the plant life, with over 100 types of mammals inhabiting the peninsula, two dozen of which are considered to be endemic.

Land Mammals

There are over 100 types of mammals on the peninsula, with over 20 endemic species. Coyotes, mountain lions, foxes, bobcats, and raccoons are fairly prevalent. The desert bighorn sheep and the peninsular pronghorn (*berrendo*) are among the endangered species on the peninsula.

Marine Mammals

Sea lions live in the Pacific and are abundant around the Coronado Islands just offshore

Previous: Valle de Guadalupe in spring.

from Rosarito. During the winter months, gray whales can be seen as they migrate to and from the warm lagoons of Baja California Sur.

Fish

To the delight of anglers and divers, thousands of species of fish ply the waters of the Pacific Ocean. Yellowtail, marlin, amberjack, corvina, roosterfish, dorado, wahoo, bluefin tuna, halibut, snapper, and sea bass are just some of the species that lure anglers to the prolific waters.

Shellfish including shrimp, clams, oysters, mussels, scallops, and lobster are all found in large numbers, making them popular dishes at restaurants and food carts. There are over 60 types of sharks around the peninsula.

Birds

With over 400 species of birds, Baja can be a birders' paradise. Coastal birds such as pelicans, blue-footed boobies, frigate birds, egrets, and gulls are commonly spotted. Inland lakes and streams are home to freshwater birds such as ducks, geese, herons, sandpipers, teals, and storks. In the desert, falcons, hawks, owls, hummingbirds, sparrows, roadrunners, and turkey vultures can be sighted. Mountain birds like eagles, red-tailed hawks, pheasants, woodpeckers, and wrens are common to the Sierras.

Reptiles and Amphibians
SNAKES
Of the 35 snakes (*serpientes*) on the peninsula, about half are nonvenomous (*culebras*), and the other half are poisonous (*víboras*). There are 18 species of rattlesnakes, including the Baja California rattler, red diamondback, and western diamondback.

History

INDIGENOUS HISTORY

Historians agree that there have been people living on the Baja California peninsula for over 11,000 years. In the north were several groups belonging to the Yuman language family: the Kiliwa, Paipai, Kumiai, Cucupá, and Quechan. The groups were adaptive to their environments and led mostly hunter-gatherer lifestyles.

SPANISH EXPLORATION

California existed as a myth for Europeans long before it was finally discovered by explorers in the early 16th century. Following Hernán Cortés's conquest of mainland Mexico, he sent three ships to explore Baja California in 1532. The peninsula was believed to be an island at this time. The ships of that first expedition disappeared without a trace. Cortés sent a follow-up expedition in 1533 that landed in La Paz, but most of the men in the expedition were killed by the indigenous people. In 1539, another expedition sponsored by Cortés was led by Captain Francisco de Ulloa and explored the entire perimeter of the Sea of Cortez as well as the Pacific coast up to Isla Cedros. It was Ulloa who is credited with naming the Mar de Cortés.

The Mission Era

The Jesuits were the first missionaries to inhabit the peninsula. Padre Juan Maria Salvatierra established the first mission in all of Alta Baja California at Loreto in 1697. The Franciscans and the Dominicans came after the Jesuits to settle the peninsula. In total, there were 27 missions as well as supporting *visitas* (visiting stations) founded on Baja. Uprisings by the indigenous people were very common, the most famous being the Pericú rebellion in 1734, which ended in extensive damage, the destruction of four missions, and the death of two padres. The history of each mission and the GPS points of the current sites (or ruins) can be found in David Kier's book *Baja California: Land of Missions.*

INDEPENDENCE FROM SPAIN

At the end of the 18th century, the Age of Enlightenment and liberal revolutions sparked the movement for independence from Spain. The revolt against the Spanish crown began on September 16, 1810, when Miguel Hidalgo shouted the *Grito de Dolores*, the cry for revolution, from the mainland city of Dolores, Guanajuato. September 16 is considered independence day in Mexico, and the reigning president reenacts the *grito* every year on the evening of September 15. It took more than a decade, but Mexico officially gained its freedom from Spain in 1821 after the Mexican War of Independence.

THE MEXICAN-AMERICAN WAR

The Mexican-American War (1846-1848) had a major impact on Baja California. President James K. Polk believed the United States had a "manifest destiny" to spread across the continent from the Atlantic to the Pacific Ocean. In 1844 Polk made an offer to Mexico to purchase the lands between the Nueces River and Rio Grande (in what is now Texas). The offer was rejected and U.S. forces invaded Mexico, starting a string of battles that would lead to the Mexican-American War and end with Mexico losing one-third of its territory. In the Treaty of Guadalupe Hidalgo ending the war, Mexico gave in to the United States and received US$15 million for the land that is now California, Nevada, Utah, and parts of Colorado, Arizona, New Mexico, and Wyoming. In the original draft of the treaty, Baja California was included in the land to be sold to the United States, but it ultimately remained with Mexico because of its proximity to Sonora.

THE MEXICAN REVOLUTION

Because of Baja's remote location in relation to the rest of Mexico, the peninsula was somewhat insulated from the political turmoil that took place in Mexico in the 19th century. But Baja California played an important part in the Mexican Revolution (1910-1920) which radically changed government and culture in Mexico. The revolution set out to end the dictatorship of President Porfirio Díaz, called for democracy, and demanded the return of lands taken unfairly from Mexican villages. Led by Francisco Madero and aided by Pancho Villa and Emiliano Zapata, rebel armies of workers and peasants rose up to fight against Díaz and his dictatorship. Baja California played a key role in the revolution in the Magonista Rebellion of 1911. This early uprising was organized by the Partido Liberal Mexicano (PLM) against the presidency of dictator Porfirio Díaz. The rebel army took control of both Mexicali and Tijuana. The success of the uprising encouraged rebel troops in other regions to join in the fight of the revolution.

The ratification of the Mexican Constitution of 1917 is largely looked upon as the end of the Mexican Revolution even though a few more years of instability followed. The constitution returned lands to the peasants in the form of cooperatively owned *ejidos,* which are still in effect today.

STATEHOOD

Northern Baja California became the 29th state of Mexico in 1952. With its sparse fishing villages and small towns, Baja California Sur remained a territory, unable to meet the population requirements to become a Mexican state. When the Transpeninsular Highway (Mexico 1) was finally completed in 1974, it opened up commerce and tourism to the southern part of the peninsula and Baja California Sur became a state later that year.

Annual Festivals and Holidays

JANUARY

- New Year's Day, January 1, is a national holiday.

- Día de los Reyes (Day of the Kings), January 6, is a Catholic holiday honoring the three kings who brought gifts to baby Jesus. The day is celebrated with a round cake called a *rosca de reyes*, inside which is hidden a plastic figurine of baby Jesus. Whoever receives the baby Jesus in their piece of cake has to make tamales for friends and family on Día de la Candelaria.

FEBRUARY

- Día de la Candelaria, February 2, is a religious holiday celebrating the Virgen of La Candelaria. Whoever received the figurine of baby Jesus on Día de los Reyes traditionally hosts a tamale party for friends and family.

- Constitution Day, February 5, is a national holiday.

MARCH

- Birthday of Benito Juárez, March 21, is a national holiday.

APRIL

- Semana Santa (Holy Week) is the week before Easter and a popular time for Mexican nationals to take their vacation.

- National Children's Day, April 30, is an observed holiday.

MAY

- Labor Day, May 1, is a national holiday.

SEPTEMBER

- Mexican Independence Day, September 16, is a national holiday celebrating Mexico's independence from Spain.

NOVEMBER

- Día de los Muertos, November 1-2, is All Saints' Day, celebrating those who have passed away.

- Revolution Day, November 20, is a national holiday.

DECEMBER

- Día de Nuestra Señora de Guadalupe (Day of the Virgin of Guadalupe), December 12, is a feast day for this patron saint.

- Las Posadas, December 16-January 6, are traditionally religious processions reenacting Mary and Joseph trying to find accommodations before the birth of Jesus. Today, they have become a time for holiday parties.

- Navidad (Christmas Day), December 25, is a national holiday.

Government and Economy

GOVERNMENT
Organization

Mexicali is the capital of Baja California (Norte) and the state is divided into five municipalities: Tijuana, Rosarito, Ensenada, Tecate, and Mexicali. The northern state of Baja California was accepted as a state of Mexico in 1952. The 28th parallel divides the two states of Baja California (Norte) and Baja California Sur.

Political System

There are 31 states in Mexico that form a representative democracy. There are three branches to the government: executive, legislative, and judicial. Mexican presidents serve a six-year term with no reelection. The legislature comprises two houses, the Senate and the Chamber of Deputies.

The three main political parties in Mexico are: Partido Acción Nacional (PAN), Mexico's conservative political party; Partido Revolucionario Institucional (PRI), Mexico's centrist political party; and Partido de la Revolución Democrática (PRD), Mexico's leftist political party.

ECONOMY

Tourism is one of the driving factors in Baja's economy. Regions such as the northern border zone around Tijuana heavily rely on tourism from the United States and Canada. Baja's other industries include fishing, agriculture, and manufacturing at *maquiladoras* in the northern border regions. The North American Free Trade Agreement (NAFTA) went into effect in 1994 and opened the door for large auto and electronics manufacturers to develop factories in northern Baja and easily import the items produced into the United States. Because of the close ties with the United States, the economy of Baja California is intertwined with that of its northern neighbor.

Economic inequality is a large problem in Mexico. The whole Baja California peninsula is in the higher wage zone for the country, but the minimum is still low, starting at US$5 per day for unskilled workers.

People and Culture

The population of the Baja peninsula is around four million, with most inhabitants living in the northern state of Baja California, and more specifically in the cities of Tijuana and Mexicali. Most of the rest of the peninsula remains sparsely populated. There are very few true indigenous people left on the peninsula today, and most Baja residents are a mix of Spanish and native cultures as well as descendants from Europe and Asia. In more recent decades, the peninsula has become home to a growing number of U.S. and Canadian retiree expats.

RELIGION

The Spanish missionaries first brought Catholicism to the peninsula, and it remains the dominant religion. Catholic holidays hold the same importance (or more) than secular national holidays. Missions and churches are prevalent everywhere on the peninsula, and although church and state are separate, Catholicism plays a large part in Mexican culture. One of the most important figures in Mexican Catholicism is the Virgin of Guadalupe, or Our Lady of Guadalupe, a title for the Virgin Mary associated with an apparition at the Basilica of Our Lady of

Guadalupe in Mexico City. Representations of the Virgin of Guadalupe are prevalent throughout the peninsula.

LANGUAGE

Latin American Spanish is the primary language spoken in Baja California. Mexicans who work in the tourism industry in large cities do speak at least some English. All travelers heading to Baja should learn at least a few basic greetings and phrases, which will go a long way in providing a better travel experience.

VISUAL ART

Rosarito and Tijuana have vibrant art scenes, ranging from colorful street art to local galleries. The arts and cultural centers in both cities are home to a variety of exhibits and festivals throughout the year featuring local artists.

MUSIC

Mexico has a vibrant tradition of music. Mariachi music is probably the first thing that comes to mind for most people, and mariachi groups can be found throughout the peninsula, especially in the larger, more touristy towns. The ensemble usually consists of a trumpet, violin, guitar, and *vihuela* (five-string guitar), and performers are distinguished by their silver-studded *charro* suits. Another popular type of music in Baja is Norteño. Norteño music is mostly easily identified for its use of the accordion and polka-like sound. European migrants brought the accordion, along with the waltz and polka, to northern Mexico (hence the designation Norteño) in the late 19th century.

DANCE

The folk dancing of Mexico, the *ballet folklórico,* can be seen in various places along the peninsula. The highly choreographed dance includes both men and women and is characterized by lively music and bold movements. The women wear colorful traditional Mexican dresses with ruffled skirts that they hold while they dance, which are an integral part of the spectacle.

Essentials

Transportation

GETTING THERE
Air

The only commercial airport in this region is Tijuana's General Abelardo L. Rodríguez International Airport (TIJ). There are rental car facilities as well as taxis at the airport. Uber is also available to pick up passengers at the airport. For those coming from San Diego and flying out of the Tijuana airport, the **Cross Border Xpress** pedestrian bridge (www.crossborderxpress.com) allows ticketed passengers to park in San Diego and walk across the bridge directly to the Tijuana airport

(US$16, one-way). CBX is located on the eastern side of Tijuana near Otay Mesa and connects directly to Tijuana's Rodriguez airport.

Bus

Greyhound (tel. 800/890-6821, www.greyhound.com.mx) has cross-border bus service between Los Angeles, Long Beach, and San Diego in the United States and Tijuana in Mexico. Service costs between US$12 and US$25 one-way, depending on exact origin.

Car

Many travelers choose to explore this region by driving their own car across the border, since everything is so close to Southern California. If you'll be traveling outside of Tecate or Tijuana, having a car is the only way to easily and thoroughly sample all that the region has to offer. Don't forget to obtain the mandatory Mexican auto insurance before driving south.

Mexico recognizes U.S. and Canadian driver's licenses, so an international license is not required.

MEXICAN AUTO INSURANCE

Mexican auto insurance is required by law when driving in Mexico. Even if you have U.S. insurance that covers you in Mexico, this is not sufficient, and you must additionally get a Mexican insurance policy. This is because Mexico does not recognize U.S. insurance and requires that you be financially responsible for any physical and bodily injuries caused by an accident. Therefore, all drivers must have at least liability coverage from a Mexican insurance provider. Mexican auto insurance policies are available for short trips by the day or can be purchased to cover you for the year. Liability-only policies are the minimum required by the law and will cover damages you may cause to other property or people. Full coverage will additionally cover damages that happen to your own vehicle. While the law does not require full coverage, it's always recommended.

There are a handful of Mexican auto insurance vendors on the U.S. side of border towns, but it's better to get a policy in advance with a reputable company. There are a number of options for this. **Discover Baja Travel Club** (8322 Clairemont Mesa Blvd., San Diego, U.S. tel. 619/275-4225, toll-free U.S. tel. 800/727-2252, www.discoverbaja.com) has been in business for over 25 years. Daily or yearly policies are available by going online to print at home, or you can call them or go to their office in San Diego.

TEMPORARY VEHICLE IMPORTATION PERMITS

Temporary Vehicle Importation Permits are not required for driving in Baja California, but if you are planning on crossing over to mainland Mexico, they are mandatory. Your car can be impounded permanently if you are caught driving in mainland Mexico without the permit. Temporary vehicle import permits can be obtained at the border crossings between the United States and Mexico.

Sea

Ensenada is an official Mexico port of entry, so if you have your own boat and are arriving from U.S. waters, you must check in with the port captain's office. You must complete a crew list document and get FMM tourist permits for all passengers on the vessel, as well as a temporary importation permit for the vessel to clear customs. If you will be entering Mexican waters for sportfishing, but not making landfall, you must obtain a **nautical FMM** (www.gob.mx).

BORDER CROSSING

There are three border crossings in this region, two in Tijuana and one in Tecate.

• The **San Ysidro border crossing** (24

hours daily) in Tijuana is the world's busiest, with 50 million people crossing every year. If you don't have an expedited crossing via SENTRI, Ready Lane, or Fast Pass, expect long lines heading northbound whether you are crossing by car or on foot. The border crossing is located on the southern end of the I-5 and I-805 freeways, 20 miles (33 km) and 25 minutes from downtown San Diego.

• Still in Tijuana but farther east is the **Otay Mesa border crossing** (24 hours daily). This border crossing is generally less busy and more relaxed than San Ysidro. It's located off of the I-905 freeway, 25 miles (40 km) and 30 minutes from downtown San Diego.

• Even more tranquil, and usually with the shortest wait, is the **Tecate border crossing** (5am-11pm daily). There are no expedited lanes here, but northbound car crossings can be a quarter of the wait compared to San Ysidro, and there's rarely any wait at all for northbound pedestrians. It takes about 50 minutes to drive the 40 miles (64 km) from downtown San Diego to the Tecate border, taking CA-94 east to CA-188 south.

Southbound crossings into Mexico are generally very quick, with the exception being Friday evening at the San Ysidro border. The **northbound** crossing back to the United States takes more time. Tijuana is the busiest land border crossing in the world, and northbound travelers should expect waits of up to 4-5 hours when crossing at peak times in a vehicle. Sunday evenings are the busiest time of the week to cross the northbound border.

Crossing on Foot
TIJUANA
Many San Diego residents park in San Diego and cross San Ysidro by foot to explore Tijuana for the day. Those crossing by foot at the **San Ysidro El Chaparral** border crossing will need to fill out a *forma migratoria multiple* (FMM) tourist permit. Visitors staying for seven days or fewer can get an FMM for

free; stays of more than seven days require a payment of US$30.

There are two **pedestrian crossings** at the San Ysidro El Chaparral border crossing—the **Pedestrian West (PedWest)** crossing, on the western side of the border crossing, and the **Pedestrian East (PedEast)** border crossing, which is on the eastern side of the northbound vehicle crossing.

The **San Diego Trolley** (U.S. tel. 619/233-3004, www.sdmts.com, US$2.50) blue line stops in San Ysidro at the border right next to San Ysidro's PedEast crossing. The trolley operates 5am-2am daily, with trolleys running every 7-30 minutes depending on the time of day.

TECATE
Tecate is a popular day trip for San Diego residents who enjoy parking their car on the U.S. side of the border (for US$5) and walking across to spend the day. Pedestrians often have no wait at this border crossing.

Expedited Reentry to the United States
Certain borders have **special lanes** offering expedited crossing for both vehicles and pedestrians.

Trusted Travelers who have a SENTRI, NEXUS, or Global Entry card may use the **SENTRI lane.** Note that, in order to use the SENTRI vehicle lane, the vehicle you are in must be SENTRI-approved as well.

The **Ready Lane** may be used by travelers with an RFID-enabled identification such as a U.S. Passport Card, Enhanced Driver's License, Trusted Traveler Card (SENTRI, NEXUS, Global Entry), Border Crossing Card (BCC), or new Permanent Resident Card (PRC).

At the San Ysidro border only, a **Fast Pass lane** offers expedited crossing for people who have obtained a pass from a medical office or hotel in northern Baja.

For more information about these programs, and to find out which borders have which lanes, see the **U.S. Customs and Border Protection** website (www.cbp.gov).

GETTING AROUND
Car

Most travelers choose to explore Baja by car—whether flying into an airport and renting a car or driving their own into Mexico. Roads in this region are generally in good shape and multilane toll roads connect the large cities, making for safe and fast travel.

DRIVING PRECAUTIONS

It's extremely important to only drive during the daylight in Baja. Driving at night is dangerous for a number of reasons. There are no streetlights on the highway, and cows and other animals come to sleep on the warm asphalt at night, causing many accidents for unsuspecting drivers. It's not uncommon for cars in Mexico to not have functioning brake lights, blinkers, or headlights, which can also be dangerous. It's important to keep all this in mind when planning your road trip in the winter, as the days are shorter, giving you less drive time.

It's important to never speed when driving in Baja. *Topes* (speed bumps) and *vados* (dips where the river crosses the road) are often unmarked, and road conditions can deteriorate without any notice, causing a number of potholes in the road. There are no shoulders for some roads, which is another good reason to take it slow.

TOLL ROADS AND FREE ROADS

There are a few toll roads in the area, with the Mexico 1D toll road running from Tijuana to Ensenada and the Mexico 2D toll road running from Tijuana to Tecate. These large divided highways are two lanes in each direction and are usually well maintained. The tolls in this region range US$2-4. There are public restrooms near each of the tollbooths on Mexico 1D. Always keep your receipt from paying the toll, as it serves as insurance in certain instances if you are involved in an accident while on the toll road.

There are free roads (Mexico 1 from Tijuana to Ensenada and Mexico 2 from Tijuana to Tecate) that may be taken as alternatives, but be aware that they take different routes than the toll roads. These two-lane, undivided roads will meander through towns and cities and take more time to travel.

OFF-HIGHWAY TRAVEL

Although Mexico 1 has been paved since 1974, much of Baja driving still consists of traveling on dirt roads, especially throughout Valle de Guadalupe. The condition of the unpaved roads can vary greatly and change quickly, so it's always best to ask locally about road conditions before taking an off-highway adventure. Mexican auto insurance will cover travel on dirt roads (the road must lead to a destination), but will not cover you when off-roading.

KILOMETER MARKINGS

The major highways in Baja use kilometer markings. People use these kilometer markings when giving distances and directions. You'll find that many businesses use their kilometer marking as their address. In Baja California (Norte), the kilometers start at 0 in Tijuana and ascend as you head south.

ROAD SIGNS

All speed limits are posted in kilometers. Many Baja road signs are accompanied by symbols, allowing even non-Spanish speakers to understand. Here are some common phrases seen on road signs:

- *Alto*: Stop
- *Tope*: Speed Bump
- *Vado*: Dip
- *Ceda el Paso*: Yield
- *Despacio*: Slow
- *Entrada*: Entrance
- *Salida*: Exit
- *Curva Peligrosa*: Dangerous Curve
- *Desviación*: Detour
- *No Tire Basura*: Don't Throw Trash
- *Conserve Su Derecha*: Keep to the Right
- *No Rebase*: No Passing

- *Un Solo Carril*: Single Lane Ahead
- *Conceda Cambio de Luces*: Dim Your Lights
- *No Deje Piedras Sobre el Pavimento*: Don't Leave Rocks on the Road
- *Este Camino No Es De Alta Velocidad*: Not a High-Speed Road

FUEL

Mexico's gas industry has been state-owned and operated since 1938, but opened up to deregulation in 2016. The ubiquitous Pemex (Petroleos Mexicanos) gas stations, which were once the only stations on the peninsula, are now joined by other brands of gas stations, and the prices that were once fairly fixed now vary from station to station.

There are two types of regular gas: Magna (87 octane) with the green handle, and Premium (93 octane) with the red handle. Diesel will be available at a separate pump with a black handle. Ultra low sulfur diesel (ULSD) is available throughout the northern state of Baja California.

The price for gas will always be shown at the pump. When you pull up to the station, you'll need to let them know how much gas you want and of what type. It's normal to refer to the grade of gas by the color of the handle. *Lleno con verde* (full with green) is a common request when pulling up to the pump.

Gas stations in Mexico are full-service, so the attendant will pump the gas for you. They will often clean your window as well. You should give them a few pesos (US$0.50) as a tip for the service. Even though stations are full-service, it's always a good idea to get out and watch them at the pump to ensure that the attendant isn't trying to take advantage of you. Make sure that the pump is zeroed out before they pump gas, and don't let them top off your tank.

As Mexico is on the metric system, gas is sold by the liter. It's always best to pay in pesos for gas, as doing the peso-to-dollar conversion can get tricky on top of trying to figure out liters to gallons. It's becoming more common for gas stations on the peninsula to accept foreign credit cards, but you should never rely on this. It's always best to have pesos ready to pay for your gas.

TRAFFIC OFFENSES

In general, the same rules apply in Mexico as do in the United States. You must wear your seat belt, license and registration must be current, no speeding, no drinking and driving, no cell phone usage while driving, and you must have at least liability coverage for Mexican auto insurance. The fines for these infractions vary from region to region but can be very expensive.

In large cities that you're unfamiliar with, it can be challenging to navigate the busy areas of town, especially knowing when to stop at intersections, as stop signs can often be difficult to see. It's also important to know that in urban areas you must stop for pedestrians in the crosswalk.

If you're pulled over by a police officer, remember to be polite and courteous. If you are in a large city (Tijuana, Rosarito, Ensenada, or Tecate), you are able to take your ticket and pay the fee by mail from the United States. The instructions will be on the ticket. If you are in any other area of the region, you will need to follow the police officer to the local station to pay the fine. If the officer is asking you to pay on the spot, he is illegally asking you for a *mordida,* or bribe. Giving him the bribe is illegal on your behalf and can get you into big trouble. It also perpetuates a cycle of police officers targeting foreigners in the hopes of getting some cash. Don't do it.

ROADSIDE ASSISTANCE

The **Angeles Verdes** (Green Angels) have come to the rescue of many Baja road-trippers who experience a breakdown or trouble on the road. The green trucks are sponsored by the Secretary of Tourism and can assist if you get into an accident, have a flat tire, run out of gas, or break down. They offer free labor, service, and towing. Gas and spare parts are available for a charge. The service of the Green Angels is free, but tips are appreciated.

The Green Angels patrol the roads on a regular basis. If you break down, pull over to the side and lift your hood to signal that you need help. If you have cell phone service, you can call 078, which will get you the 24/7 bilingual tourist assistance, who will send roadside assistance.

MILITARY CHECKPOINTS

Road-trippers will encounter a number of military checkpoints on Mexico 1 throughout the peninsula. The soldiers will be dressed in full army fatigues with large guns and may seem intimidating at first, but they are there to keep you safe and are just checking that you aren't transporting drugs or arms. They will likely ask you where you are coming from and where you are going. They may ask to look through your vehicle. Tell them that you are on *vacaciones* (vacation). It's best to be polite and respectful, and you'll be on your way in no time.

MAPS

If you can get a copy of the currently out-of-print *Baja California Almanac* (www.baja-almanac.com), this is the only map you'll need for a road trip on the peninsula. The *Baja Almanac* is considered the ultimate map for Baja and by far the most detailed and accurate navigation tool. Even older editions will still be useful.

CAR RENTAL

There are car rental companies in Tijuana and Ensenada. Some car rental companies in San Diego will allow you to take the rental car to Mexico, but make sure in advance. Understand that you'll need to purchase Mexican auto insurance through them, which will be an additional charge. If renting a car in Baja, be aware that the insurance is not included in the rate at which you rent the car.

Bus

There is bus service between Tijuana, Tecate, Rosarito, and Ensenada as well as to other cities and parts of the peninsula. **Autobuses de la Baja California** (ABC, tel. 664/104-7400, www.abc.com.mx) and **Aguila** (toll-free Mex. tel. 800/026-8931, www.autobusesaguila.com) are two of the largest companies that operate along the entire peninsula. Buses tend to be large and modern, with air-conditioning and comfortable seats. It's generally not necessary to make a reservation in advance, but it's a good idea to stop by the bus depot a day or so ahead of time to check out the schedule and current fares.

Taxi

Taxis can be found around larger cities, especially in the central tourist areas, at taxi stands, and at larger hotels. There are no meters in taxis in Baja, so always negotiate the fare with the driver before getting in the taxi. **Uber** (www.uber.com) is now available in Tijuana, and can be found as far south as Ensenada.

Motorcycle

More and more riders are being lured by the adventure of cruising on their motorcycle down the Baja peninsula. Specifically motorcycle mechanics are less common than auto mechanics, so it's wise to be self-sufficient in this aspect. There are a number of guided motorcycle trips on the peninsula if you don't want to travel alone. **Adventure Rider Motorcycle Forum** (www.advrider.com) has some of the best information about riding on the peninsula.

Bicycle

Bicycling along Baja's Mexico 1 is a dangerous feat that should not be attempted by any cyclists who are not experts. The lack of shoulders and guardrails on the windy highway, coupled with the large trucks and many drivers that speed, make for a dangerous situation for any cyclist. The **Baja Divide** (www.bajadivide.com) is a new self-guided route that links 2,000 miles of dirt roads from Tecate to Cabo for cyclists looking to explore the Baja peninsula, without having to take the harrowing highway option.

Visas and Officialdom

PASSPORTS AND VISAS

A passport is required for travel in Baja. If you are crossing in and out of Mexico by land, you can use a passport card. If traveling by air, a passport book is required.

There is a lot of confusion about the visa situation for U.S. and Canadian travelers headed into Mexico. A visa is not required for U.S. and Canadian citizens. However, a *forma migratoria múltiple* (FMM) tourist permit is mandatory for all non-Mexican citizens traveling in Baja. Many people will refer to the FMM as a visa, which causes an extreme amount of confusion about the issue. An FMM is required for all U.S. and Canadian citizens every time they enter Baja, regardless of where they will be going and how long they will be staying. The previous exceptions for trips under 72 hours and/or within the border zone no longer apply. For trips seven days or fewer, there is no charge for the FMM.

Visas are required for citizens traveling to Mexico from certain countries. For a full list, see www.gob.mx.

FMM TOURIST PERMITS

All U.S. and Canadian citizens are required to have a *forma migratoria múltiple* (FMM) tourist permit every time they enter Baja. The previous exceptions for trips under 72 hours and/or within the border zone no longer apply. To be clear, the FMM tourist permit is not a visa, although many people refer to it as a visa, creating much confusion about the topic.

If crossing by land, travelers must stop at the border to complete the FMM form, pay the US$30 fee, and then have the form stamped with the date of entry. You must present your passport book or passport card when getting your FMM. FMM tourist permits are valid for up to 180 days. If you will be spending seven days or less in Baja, free FMM tourist permits are available as well.

If you are driving into Mexico, they will not stop you at the border to get your FMM; you must find the SAT/Aduanas building and stop on your own at the border crossing. At the San Ysidro-Tijuana border crossing, you will need to stop before crossing the border. Stay to the far right and follow the "something to declare" signs, which will take you into a side parking lot where you can park and enter the large blue SAT building. At both the Otay Mesa and the Tecate border crossings, you will first cross the border and then immediately pull to the right where you can park and enter the SAT/Aduanas building to get your FMM.

Travelers arriving in Baja by commercial flight from outside Mexico will have the cost of their FMM included in their plane ticket and will be provided with all the paperwork to clear when arriving in Baja at the airport. Travelers crossing by sea into Baja must stop at the port captain's office to have their FMM stamped. If you will be entering Baja by boat and will not be stopping on land, but will be in Mexican waters, you must get a nautical FMM, which is a separate process. For more information go to www.gob.mx.

EMBASSIES AND CONSULATES

There is a **Mexican Consulate** (1549 India St., San Diego, tel. 619/231-8414, info@consulmexsd.org, 8am-6pm Mon.-Fri.) in San Diego that can assist with visas, permanent and temporary residency for Mexico, special import permits, and questions about Mexican customs.

The **U.S. Consulate** (Paseo de la Culturas, Mesa de Otay, tel. 664/977-2000, 7:30am-4:15pm Mon.-Fri) is in Tijuana near the airport and can help with lost passports, visa issues, or emergency services. They can also assist with notaries, births and deaths of U.S. citizens, and arrests of U.S. citizens in Baja. The **Canadian Consulate** (Germán Gedovius 10411-101, tel. 664/684-0461, tjuna@international.gc.ca, 9:30am-12:30pm Mon.-Fri.) helps Canadian citizens with passport issues and other emergency situations that may arise while traveling.

CUSTOMS
Entering Mexico

Travelers crossing into Mexico are allowed to bring items for personal use, as well as up to US$75 of new merchandise (per adult) duty-free when crossing by land. If crossing by air, US$300 of new merchandise is permitted duty-free. Adults may bring up to three liters of liquor or beer and up to six liters of wine. You may carry up to US$10,000 cash without paying duty.

Many people find themselves wanting to bring items to donate to orphanages and other charitable causes in Baja. However, bringing large amounts of used clothing and other items will be subject to paying duty. Firearms are illegal in Mexico and may only be possessed with a proper permit for hunting.

Returning to the United States

Travelers may bring up to US$800 worth of new merchandise into the United States from Mexico every 30 days without paying a duty. Adults may bring back one liter of alcohol and 200 cigarettes. Some foods are allowed into the United States from Mexico; however, most fruits, vegetables, nuts, and meat products are prohibited. The specific list changes often, so check with www.cbp.gov for a complete rundown.

Recreation

HIKING AND BACKPACKING

Baja has captured the hearts of many hikers and explorers. From the high peaks of the northern Sierra to the sands of the *Desierto Central*, the peninsula offers a wide variety of options. One thing that's common throughout the peninsula is the lack of well-marked trails, if there are any trails at all. **Mexico Maps** (www.mexicomaps.com) has topographic maps available for the entire peninsula.

You will need to be prepared for self-sufficient camping, and please be respectful by carrying out all your trash and abiding by low-impact camping principles. Make sure to bring plenty of water and a first-aid kit, in addition to the usual hiking and camping essentials.

HUNTING

Many hunters come to Baja to hunt quail, dove, pheasant, and waterfowl in northern Baja in regions around Tecate and south of Ensenada. Hunting season runs from the beginning of September and extends through the end of February for certain species.

Guns and ammunition are highly regulated in Mexico, and permits can be expensive (US$350 for the year). Most hunters rent guns by the day from the hunting outfitter they are using. A hunting license and game tags are required. All non-Mexicans must be accompanied by a licensed Mexican hunting guide while in the field. **Baja Hunting** (www.bajahunting.com) can assist with permits and arrangements.

FISHING

Sportfishing is popular all over the peninsula, and anglers come for the thrill of catching yellowtail, dorado, tuna, roosterfish, and more. Mexican fishing licenses are required when fishing on the water. Everyone who is on board a boat with tackle, whether or not they are fishing, must have a fishing license. They are available by the day, week, month, or year. You can obtain a fishing permit in advance online through the website of the **Mexico**

Department of Fisheries (PESCA) (www.sportfishingbcs.gob.mx). If you are paying to take a fishing charter, they will often take care of the fishing permit for you, but be sure to ask in advance. Fishing permits are not required if you are fishing from shore.

BOATING

Recreational boating is an enjoyable way to experience Baja and grants access to remote beaches and places that other travelers can't easily get to. **Temporary Import Permits** (TIPs) for boats are now required for Baja. The permits are good for 10 years. You can start the process online at www.gob.mx/banjercito.

Ensenada is an official Mexico port of entry. You must check in with the port captain's office and complete a crew list document and get FMMs for all passengers on the vessel. If you will be entering Mexican waters for sportfishing, but not making landfall, you must obtain a **nautical FMM** (www.gob.mx).

SURFING

Baja is full of surf breaks on the Pacific side of the peninsula around Rosarito and Ensenada. Surf shops, rentals, and lessons can be found in Ensenada and throughout the Rosarito area.

SNORKELING AND SCUBA DIVING

The peninsula has a diverse marinelife, which makes for interesting snorkeling and diving. Rosarito and Ensenada both have some diving sites and dive shops that can assist with trips and equipment. The water is cold here and wetsuits will be necessary.

Food and Accommodations

FOOD
Food and Water Safety

The most frequently asked question among first-time Baja travelers is "Is it safe to drink the water?" The tap water in Mexico contains different bacteria than that found in the water in the United States, and for this reason can cause upset stomachs for travelers. It's safe to drink the water and ice that is served at restaurants and hotels in cities, as they use purified water. The Mexicans do not drink water from the tap either, so you can be assured that when you are served water or ice at a restaurant or hotel, it is purified. You should brush your teeth with bottled water to be safe. There are water purification stations at grocery stores and convenience stores where you can refill bottles with potable water.

As when traveling in any developing country, it's a good idea to carry some Imodium with you. Most towns in Baja have pharmacies where they can give you something like Lomotil over the counter if needed.

Where to Eat

Foodies from around the world are flocking to northern Baja, where Tijuana and Ensenada are leading the way in an incredible culinary scene. The fresh local seafoods, meats, and Mexican flavors are being combined with Asian and Mediterranean influences. This new Baja California style of cooking is now catching on all over, with "Baja California"-style restaurants opening in places like New York and Chicago.

Throughout the entire region, fresh seafood, rich traditional Mexican dishes, and savory *antojitos* like tacos and tamales are the staples. Don't miss picking up a bag of fresh tortillas, either *harina* (flour) or *maíz* (corn), whenever you pass a *tortillería*.

What to Eat
ANTOJITOS AND STREET FOOD

Antojitos (little whims) are traditional Mexican fast-food dishes such as tacos, tortas, tamales, tostadas, and quesadillas. You can find these served on menus at many casual sit-down restaurants (either à la carte or served as a meal with rice and beans on the side) and also at street food carts.

SEAFOOD

Because the peninsula is surrounded by water, *mariscos* are practically a dietary staple in Baja. You can enjoy seafood at all different price ranges and settings. At street carts and cheap *mariscos* stands, you'll find items like fish tacos, ceviche (raw fish "cooked" in lime juice), and *cocteles de mariscos* (seafood cocktails where the seafood is served chilled in a tomato-based broth). A favorite among locals are *almejas gratinadas* (clams au gratin), where the clam is topped with cheese and then grilled. At sit-down restaurants, you'll find items like *pescado del día* (fish of the day), *camarones* (shrimp), *langosta* (lobster), and *pulpo* (octopus).

MEAT

Carne is a large part of Mexican food, whether served by itself or as part of a dish. You'll find *pollo* (chicken), *puerco* (pork), and *res* (beef) on many menus as well as less-traditional meats like *chiva* (goat) and *borrego* (lamb).

SALSAS

No meal in Mexico is complete without adding some kind of salsa. Many restaurants and food stands make their own, adding to the unique flavors of the food. Pico de gallo (also called *salsa fresca* or *salsa bandera*) is a combination of chopped tomatoes, onions, cilantro, and jalapeño. *Crema* (a thinned sour cream), guacamole, and other salsas are common as well. If you don't like hot flavors, ask how hot the salsas are before trying them; you don't want to be caught off-guard by a habanero salsa!

BEVERAGES

A standard selection of sodas can be found around the peninsula. Coca-Cola here is made with cane sugar instead of corn syrup,

Seafood Guide

- *almejas:* clams
- *atún:* tuna
- *camarón:* shrimp
- *cangrejo:* crab
- *caracol:* sea snail
- *erizo:* sea urchin
- *jurel:* yellowtail
- *langosta:* lobster
- *mejillones:* mussels
- *ostiones:* oysters
- *pargo:* red snapper
- *tiburón:* shark

giving it a different taste and making it somewhat of a sought-after beverage over the years. *Aguas frescas* (literally fresh waters) are infused waters, served around Mexico. The most traditional flavors are *jamaica* (hibiscus), *horchata* (rice milk), and *tamarindo* (tamarind), although hip restaurants will serve other refreshing and creative flavors. *Limonada* is Mexico's version of lemonade. It is made with simple syrup and *limones*, which are limes in Mexico. You can order it *natural,* made with still water, or *mineral* with sparkling water.

ALCOHOLIC BEVERAGES

Even those uninitiated with Mexico are likely familiar with the margarita and tequila. Mexico makes a number of good beers, and beers like Tecate, Dos Equis, and Pacífico can be found all along the peninsula. In northern Baja there's a growing craft beer scene as well. Baja's main wine region, the Valle de Guadalupe, has helped wine become more popular around Mexico, and you'll see wines from the region on the menus of nicer restaurants throughout the peninsula.

La Cuenta, Por Favor

Mexicans consider it rude to bring the check to the table before it's asked for. When you eat at a restaurant in Mexico, you are welcomed with a warm hospitality that invites you to come eat, drink, relax, and enjoy. They would never dream of kicking you out in order to turn tables. Many foreigners may be frustrated with this at first, but most come to enjoy it. When you're ready for the check, you'll have to ask for it: *la cuenta, por favor.*

ACCOMMODATIONS

There are a wide variety of accommodations found on the peninsula. The options depend on your destination and personal preference.

Camping and RV Parks

There are plenty of places to camp in the region, ranging from isolated sites with no services to fancy RV parks with full hookups.

Motels

Budget motels are found throughout the region and are a good option for travelers looking to save on accommodations. It's common at many of the affordable motels and hotels for them to ask for a deposit of a few hundred pesos as collateral for the TV remote control.

Bed-and-Breakfasts and Boutique Hotels

There are a number of B&Bs and small boutique hotels in the Valle de Guadalupe, where there are no large hotels. For some of the more exclusive properties, expect to pay prices similar to what you would see in the United States.

Vacation Rentals

Vacation rentals abound all along the peninsula, and these can be a good option for travelers planning to stay for an extended period of time or for locations where there are very few options in terms of hotels or motels. It can also be convenient to have access to a full kitchen to avoid having to eat all meals out at restaurants. **Vacation Rentals by Owner** (VRBO, www.vrbo.com) and **Airbnb** (www.airbnb.com) both have rentals along the peninsula.

Travel Tips

CONDUCT AND CUSTOMS
Time

Many foreigners may experience frustration with the fact that things happen at a much slower pace in Baja than at home. It's not abnormal for service to be slower than you are used to and for everything in general to take longer. Punctuality among friends may fall to the wayside in Mexico, but you should be on time for any business-related matters. Most professionals are aware of foreigners' adherence to punctuality and put in the extra effort to be prompt.

Polite Interactions

Mexican people are far more polite and less direct than stereotypical U.S. people. They always exchange niceties and ask about your well-being and your family before getting to the matter at hand. You should begin all conversations with at least a polite *Hola, buenos días* (or *buenas tardes,* depending on time of day) before delving into matters.

A cultural difference that foreigners may find frustrating is that Mexicans have a hard time delivering bad news or saying "no." They often consider it rude and will skirt the issue, which can lead to much confusion and irritation. Mexicans will rarely give you a "no" for an RSVP; they are far more likely to say "yes" and then not show up, as they consider this to be more acceptable than declining from the beginning. Likewise, if you are waiting on something they don't have, the common response is that they will have it *mañana,* tomorrow. Many foreigners have learned to accept the fact that in Mexico *mañana* doesn't necessarily mean tomorrow, it just means not today.

If you sense that you are not getting a direct answer, it's best to rephrase the question or to ask again in a different manner, to make sure that you are getting the whole story.

Tipping

You should tip a few pesos to the attendants at the gas station, the baggers at the grocery store, and parking lot attendants. At restaurants, 10 percent is standard, and you should give 15 percent for a fancy fine-dining experience. Just a few pesos will be sufficient as a tip at taco stands and food carts.

WHAT TO PACK

If it's your first time road-tripping down the peninsula, here are a few items to bring along:

Electronics: A GPS unit will be your most valuable tool for navigating the peninsula. Street names and addresses don't exist in many areas, so using GPS coordinates is often the most reliable way to find your destination. There are stretches of the peninsula where you won't get music on the radio, so an auxiliary cable and portable music player are a good idea. A camera and cell phone are a must for most Baja travelers. Expensive larger electronic items like laptops should be left at home unless you absolutely need them. The more you bring along, the more you need to keep track of, and most hotels on the peninsula don't have safes. Mexico uses the same outlets as the United States and Canada, so you don't need to bring along a converter for your chargers.

Toiletries and First Aid: Don't forget items like sunscreen, aloe vera, bug spray, and hand sanitizer in addition to your usual toiletry items. Most Baja hotels do not provide toiletries like shampoo, conditioner, or lotion, so you should bring your own from home. Hair dryers are another item not usually provided by hotels, so you should bring one from home if you need one for daily use. Pack a small first-aid kit with Neosporin and Band-Aids. You can get the generic version of most over-the-counter medications and items at any pharmacy on the peninsula, but if there's a specific medication or product you like to have on hand, bring it from home. Most Baja travelers carry Pepto-Bismol and Imodium A-D to help soothe an upset stomach. An extra roll of toilet paper is always valuable to have on hand for pit stops and because many gas station and public restrooms will not provide it.

Personal Items: Bring sturdy footwear for hiking and sandals for the beach. Water shoes can come in handy for hikes where you'll be crossing streams and for swimming in natural pools or rivers. Swimsuits, sunhats, sunglasses, and beach towels are necessary for beach time. Pack clothing that can be layered for hot days and cool nights. Leave expensive jewelry at home. Bring along plenty of reading material because English books and magazines can be difficult to find and expensive.

Sports Equipment: The equipment you bring with you depends on your interests and the size of your vehicle. Most sports enthusiasts secure gear on the top of their car with sturdy straps. You'll be able to rent equipment like kayaks, surfboards, stand-up paddleboards, bicycles, fishing rods, snorkels, and scuba gear in more developed towns. Many road-trippers bring along their own coolers, beach chairs, and umbrellas. Camping equipment will all need to be brought with you.

Vehicle: Be sure to have a standard emergency road kit, tow straps, flashlight, jack, and spare tire at the very minimum. Duct tape and a tire repair kit can help if you're in a desperate situation. It's always a good idea to carry a gas can and extra water.

SANITATION

Gas station and public restrooms do not usually provide toilet paper, so it's a good idea to always carry your own with you. In many rural areas, bathrooms will be on septic systems and you should place the toilet paper in the wastebasket. There will usually be a sign directing you to do so, typically in both Spanish and English. In the cities, the systems can usually handle toilet paper, so it's OK to put it into the toilet unless there's a sign asking you specifically to use the wastebasket. You can usually rely on a sign to tell you what to do. If there's no sign but a wastebasket next to the toilet, it's best to play it safe and use the trash.

ACCESS FOR TRAVELERS WITH DISABILITIES

Baja California is a region that can be difficult to explore independently for visitors with disabilities. Uneven sidewalks (if there are sidewalks at all), stairs without ramps, and dirt roads and floors can make getting around in a wheelchair nearly impossible in most areas. Buses and shuttles are generally not wheelchair accessible. Check in advance with your hotel to ask about accessibility and to make any special advance arrangements.

There are very few provisions in Baja for blind or hearing-impaired travelers. A few new intersections in Tijuana now have audio assistance for the blind, but they are rare exceptions on the peninsula.

TRAVELING WITH CHILDREN

Baja is a great place to travel with children, and there are plenty of activities for kids of all ages and interests. Many hotel rooms along the peninsula are equipped with multiple beds to suit families. Some of the wineries and boutique accommodations in Valle de Guadalupe may not accept children, so it's best to check ahead. Otherwise, kids are warmly welcomed in other areas of the region.

TRAVELING WITH PETS

Road-trippers traveling with their dogs will find a number of motels and campsites in Baja that are pet friendly. You should carry current vaccinations and registration for your dog.

TRAVELING ALONE

Solo travelers heading to the region shouldn't have any hesitation in doing so. The northern region of Baja is relatively easy to drive in and English is readily spoken throughout the area.

SENIOR TRAVELERS

A large number of senior travelers are attracted to Baja California because of the warm weather and affordable prices. There are a growing number of retired expats who have made Baja their full-time or part-time home.

GAY AND LESBIAN TRAVELERS

LGBT travelers should have no problems traveling in Baja. Larger cities like Tijuana and Ensenada will have more options for nightlife and entertainment.

Health and Safety

MEDICAL ASSISTANCE AND EMERGENCY EVACUATION

Travelers will find knowledgeable doctors and modern medical facilities in nearly every sizable town in Baja. Large, modern hospitals operate in larger cities, and clinics and Red Cross facilities are available in smaller towns.

There are a number of companies that provide emergency evacuation from Baja. **Medical Air Services Association** (MASA, toll-free tel. 800/423-3226, www.masamts.com

Emergency Phone Numbers and Resources

These numbers can be dialed from any cell phone or landline in order to reach emergency services in Baja:

- **911:** All of Mexico uses 911 as their emergency phone number.
- **078:** Tourist assistance hotline. Travelers can call from anywhere in Baja California to get 24/7 bilingual assistance, from roadside assistance to emergency services or travel information.
- **074:** Roadside assistance

com) and **Aeromedevac** (Mex. tel. 800/832-5087, toll-free U.S. tel. 800/462-0911, www. aeromedevac.com) are two such services. It's always a good idea to purchase extra travel insurance when traveling to help cover any medical payments or emergency evacuation.

SUNBURN AND DEHYDRATION

The Baja sun can be intense and is prone to catching travelers off-guard. Sunburns and dehydration are common afflictions for unsuspecting tourists who have spent too much time out in the sun and heat. Sunscreen and hats should be worn outside. Always make sure you have plenty of drinking water and are staying well hydrated.

STINGS AND BITES

Stingrays and jellyfish are often the culprits for any stings in the ocean. Although the stings may hurt, they are not life-threatening. When entering the water from the shore, always do the "stingray shuffle" to frighten off any unsuspecting rays hiding under the sand. Seek medical attention for any allergic reactions.

On land, scorpions are common throughout the peninsula. They like to hide in cool, dark places like under rocks or in piles of wood. Always shake out towels, blankets, clothing, and shoes that have been outside and may have become a hiding spot for scorpions. A scorpion sting is painful, but rarely dangerous for adults. If your child is stung, seek medical attention.

CRIME

Mexico has been in the news the past decade for drug cartel-related violence. The violence, which was never targeted at tourists, usually takes place in neighborhoods far away from tourist areas. That said, it's always a good idea when traveling to be aware of your surroundings and to avoid drawing attention to yourself. Expensive electronics and flashy jewelry should stay at home. Don't leave items in your car that could be a target for petty theft.

Tourist Information

MONEY

The Mexican currency is the peso, abbreviated MXN or sometimes MN. It uses the same symbol as the U.S. dollar ($), which can cause some confusion at times. Establishments in Mexico are legally required to post their prices in pesos, but at some tourist-centered restaurants and hotels the prices are listed in U.S. dollars. Mexico has a 16 percent IVA (sales tax) that is also supposed to be included in the listed price of items, but sometimes isn't.

Dollars or Pesos?

While U.S. dollars are accepted in some tourist areas of Baja, it's always advisable to pay with pesos so that you get the best exchange rate. There are a number of exchange houses in large cities, but these days most travelers get cash out of the ATMs in Baja for the best exchange rate. Be aware that you'll pay a fee at the ATM and will possibly pay another fee with your bank in the United States, depending on how your bank operates with foreign transaction fees.

Foreign credit cards are commonly accepted in larger cities in northern Baja, but it's always best to have enough cash on you in case businesses don't take cards or the machine is not working (which is common). There are many small towns in the middle of the peninsula where credit cards are not accepted and there are no ATMs, so you'll need to have cash. Always remember to call your bank ahead of time to let them know you will be using your debit or credit card in Mexico, so that they can put a travel alert on your account. Travelers checks are not widely accepted, so it's best to have credit cards or cash.

Bargaining is accepted, and expected, in markets and at street stalls. Start by asking how much the item costs (*¿Cuanto cuesta?*) and then counteroffer with a lower price (go down to about half of the initial asking price). You can go back and forth from there until you settle on a mutually acceptable price. Always be polite and kind while bargaining. Never insult the merchandise or the vendor in attempt to get a lower price. For brick-and-mortar stores, the set price will likely be posted.

COMMUNICATIONS

Phones and Cell Phones

Because of the growing numbers of cross-border travelers and citizens, many of the large U.S. phone carriers have plans that will give you data, minutes, and texting in Baja. Always make sure to call your carrier to learn about your options before traveling.

Phone numbers in Baja follow the same format as numbers in the United States, with a three-digit area code followed by a seven-digit number. There's no standard format for hyphenating the phone numbers in Mexico, so they may at times look different than presented in this book. The area code for Mexico is 52. For dialing a Mexican phone number from the United States, you will need to dial 011-52 before the area code and phone number.

Internet Access

Many hotels along the peninsula now offer wireless access. The service is not guaranteed and the signal is not always strong enough to extend everywhere around a property. But it's usually sufficient for light Internet use and will be available at least in the lobby area. More restaurants are also offering wireless Internet, especially in larger cities. Internet cafés are few and far between along the peninsula because of the prevalence of wireless Internet access.

WEIGHTS AND MEASURES

Mexico is on the metric system for weights, volumes, temperature, and distances. Driving directions and speed limits are given in kilometers. Gas is sold in liters, and temperature is measured in degrees Celsius.

TIME ZONE

The state of Baja California (Norte) is on Pacific Standard Time and observes daylight saving time.

TOURIST OFFICES

Most large cities in Baja have at least one tourist office where travelers can speak to someone in English and gather brochures and information about the region. The **Baja California (Norte) website** (www.bajanorte.com) has helpful information.

TRAVEL CLUBS

Whether you are a first-time tourist or a seasoned Baja traveler, there are a number of advantages to joining a Baja-specific travel club. They offer up-to-date information, travel discounts, services and assistance, and premium Mexican auto insurance. **Discover Baja Travel Club** (8322 Clairemont Mesa Blvd., San Diego, U.S. tel. 619/275-4225, toll-free U.S. tel. 800/727-2252, www.discoverbaja. com, US$39 per year) is conveniently located in San Diego, where you can stop in to get your auto insurance, prepaid FMM tourist permit, fishing license, and Baja books and maps, before heading south.

MAPS

For driving the peninsula, the currently out-of-print *Baja California Almanac* (www. baja-almanac.com) is considered the ultimate map of Baja and by far the most detailed and accurate navigation tool. Even older editions are still useful.

Resources

Glossary

abarrotes: groceries
aduana: customs
aguas termales: hot springs
alberca: swimming pool
antojitos: literally "little whims," casual Mexican dishes like tacos or tortas
bahía: bay
BCN: the state of Baja California (Norte)
BCS: the state of Baja California Sur
birria: a traditional meat stew often served as a taco using just the meat
calle: street
callejón: alley
campestre: literally "country," used to refer to outdoor country restaurants
cañon: canyon
cardón: a large cactus native to northwestern Mexico
caseta: tollbooth or guard shack
cervecería: brewery
cerveza: beer
colectivo: taxi van that picks up several passengers at a time, operating like a small bus; also used to refer to a collection of food stalls or food trucks
efectivo: cash
ejido: communally held land
farmacia: pharmacy
federales: nickname for the federal police
FMM (*forma migratoria múltiple*): tourist permit required for non-Mexican citizens traveling in Baja
Green Angels: a group providing free roadside assistance

gringo: a foreigner in a Spanish-speaking country who is not Latino or Hispanic
INM (Instituto Nacional de Migración): unit of the Mexican government that controls migration
malecón: waterfront promenade
mariscos: seafood
mercado: market
mordida: literally "bite," a bribe
palapa: structure with a thatched roof
PAN (Partido Acción Nacional): Mexico's conservative political party
panga: aluminum fishing boat
Pemex: the government-regulated gas stations in Mexico
playa: beach
PRD (Partido de la Revolución Democrática): Mexico's leftist political party
PRI (Partido Revolucionario Institucional): Mexico's centrist political party
punta: point
SAT (Servicio de Administración Tributaria): unit of Mexican government that controls customs
SECTUR (Secretaria de Turismo): Secretary of Tourism
tienda: store
tinaja: pool or spring
tope: speed bump
ultramarine: mini market/liquor store
vino: wine
zocalo: a public town plaza; also used to refer to the gazebo structure in the plaza

ABBREVIATIONS

Av.: Avenida
Blvd.: Boulevard
Col.: Colonia

Km.: Kilometer
s/n: *sin número* (without number, used for addresses without building numbers)

Spanish Phrasebook

Spanish commonly uses 30 letters—the familiar English 26, plus four straightforward additions: ch, ll, ñ, and rr, which are explained in "Consonants," below.

PRONUNCIATION

Once you learn them, Spanish pronunciation rules—in contrast to English—don't change. Spanish vowels generally sound softer than in English. (*Note:* The capitalized syllables below receive stronger accents.)

Vowels

a   like ah, as in "hah": *agua* AH-gooah (water), *pan* PAHN (bread), and *casa* CAH-sah (house)

e   like ay, as in "may": *mesa* MAY-sah (table), *tela* TAY-lah (cloth), and *de* DAY (of, from)

i   like ee, as in "need": *diez* dee-AYZ (ten), *comida* ko-MEE-dah (meal), and *fin* FEEN (end)

o   like oh, as in "go": *peso* PAY-soh (weight), *ocho* OH-choh (eight), and *poco* POH-koh (a bit)

u   like oo, as in "cool": *uno* OO-noh (one), *cuarto* KOOAHR-toh (room), and *usted* oos-TAYD (you); when it follows a "q" the u is silent; when it follows an "h" or has an umlaut, it's pronounced like "w"

Consonants

b, d, f, k, l, m, n, p, q, s, t, v, w, x, y, z, ch
pronounced almost as in English; h occurs, but is silent—not pronounced at all

c   like k as in "keep": *cuarto* KOOAR-toh (room), Tepic tay-PEEK (capital of Nayarit state); when it precedes "e" or "i," pronounce c like s, as in "sit": *cerveza* sayr-VAY-sah (beer), *encima* ayn-SEE-mah (atop)

g   like g as in "gift" when it precedes "a," "o," "u," or a consonant: *gato* GAH-toh (cat), *hago* AH-goh (I do, make); otherwise, pronounce g like h as in "hat": *giro* HEE-roh (money order), *gente* HAYN-tay (people)

j   like h, as in "has": *Jueves* HOOAY-vays (Thursday), *mejor* may-HOR (better)

ll   like y, as in "yes": *toalla* toh-AH-yah (towel), *ellos* AY-yohs (they, them)

ñ   like ny, as in "canyon": *año* AH-nyo (year), *señor* SAY-nyor (Mr., sir)

r   is lightly trilled, with tongue at the roof of your mouth like a very light English d, as in "ready": *pero* PAY-doh (but), *tres* TDAYS (three), *cuatro* KOOAH-tdoh (four)

rr   like a Spanish r, but with much more emphasis and trill. Let your tongue flap. Practice with *burro* (donkey), *carretera* (highway), and Carrillo (proper name), then really let go with *ferrocarril* (railroad)

Note: The single small but common exception to all of the above is the pronunciation of Spanish y when it's being used as the Spanish word for "and," as in "Ron y Kathy." In such case, pronounce it like the English ee, as in "keep": Ron "ee" Kathy (Ron and Kathy).

Accent

The rule for accent, the relative stress given to syllables within a given word, is straightforward. If a word ends in a vowel, an n, or an s, accent the next-to-last syllable; if not, accent the last syllable.

Pronounce *gracias* GRAH-seeahs (thank you), *orden* OHR-dayn (order), and *carretera* kah-ray-

TAY-rah (highway) with stress on the next-to-last syllable.

Otherwise, accent the last syllable: *venir* vay-NEER (to come), *ferrocarril* fay-roh-cah-REEL (railroad), and *edad* ay-DAHD (age).

Exceptions to the accent rule are always marked with an accent sign: (á, é, í, ó, or ú), such as *teléfono* tay-LAY-foh-noh (telephone), *jabón* hah-BON (soap), and *rápido* RAH-pee-doh (rapid).

BASIC AND COURTEOUS EXPRESSIONS

Most Spanish-speaking people consider formalities important. Whenever approaching anyone for information or some other reason, do not forget the appropriate salutation—good morning, good evening, etc. Standing alone, the greeting *hola* (hello) can sound brusque.

Hello. *Hola.*
Good morning. *Buenos días.*
Good afternoon. *Buenas tardes.*
Good evening. *Buenas noches.*
How are you? *¿Cómo está usted?*
Very well, thank you. *Muy bien, gracias.*
Okay; good. *Bien.*
Not okay; bad. *Mal or feo.*
So-so. *Más o menos.*
And you? *¿Y usted?*
Thank you. *Gracias.*
Thank you very much. *Muchas gracias.*
You're very kind. *Muy amable.*
You're welcome. *De nada.*
Goodbye. *Adios.*
See you later. *Hasta luego.*
please *por favor*
yes *sí*
no *no*
I don't know. *No sé.*
Just a moment, please. *Momentito, por favor.*
Excuse me, please (when you're trying to get attention). *Disculpe* or *Con permiso.*
Excuse me (when you've made a mistake). *Lo siento.*
Pleased to meet you. *Mucho gusto.*

How do you say . . . in Spanish? *¿Cómo se dice . . . en español?*
What is your name? *¿Cómo se llama usted?*
Do you speak English? *¿Habla usted inglés?*
Is English spoken here? (Does anyone here speak English?) *¿Se habla inglés?*
I don't speak Spanish well. *No hablo bien el español.*
I don't understand. *No entiendo.*
My name is . . . *Me llamo . . .*
Would you like . . . *¿Quisiera usted . . .*
Let's go to . . . *Vamos a . . .*

TERMS OF ADDRESS

When in doubt, use the formal *usted* (you) as a form of address.

I *yo*
you (formal) *usted*
you (familiar) *tu*
he/him *él*
she/her *ella*
we/us *nosotros*
you (plural) *ustedes*
they/them *ellos* (all males or mixed gender); *ellas* (all females)
Mr., sir *señor*
Mrs., madam *señora*
miss, young lady *señorita*
wife *esposa*
husband *esposo*
friend *amigo* (male); *amiga* (female)
sweetheart *novio* (male); *novia* (female)
son; daughter *hijo; hija*
brother; sister *hermano; hermana*
father; mother *padre; madre*
grandfather; grandmother *abuelo; abuela*

TRANSPORTATION

Where is . . . ? *¿Dónde está . . . ?*
How far is it to . . . ? *¿A cuánto está . . . ?*
from . . . to . . . *de . . . a . . .*
How many blocks? *¿Cuántas cuadras?*
Where (Which) is the way to . . . ? *¿Dónde está el camino a . . . ?*
the bus station *la terminal de autobuses*
the bus stop *la parada de autobuses*

Where is this bus going? *¿Adónde va este autobús?*
the taxi stand *la parada de taxis*
the train station *la estación de ferrocarril*
the boat *el barco*
the launch *lancha; tiburonera*
the dock *el muelle*
the airport *el aeropuerto*
I'd like a ticket to . . . *Quisiera un boleto a . . .*
first (second) class *primera (segunda) clase*
round-trip *ida y vuelta*
reservation *reservación*
baggage *equipaje*
Stop here, please. *Pare aquí, por favor.*
the entrance *la entrada*
the exit *la salida*
the ticket office *la oficina de boletos*
(very) near; far *(muy) cerca; lejos*
to; toward *a*
by; through *por*
from *de*
the right *la derecha*
the left *la izquierda*
straight ahead *derecho; directo*
in front *en frente*
beside *al lado*
behind *atrás*
the corner *la esquina*
the stoplight *la semáforo*
a turn *una vuelta*
right here *aquí*
somewhere around here *por acá*
right there *allí*
somewhere around there *por allá*
road *el camino*
street; boulevard *calle; bulevar*
block *la cuadra*
highway *carretera*
kilometer *kilómetro*
bridge; toll *puente; cuota*
address *dirección*
north; south *norte; sur*
east; west *oriente (este); poniente (oeste)*

ACCOMMODATIONS

hotel *hotel*
Is there a room? *¿Hay cuarto?*

May I (may we) see it? *¿Puedo (podemos) verlo?*
What is the rate? *¿Cuál es el precio?*
Is that your best rate? *¿Es su mejor precio?*
Is there something cheaper? *¿Hay algo más económico?*
a single room *un cuarto sencillo*
a double room *un cuarto doble*
double bed *cama matrimonial*
twin beds *camas gemelas*
with private bath *con baño*
hot water *agua caliente*
shower *ducha*
towels *toallas*
soap *jabón*
toilet paper *papel higiénico*
blanket *frazada; manta*
sheets *sábanas*
air-conditioned *aire acondicionado*
fan *abanico; ventilador*
key *llave*
manager *gerente*

FOOD

I'm hungry. *Tengo hambre.*
I'm thirsty. *Tengo sed.*
menu *carta; menú*
order *orden*
glass *vaso*
fork *tenedor*
knife *cuchillo*
spoon *cuchara*
napkin *servilleta*
soft drink *refresco*
coffee *café*
tea *té*
drinking water *agua pura; agua potable*
bottled carbonated water *agua mineral*
bottled uncarbonated water *agua sin gas*
beer *cerveza*
wine *vino*
milk *leche*
juice *jugo*
cream *crema*
sugar *azúcar*
cheese *queso*
snack *antojo; botana*

breakfast *desayuno*
lunch *almuerzo*
daily lunch special *comida corrida* (or *el
menú del día* depending on region)
dinner *comida* (often eaten in late
afternoon); *cena* (a late-night snack)
the check *la cuenta*
eggs *huevos*
bread *pan*
salad *ensalada*
fruit *fruta*
mango *mango*
watermelon *sandía*
papaya *papaya*
banana *plátano*
apple *manzana*
orange *naranja*
lime *limón*
fish *pescado*
shellfish *mariscos*
shrimp *camarones*
meat (without) *(sin) carne*
chicken *pollo*
pork *puerco*
beef; steak *res; bistec*
bacon; ham *tocino; jamón*
fried *frito*
roasted *asada*
barbecue; barbecued *barbacoa; al carbón*

SHOPPING

money *dinero*
money-exchange bureau *casa de cambio*
I would like to exchange traveler's
checks. *Quisiera cambiar cheques de
viajero.*
What is the exchange rate? *¿Cuál es el
tipo de cambio?*
How much is the commission? *¿Cuánto
cuesta la comisión?*
Do you accept credit cards? *¿Aceptan
tarjetas de crédito?*
money order *giro*
How much does it cost? *¿Cuánto cuesta?*
What is your final price? *¿Cuál es su último
precio?*
expensive *caro*
cheap *barato; económico*

more *más*
less *menos*
a little *un poco*
too much *demasiado*

HEALTH

Help me please. *Ayúdeme por favor.*
I am ill. *Estoy enfermo.*
Call a doctor. *Llame un doctor.*
Take me to ... *Lléveme a ...*
hospital *hospital; sanatorio*
drugstore *farmacia*
pain *dolor*
fever *fiebre*
headache *dolor de cabeza*
stomachache *dolor de estómago*
burn *quemadura*
cramp *calambre*
nausea *náusea*
vomiting *vomitar*
medicine *medicina*
antibiotic *antibiótico*
pill; tablet *pastilla*
aspirin *aspirina*
ointment; cream *pomada; crema*
bandage *venda*
cotton *algodón*
sanitary napkins use brand name (e.g.,
Kotex)
birth control pills *pastillas anticonceptivas*
contraceptive foam *espuma
anticonceptiva*
condoms *preservativos; condones*
toothbrush *cepilla dental*
dental floss *hilo dental*
toothpaste *crema dental*
dentist *dentista*
toothache *dolor de muelas*

POST OFFICE AND
COMMUNICATIONS

long-distance telephone *teléfono larga
distancia*
I would like to call ... *Quisiera llamar a ...*
collect *por cobrar*
station to station *a quien contesta*
person to person *persona a persona*
credit card *tarjeta de crédito*

post office *correo*
general delivery *lista de correo*
letter *carta*
stamp *estampilla, timbre*
postcard *tarjeta*
aerogram *aerograma*
airmail *correo aereo*
registered *registrado*
money order *giro*
package; box *paquete; caja*
string; tape *cuerda; cinta*

AT THE BORDER

border *frontera*
customs *aduana*
immigration *migración*
tourist card *tarjeta de turista*
inspection *inspección; revisión*
passport *pasaporte*
profession *profesión*
marital status *estado civil*
single *soltero*
married; divorced *casado; divorciado*
widowed *viudado*
insurance *seguros*
title *título*
driver's license *licencia de manejar*

AT THE GAS STATION

gas station *gasolinera*
gasoline *gasolina*
unleaded *sin plomo*
full, please *lleno, por favor*
tire *llanta*
tire repair shop *vulcanizadora*
air *aire*
water *agua*
oil (change) *aceite (cambio)*
grease *grasa*
My ... doesn't work. *Mi ... no sirve.*
battery *batería*
radiator *radiador*
alternator *alternador*
generator *generador*
tow truck *grúa*
repair shop *taller mecánico*
tune-up *afinación*
auto parts store *refaccionería*

VERBS

Verbs are the key to getting along in Spanish. They employ mostly predictable forms and come in three classes, which end in *ar, er,* and *ir,* respectively:
to buy *comprar*
I buy, you (he, she, it) buys *compro, compra*
we buy, you (they) buy *compramos, compran*
to eat *comer*
I eat, you (he, she, it) eats *como, come*
we eat, you (they) eat *comemos, comen*
to climb *subir*
I climb, you (he, she, it) climbs *subo, sube*
we climb, you (they) climb *subimos, suben*

Here are more (with irregularities indicated):
to do or make *hacer* (regular except for *hago,* I do or make)
to go *ir* (very irregular: *voy, va, vamos, van*)
to go (walk) *andar*
to love *amar*
to work *trabajar*
to want *desear, querer*
to need *necesitar*
to read *leer*
to write *escribir*
to repair *reparar*
to stop *parar*
to get off (the bus) *bajar*
to arrive *llegar*
to stay (remain) *quedar*
to stay (lodge) *hospedar*
to leave *salir* (regular except for *salgo,* I leave)
to look at *mirar*
to look for *buscar*
to give *dar* (regular except for *doy,* I give)
to carry *llevar*
to have *tener* (irregular but important: *tengo, tiene, tenemos, tienen*)
to come *venir* (similarly irregular: *vengo, viene, venimos, vienen*)

Spanish has two forms of "to be":
to be *estar* (regular except for *estoy,* I am)
to be *ser* (very irregular: *soy, es, somos, son*)

Use *estar* when speaking of location or a temporary state of being: "I am at home." *"Estoy en casa."* "I'm sick." *"Estoy enfermo."* Use *ser* for a permanent state of being: "I am a doctor." *"Soy doctora."*

NUMBERS

zero *cero*
one *uno*
two *dos*
three *tres*
four *cuatro*
five *cinco*
six *seis*
seven *siete*
eight *ocho*
nine *nueve*
10 *diez*
11 *once*
12 *doce*
13 *trece*
14 *catorce*
15 *quince*
16 *dieciseis*
17 *diecisiete*
18 *dieciocho*
19 *diecinueve*
20 *veinte*
21 *veinte y uno* or *veintiuno*
30 *treinta*
40 *cuarenta*
50 *cincuenta*
60 *sesenta*
70 *setenta*
80 *ochenta*
90 *noventa*
100 *ciento*
101 *ciento y uno* or *cientiuno*
200 *doscientos*
500 *quinientos*
1,000 *mil*
10,000 *diez mil*
100,000 *cien mil*

1,000,000 *millón*
one-half *medio*
one-third *un tercio*
one-fourth *un cuarto*

TIME

What time is it? *¿Qué hora es?*
It's one o'clock. *Es la una.*
It's three in the afternoon. *Son las tres de la tarde.*
It's 4 a.m. *Son las cuatro de la mañana.*
six-thirty *seis y media*
a quarter till eleven *un cuarto para las once*
a quarter past five *las cinco y cuarto*
an hour *una hora*

DAYS AND MONTHS

Monday *lunes*
Tuesday *martes*
Wednesday *miércoles*
Thursday *jueves*
Friday *viernes*
Saturday *sábado*
Sunday *domingo*
today *hoy*
tomorrow *mañana*
yesterday *ayer*
January *enero*
February *febrero*
March *marzo*
April *abril*
May *mayo*
June *junio*
July *julio*
August *agosto*
September *septiembre*
October *octubre*
November *noviembre*
December *diciembre*
a week *una semana*
a month *un mes*
after *después*
before *antes*

(Courtesy of Bruce Whipperman, author of *Moon Pacific Mexico*.)

Suggested Reading

TRAVELOGUES

Berger, Bruce. *Almost an Island: Travels in Baja California.* Tucson: University of Arizona Press, 1998. With his rich and descriptive writing, Berger recounts his three decades spent traveling in Baja California.

Hazard, Ann. *Agave Sunsets: Treasured Tales of Baja.* San Diego: Sunbelt Publications, 2002. This collection of spirited Baja tales will introduce you to colorful characters and erase barriers between Mexican and gringo cultures.

Hill, Herman, and Silliman, Roger. *Baja's Hidden Gold: Treasure Along the Mission Trail*, 2nd ed. Oaxaca: Carpe Diem Publishing, 2014. A collection of the stories of Herman Hill, a prospector, dreamer, and adventurer seeking gold in Baja California.

Mackintosh, Graham. *Into a Desert Place.* New York: W. W. Norton & Co., 1995. One of the most widely read Baja books chronicling the journey of a British self-described "couch potato" who walks the entire coastline of the Baja peninsula.

Smith, Jack. *God and Mr. Gomez.* Santa Barbara: Capra Press, 1997. A comedic account of the author's experience purchasing land and building a house along Baja's northern coast.

HISTORY AND CULTURE

Kier, David. *Baja California: Land of Missions.* El Cajon, CA: M&E Books, 2016. This comprehensive guide covering the history and information about all of the Spanish missions in Baja California is an invaluable tool for any Baja traveler.

Niemann, Greg. *Baja Legends.* San Diego: Sunbelt Publications, 2002. The useful book explains some of the most prominent Baja establishments, personalities, and legends region by region.

NATURAL HISTORY AND FIELD GUIDES

Minch, Jason and John. *Roadside Geology and Biology of Baja California*, 2nd ed. San Diego: Sunbelt Publications, 2017. This guide explains the biology and geology kilometer-by-kilometer down the Baja peninsula.

Rebman, Jon P., and Roberts, Norman C. *Baja California Plant Field Guide*, 3rd ed. San Diego: Sunbelt Publications, 2012. This must-have field guide is the definitive book for identifying Baja's diverse flora.

SPORTS AND RECREATION

Church, Mike and Terry. *Traveler's Guide to Camping Mexico's Baja*, 6th ed. Rolling Homes Press, 2017. This indispensable guide gives all of the most accurate information for all the campsites and RV parks on the peninsula.

Parise, Mike. *The Surfer's Guide to Baja.* Surf Press Publishers, 2012. This guide gives detailed directions and maps to the best surf spots along the peninsula.

Internet Resources

Many establishments in Baja now have websites or at least Facebook pages where you can find information about hours and location. For general Baja travel, there are a number of online forums and even Facebook groups, but always double-check the information that you find, as it's not always accurate. The websites below have reliable and accurate information about travel in Baja.

Baja California State Tourism
www.bajanorte.com
The state tourism website for Baja California (Norte) gives specific and helpful information about hotels, sights, and restaurants for each region.

Baja Insider
www.bajainsider.com
This comprehensive website covers valuable information for Baja residents and visitors.

Discover Baja
www.discoverbaja.com
Not only do they offer Mexican auto insurance, but this website is a wealth of information about travel regulations and the best places to go and things to do in Baja.

INAH
http://inah.gob.mx
INAH (Instituto Nacional de Antropología e Historia) is responsible for protecting Baja's cultural sites, including rock art and the Spanish missions.

INM
www.gob.mx
The Mexican migration website, where non-Mexican citizens can obtain FMM tourist permits online.

Smart Traveler Enrollment Program (STEP)
https://step.state.gov
The U.S. Department of State runs the Smart Traveler Enrollment Program (STEP) as a free service that allows U.S. citizens traveling abroad to enroll their trip with the nearest U.S. embassy or consulate.

U.S. Customs and Border Protection
www.cbp.gov
Has customs information about items allowed back into the United States from Mexico.

U.S. Embassy
https://mx.usembassy.gov
The website for the U.S. embassy in Mexico City has information about services for U.S. citizens.

ONLINE NEWSLETTERS

There are a few Baja websites that send out regular online newsletters with helpful travel information. **Discover Baja** (www.discoverbaja.com) offers a newsletter that travelers can sign up for to receive monthly emails with quality articles about all areas of Baja.

Baja Times (www.bajatimes.com.mx) is a free publication focusing on Tijuana, Rosarito, and Ensenada that is printed twice a month and also has an online version.

Gringo Gazette (www.gringogazette.com) has a northern edition with a printed version that can be found in establishments around town and an online version as well.

Rosarito Town Crier (www.rosaritotown-crier.com) is an email newsletter covering cultural and nonprofit events in the Rosarito area.

Index

UV

WXYZ

List of Maps

Photo Credits

Trips to Remember

BALI & LOMBOK
CHANTAE REDEN

ECUADOR
& THE GALÁPAGOS ISLANDS
BETHANY PITTS

GREEK ISLANDS & ATHENS
SARAH SOULI

ICELAND
JENNA GOTTLIEB

TRIP OF A LIFETIME
MACHU PICCHU
INCLUDING CUSCO & THE INCA TRAIL
RYAN DUBÉ

MOROCCO
LUCAS PETERS

NEW ZEALAND
JAMIE CHRISTIAN DESPLACES

OAXACA
ANNE COPELAND

TRIP OF A LIFETIME
PATAGONIA
INCLUDING THE FALKLAND ISLANDS
WAYNE BERNHARDSON

PRAGUE, VIENNA & BUDAPEST
JENNIFER WALKER & AUĎREA SCHELLON

ROME, FLORENCE & VENICE
ALEXEI J. COHEN

Epic Adventure

PACIFIC COAST HIGHWAY
Road Trip
CALIFORNIA, OREGON & WASHINGTON
IAN ANDERSON

ROUTE 66
Road Trip
JESSICA DUNHAM

YELLOWSTONE TO GLACIER NATIONAL PARK
Road Trip
JACKSON HOLE, CODY, THE GRAND TETONS
& THE ROCKY MOUNTAIN FRONT
CARTER G. WALKER

AMALFI COAST
With Capri, Naples & Pompeii
LAURA THAYER

ARUBA

BAHAMAS
MARIAN LAINE MOYLE

Beachy Getaways

BAJA
Tijuana to Los Cabos
JENNIFER KRAMER

BELIZE
LEBAWIT LILY GIRMA

BERMUDA
ROSEMARY JONES

COSTA RICA
NIKKI SOLANO

DOMINICAN REPUBLIC
LEBAWIT LILY GIRMA

FIJI
ROBERT KAY

FLORIDA KEYS
With Miami & the Everglades
JOSHUA LAWRENCE KINSER

JAMAICA

MAUI
With Molokai & Lanai
GREG ARCHER

PUERTO RICO
SUZANNE VAN ATTEN

FRENCH RIVIERA:
NICE, CANNES, MONACO & ST-TROPEZ
JON BRYANT

PUERTO VALLARTA
With Sayulita, the Riviera Nayarit & Costalegre
MADELINE MILNE

MAP SYMBOLS

═══	Expressway	○	City/Town	✈	Airport	⚲	Golf Course
────	Primary Road	◉	State Capital	✈	Airfield	🅿	Parking Area
～～～	Secondary Road	⊛	National Capital	▲	Mountain	▱	Archaeological Site
═ ═ ═	Unpaved Road	◎	Highlight	✦	Unique Natural Feature	⛪	Church
─ ─ ─	Trail	★	Point of Interest				
··········	Ferry	•	Accommodation	≋	Waterfall	⛽	Gas Station
━ ━ ━	Railroad	▾	Restaurant/Bar	⚑	Park	◠	Glacier
▨▨▨	Pedestrian Walkway	▪	Other Location	TH	Trailhead	▨	Mangrove
▥▥▥	Stairs	⋀	Campground	⛷	Skiing Area	⬡	Reef
						⬛	Swamp

CONVERSION TABLES

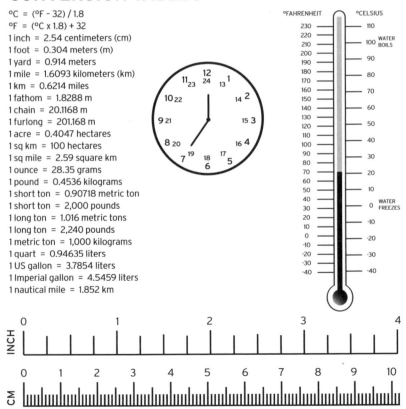

°C = (°F - 32) / 1.8
°F = (°C x 1.8) + 32
1 inch = 2.54 centimeters (cm)
1 foot = 0.304 meters (m)
1 yard = 0.914 meters
1 mile = 1.6093 kilometers (km)
1 km = 0.6214 miles
1 fathom = 1.8288 m
1 chain = 20.1168 m
1 furlong = 201.168 m
1 acre = 0.4047 hectares
1 sq km = 100 hectares
1 sq mile = 2.59 square km
1 ounce = 28.35 grams
1 pound = 0.4536 kilograms
1 short ton = 0.90718 metric ton
1 short ton = 2,000 pounds
1 long ton = 1.016 metric tons
1 long ton = 2,240 pounds
1 metric ton = 1,000 kilograms
1 quart = 0.94635 liters
1 US gallon = 3.7854 liters
1 Imperial gallon = 4.5459 liters
1 nautical mile = 1.852 km

MOON TIJUANA, ENSENADA & VALLE DE GUADALUPE WINE COUNTRY

Avalon Travel
Hachette Book Group
1700 Fourth Street
Berkeley, CA 94710, USA
www.moon.com

Editor and Series Manager: Kathryn Ettinger
Acquiring Editor: Grace Fujimoto
Copy Editor: Brett Keener
Graphics Coordinator: Lucie Ericksen
Production Coordinator: Lucie Ericksen
Cover Design: Faceout Studios, Charles Brock
Interior Design: Domini Dragoone
Moon Logo: Tim McGrath
Map Editor: Albert Angulo
Cartographers: Albert Angulo and John Culp
Indexer: Greg Jewett

ISBN-13: 978-1-64049-772-6

Printing History
1st Edition — October 2020
5 4 3 2 1

Front cover photo: Adobe Guadalupe winery on the Ruta del Vino © Giovanni Simeone / Sime / eStock Photo
Back cover photo: Valle de Santo Tomás © Jennifer Kramer

Printed in China by R.R. Donnelley

Avalon Travel is a division of Hachette Book Group, Inc. Moon and the Moon logo are trademarks of Hachette Book Group, Inc. All other marks and logos depicted are the property of the original owners.